# Core Economics

## Concepts & Applications Volume I

# Core Economics

## Concepts & Applications Volume I

### Subodh Mathur

Subodh (Ph. D. Economics MIT) has taught graduate and undergraduate courses in Economics and supervised doctoral dissertations for several years. He has more than thirty-five years of worldwide experience in applying economic concepts to resolve real-world issues.

My mother Dayavanti Khemchand
To my enduring sorrow, she did not live long enough to enjoy
the fruits of her hard work.


My mother-in-law Lata Deolalikar
She pampered me as a son-in-law and loved me like a son.

These remarkable mothers transcended their traditional
upbringing and paved the way for their children and
grandchildren to become citizens of a global world.

*They would have loved to see this*

Laxmi Devi, my dadi, my grandmother, who was brought up in purdah. My oldest brother called her a traditional unorthodox woman. She had no trouble in communicating with Anne, her German granddaughter-in-law, though they spoke no common language.

Khemchand, my father, a fearless, dedicated civil servant. He brought books, learning, and the whole world into the family when we lived in places that were remote back then, and remain so even today.

Prakash, my oldest brother, whom we called Titi and colleagues called PC. He did not let his cleft palate handicap or small-town upbringing hold him back, and led his siblings on the path to academic success.

Anne, my German bhabi, my sister-in-law. A daunting challenge for her to inter-mingle with so many in-laws from another culture, but she made it.

Manmohini, my older sister, whom we called Dolly. A regional-level athlete, she grew up to be a college professor.

Rakesh, my school friend, my closest compatriot, my brother-in-law. A top-ranked civil servant with a Ph.D. and many books to his credit.

# They kept me going

I begin with my pranam to Dr. Robert Smith, a Hindi-speaking Australian political scientist and civil servant, who worked with PC, my oldest brother. Bob read all my drafts, and wrote helpful and encouraging comments at every step.

Charles "Chas" Feinstein, one of the world's leading energy practitioners. He wrote, "Wow, Subodh! I really learned a lot" on one of my drafts. Wow, and thanks, Chas!

Amit Shah, my college classmate and a publishing executive. He approved my writing style – which meant so much to me.

Dr. Albert Woodward, an American health economist and one of my former students from ages ago. Read all my drafts. Quality check as a practicing economist.

Sten Bergman, a Swedish engineer with worldwide experience. I felt great when he said that my drafts made sense to him and his grandson.

Subhash and Ashok Mathur, two of my older brothers. A civil servant and a finance expert, respectively. Subhash read every word, and bluntly told me what I needed to redo. Ashok stepped in with a fresh pair of eyes.

TCA Srinvasa-Raghavan, my college classmate and a financial journalist. He said my drafts made sense in the real world. Who could ask for more?

Devajyoti "Doc" Ghose, my college classmate. An economist who became a financial market specialist. Extensive edits on my draft chapter about the bond market – a tough chapter to write.

Dr. Maithili Daphtary, a biomedical engineer. She read my drafts with a hawk's eye, catching mistakes that others totally missed.

Raj Melville, one of my friends from MIT days. An engineer with an MBA, and so much real-world experience. He wrote that the book is a must read for those who are curious about the economy. Yes!

Prof. Anil Deolalikar, my brother-in-law, distinguished economist, and Dean, School of Public Policy, University of California, Riverside. Made time to read my drafts, and said that they covered major economics principles in an accessible, conversational style. Well! That was my intent.

T. Singaravelan "Velan", one of my Internet friends and a cleantech entrepreneur in Singapore. Read my drafts with an unbiased eye, and offered his help at every step

Parul Mathur, my niece. She has always wanted me to do something like this. And she readily agreed to make the book's companion website.

Rakshat Hooja, my nephew, who doesn't believe that he has actually figured out what he wants to do with his life. He thinks I have decoded the language of economists for those who are not economists. Mission accomplished!

Sfoorti Mathur, my niece and a graphic designer. She created the cover page for this book, and was my co-editor for a different e-book.

Dr. Aditya Balasubramanian, an economist who has adopted History as his field. No generation gap here. He said he was on the same page as me.

The newest members of my extended family. Dr. Esther Hedberg, a psychiatrist, and Daniel Gottlieb, a lawyer. They are waiting to read the finished product.

My daughter, Suchita, a lawyer who is working so hard for marginalized people that she had no time to read these drafts. But she made it clear that she wanted me to succeed.

My son Abhijai, who is working on a Ph.D. in Chemistry. To my surprise, he read some of my drafts. That's not all – I accepted most of his edits.

My staunchest, dyed-in-the-wool supporter who always keeps me on my toes. My rock. My wife Anuradha Deolalikar.

I close with my father-in-law, Bapu Deolalikar. Now 93 years old and growing younger every day, he read some of my chapters with care. That means so much to me.

# About this book

*Core Economics* is in the same genre as Professor Levitt's Freakonomics and Professor Chang's Economics: The User's Guide. The focus is on the economics of real-world issues, with minimal jargon and mathematics. The difference is that Core Economics reflects my 35 years of worldwide practitioner experience in applying economic concepts to formulate real-world projects and schemes.

**The book focuses on the core ideas and principles in economics and their applications. This makes it easy to see how economics works in real life.**

**The book is one step in formulating a new learning/teaching paradigm aimed at people outside the classroom – people who want to learn without becoming students.**

It's not a textbook. Not even close. It has none of the formalisms of a textbook. Instead, the book is a bit like a chat with my readers.

I have worked in Washington, DC, and I have worked in remote villages in Asia and Africa. Not alone. As a part of a team of professionals from various disciplines. Here I learned how to discuss economic concepts in jargon-free language, and they taught me how things work in the real world.

And, then I went back to university teaching. With a difference. Instead of teaching mathematical courses in the Economics Department, I asked to teach students who were not going to be economists.

I felt that standard economics textbooks were not suitable for these students. So, I wrote my own lectures from scratch to suit their needs. The look and feel of my lectures were quite different from that of any standard economics textbook

I thought about turning my lectures into a book. But, instead of doing this, I went back to applied work. It was an exciting assignment!

In 2019, Johns Hopkins University's School of Advanced International Studies' Energy, Resources and Environment group selected me to teach a course, beginning in January 2020. I was thrilled. I cleared my work plan for January-May 2020 so that I could concentrate on my students.

But the course was canceled just a few days before it was to begin. That opened up a big gap in my work schedule.

I wrote a couple of chapters and posted them online. I liked the reaction I got. So, I decided to write this book.

When I had written about 65,000 words (around 200 pages), I had not yet reached the halfway point. Some of my advisers felt that I had already covered a lot of ground, and I should publish it.

How could I publish half a book? No conventional publisher would take it. So, I decided to call it Volume I and self-publish it. And write some more in Volume II.

I was able to find a convenient dividing point between Volume I and Volume II. **There's more than enough in Volume I to give you a good idea of what economics is about, and how economists analyze the economy.**

So here we are. The book has plenty of charts based on real-world data. These charts have not been produced by graphics professionals. Instead, they are straight out of commonly used spreadsheet software. Nor have the fonts and formats been designed by experts. All of this takes time, but I didn't want to delay the book. And all of this takes money, which increases the book's price. I didn't want this either.

I decided to focus hard on the content and speed of delivery. If you are reading this, the delivery part has been fulfilled. I hope you enjoy reading this book and learn from it.

Please write to me at prof.mathur@gmail.com if you have any comments. And, let me know if you find any typos or other mistakes. I will write them up on the Errata section of the companion website http://www.profmathur.com/.

# CONTENTS

## Section I.    A Broad Introduction to Economics

This section, consisting of Chapters 1-3, is a broad introduction to economics.

In Chapter 1, we discuss what economics is about. **First, we discuss how economists try to understand the manner in which the economic world works**. The basic approach is to develop economic models. These models don't include all the details of the real world. Instead, the models focus on the relevant principal economic forces.

**Second, we look at how economists use these models in the real world**. One major use is to forecast the future values of key economic variables, such as economic growth. Another major use is to analyze the effect of policy changes, such as changes in tax rates.

In Chapter 2, **we look at the great ideas in economics.** For this, we draw upon the work of famous economists. One small group of these economists consists of people who passed away before the Nobel Prize in Economics was instituted. The larger group consists of some of the people who won this Nobel Prize.

In Chapter 3, **we look at an idea that is at the heart of economics. This is the idea that we face a scarcity of resources.** Hence, resources have to be allocated among the potential competing uses. What is the way to ensure that these scarce resources are properly allocated? Can we leave it to market forces? Or, are there instances where markets will do a poor job?

## CHAPTER 1.    WHAT IS ECONOMICS ABOUT?

The focus of this chapter is to give you a broad introduction to economic concepts and their applications. We will look at the details in later chapters.

Let's begin by asking what do economists do. As I see it, economists do two broad things. **First, they try to understand how the economic world works.**

The economic world is complex. In a market or an economy, there are many relevant factors. If you try to look at all of them at the same time, you will find that it is hard to figure out the relationships between them. It's hard to see the forest when you are looking at the trees.

Economists avoid this problem by looking at a simplified version of the real world. We do this simplification by making assumptions. As we discuss later in this chapter, economists make assumptions because they allow us to focus on the main issues, features, and economic variables. Of course, we run the risk that some of our assumptions will give us misleading results. So, **it's an art to formulate your assumptions so that they are balanced – so that they simplify without giving you misleading conclusions.**

And it remains an art even when you use mathematics. In economics, mathematics is just a tool that helps you to be clear, explicit, and precise. In the end, the results have to make economic sense, not just be mathematically sound. Anyhow, the use or misuse of mathematics by economists is a methodological issue beyond the scope of this book. That's because you will find barely any mathematics here.

We call this simplified version of economic reality an economic model. The purpose of this model is to understand the relationships between the various economic variables, and derive conceptual insights.

Second, economists use their understanding of how the economic world works to forecast economic variables, and to figure out the impact of policy changes on the economy.

Here we expand the simplified model and add in as many as possible of the details that we had left out. The expanded models use real-world data, which could be for one country or region for several time periods, or for several countries and regions at a point of time, or over several periods. These models also use econometric techniques, which are statistical methods that are suitable for economic analysis. Econometric techniques are inherently mathematical. We will introduce them briefly in this chapter, and discuss them in some detail in Volume II of this book.

## Chapter flow

This chapter has two broad parts, corresponding to the two broad things that economists do. **The bulk of the chapter deals with the first part.** Here we begin by looking at an economic model that got Professor Akerlof an Economics Nobel Prize. I chose this model because it is easy to see from it how economists derive meaningful insights from a model that has simplifying assumptions. From here, we move to a more general look at economic models. Then, we look at the various fields within economics, with details on the core fields within economics.

In the second part, we begin by looking at the US Congressional Budget Office's (CBO) ten-year forecast of the US economy. Then we look at the impact of two different policy changes.

At the end of the chapter, and in all subsequent chapters, we summarize the main points in the form of Key Takeaways.

## PROF. AKERLOF'S NOBEL PRIZE-WINNING MODEL

Before we look at this model, let me say that if you find it to be a bit abstract, you are not alone. Economics sometimes takes a while to sink in. So, don't give up – you will get it.

Professor Akerlof won the Nobel Prize in Economics in 2001 for an academic article he published in 1970. The paper had some algebra in it, but he derived his main insights in a simple, elegant way. **He developed a model of the market for used cars. However, he said that his insights were quite general.** In his article, he showed that his conclusions could be applied to these four areas:

- medical insurance for senior citizens,
- the employment of minorities,
- the costs of dishonesty, and
- credit markets in countries like India.

Later, based on this model, regulators formulated some rules to govern the sale of used homes in the US.

Used cars, used homes – where's the similarity? The similarity is that the owners of used cars and old homes know more about them than the potential buyers. In other words, the sellers and buyers don't have the same information about the product for sale.

Formally, we say that there is an asymmetry in the knowledge that the buyers and sellers have about the used cars or old homes offered for sale.

Professor Akerlof showed that markets don't work well when there is an asymmetry of information between buyers and sellers. The implication is that markets will work better when buyers and sellers have the same or similar information about the product.

This conclusion is consistent with the behavior of various sellers, who know that they will sell more if the potential buyers feel confident about what they are buying. For example, street food sellers have known for centuries that they will sell more if they let people taste their food. Same for ice-cream shops, which let you taste their flavors. Some companies give you guarantees and warranties for their products for several years, so that you are sure that the product is reliable. Other sellers let you return their products so that you can take it home and try it out.

## Akerlof's model had simplifying assumptions

Like most economic models, Professor Akerlof's model had several simplifying assumptions. These assumptions lead to just four categories of cars: good new cars, bad new cars, good used cars, and bad used cars.

First, he classified all cars as new cars and used cars, but without any details about their features. Next, he classified both new and used cars as being either of good quality or bad quality. He left out the reality that cars have many different levels of qualities. This is a very simplified description of the car market. However, Professor Akerlof was still able to derive meaningful conclusions from this model.

People call bad cars as lemons in everyday language. When Professor Akerlof did his analysis, there were no laws about lemon cars. That has changed. Today we have laws that call new cars with significant unfixable defects as lemons. Now, in many US states, the law requires car companies to take back a lemon and replace it with a good new car.

Professor Akerlof assumed that $x\%$ of new cars are lemons, where $x$ is an unspecified number. Further, he assumed that buyers know that $x\%$ of new cars are lemons, but they do not know whether a particular new car is a lemon. And, Professor Akerlof assumed that a new car buyer's estimate of the probability of getting a lemon is $x\%$. This is the case because the buyer has no additional information other than that $x\%$ of new cars are lemons.

People get a better idea of the quality of their car after they have owned it for some time. They will know soon whether the car is a lemon or not.

## Sales of used cars in the Akerlof model

Let's look at what happens when an owner wants to sell a car after it has become a used car.

Consider the **case where the used car is of good quality, not a lemon**. This makes the car more valuable than a lemon.

Now bring a potential buyer of a used car into the picture. The buyer does not know whether a used car is a lemon. And, the buyer may not trust the seller who says that it is a good car. **Now, there is an asymmetry in information because the seller knows more about the car than the buyer.** In this sale, it is the buyer's responsibility to determine the quality of what they are buying.

With asymmetric information, a buyer may not be willing to pay a high price for a good used car because the buyer is not sure that it is a good car. A buyer thinks that the probability that the used car is a lemon is $x$%, even though the seller knows and says that it is not a lemon.

Hence, a person who bought a good new car may decide that it is not worthwhile to sell it when it becomes a used car. The reason is that since the potential buyers do not recognize the true value of the vehicle, they are not willing to pay a suitable price.

Now, let's look at the **case where the used car is a lemon.** This car is less valuable than a good car. On the other hand, buyers would still think that the probability of the car being a lemon is $x$%. An owner who has a lemon may want to sell it at a reasonable price to a buyer who cannot tell that it is a lemon. Thus, there is an incentive for car owners to sell a lemon in the used car market.

The result is that few good cars will be offered for sale in the used car market. Hence, the used-car market will tend to be dominated by lemons. And this will make buyers suspicious of the used-car market. In other words, the used-car market will not work well.

## The core message from the Akerlof model

**The core message from Akerlof's model is that it is worthwhile to reduce information asymmetries.** This will help not only the buyers but also the sellers because buyers will be more willing to buy products that are unlikely to be lemons. At the same time, we have to keep in mind that actions that reduce information asymmetries may create some additional costs.

**This message is consistent with the full disclosure requirement that is becoming more common these days**. Most sellers now have to provide some information details about what they are selling. Some restaurants have begun to include nutrition information on their menus. Cars have mileage stickers. Many appliances have energy use information. Even scientists who publish their research often declare who is funding them.

## LET'S LOOK MORE GENERALLY AT ECONOMIC MODELS

When we look at economic models, we find that they **have assumptions and variables.** In Professor Akerlof's model, there were assumptions about the types of cars. His model also had variables, such as the number of good used cars being offered for sale. **Economic models also have coefficients, as discussed below**, though Professor Akerlof's simple model did not have any coefficients.

### Role of assumptions in economic models

Economists make many assumptions in their models. These assumptions are sometimes about the features of the economy or the market. For example, Professor Akerlof had several assumptions about the type of cars. Other assumptions are about the nature of the behavior of the participants in the model.

**Why do economists make these assumptions? Why don't they just look at the real world itself?** Well, we do look at the real world when we apply our models to the real world. However, looking at real-world data is not enough. The data does show <u>what</u> is happening, but it does not provide an explicit, transparent explanation of <u>why</u> it is happening. And, economists want to understand <u>why</u> things are the way they are. For example, Professor Akerlof figured out that used car markets don't work well because of asymmetric information.

Let's look at a controversial assumption that economists usually make. This assumption is that people spend their money so that they, in colloquial terms, get the biggest bang for their money. Economists often convert this assumption into a precise mathematical formulation. Take a look at Professor Akerlof's article. You will find that after the simple discussion that we have seen above, he used mathematical equations to describe this type of behavior.

Many people find this assumption odd and unacceptable. They complain that people are human beings, not robots. What sense does it make to describe people's behavior in mathematical terms? One rationale for this assumption is that it captures the essence of the behavior of most people in most situations.

7

In other words, all people may not behave this way in all cases, but this does capture the central tendency.

Another rationale for the mathematical statement is that the analysis is explicit, precise, and transparent. That makes it easier for interested people to understand and possibly challenge the study.

In the end, what matters is whether the conclusions are consistent with what we see in the real world, and the extent to which the analysis helps understand the real world.

## Economic models have two types of variables: endogenous and exogenous

Unfortunately, I have to introduce some jargon here. Don't skip this part – this jargon is intrinsic to economics.

Let me first bring in a simple way to keep track of the jargon. We usually use the term ex to mean former. I want you to **think about ex as outside – as in exit**.

For us, the opposite of ex is en. Think of en as similar to in - inside or internal.

The variables in an economic model are classified as exogenous or endogenous. Remember, ex indicates outside, and en indicates inside.

We call a variable **endogenous if its value is determined by the actions of the economic participants in the economic model.** For example, in Professor Akerlof's model, the number of good used cars offered for sale is an endogenous variable. Generally, since the price of a commodity in a market is determined by the buyers and sellers, it is an endogenous variable.

In contrast, we call a variable exogenous if its value is not determined by the actions of the participants in the model. Instead, the values of exogenous models are outside the domain of the economic model. For example, in Professor Akerlof's model, the percentage of lemons is exogenous because it is not determined by the interaction of buyers and sellers of cars. Another example of an exogenous variable would be a sales tax rate, which is set by the government.

**A variable may be endogenous in one model and yet be exogenous in another model.** As we will see below, the market interest rate is an endogenous variable when economists analyze the full economy. However, when the analysis is about a particular market, say for cars, the interest rate is an exogenous variable. The reason is that the interest rate is not determined by what happens in the car market. For example, people who take a loan to buy a car have to pay the prevailing interest rate, which applies to all loans.

## Economic models have coefficients

Unlike in Professor Akerlof's simple model, economists usually specify the relationships between endogenous and exogenous variables in terms of mathematical equations. **These equations have coefficients, which measure the strength of the relationships between the model's variables**.

For example, consider the relationship between the demand for a commodity and its price. All of us know that if a commodity's price goes up, then its quantity demanded comes down. But by how much? Will the demand come down a lot? Or, just a little bit? This depends upon the market we are looking at.

To understand coefficients, let's write the relationship between demand and price in mathematical terms. This will lead to a demand equation. It's not complicated algebra, so stick with me.

We start by writing $Q$ to represent the quantity demanded of a commodity – say bananas. Then, $Q$ depends on four factors.

- <u>Price of bananas</u>. Let $P$ represent the price in the demand equation. $P$ is an endogenous variable.

- <u>Price of a substitute commodity</u> that consumers can switch to, such as apples. Let $S$ represent the price of apples – the substitute commodity – in the demand equation. $S$ is an exogenous variable because the model's focus is bananas, not apples.

- <u>Incomes of the buyers</u>. Let $I$ represent income in the demand equation. $I$ is an exogenous variable.

- <u>Tastes of the buyers</u>. Tastes are exogenous. However, economists have no way to quantify tastes. Hence, tastes cannot be written directly as a variable in the demand equation. However, economists have other ways to handle tastes, so this critical factor is not ignored.

In mathematical terms, $Q$ depends upon $P$, $S$, and $I$. A simple form of this dependence leads to this demand equation:

$$Q = a + b*P + c*S + d*I$$ Demand equation, where * indicates multiplication

In applying this equation to the real world, economists will have actual data for the variables $Q$, $P$, $S$, and $I$. **The terms $a$, $b$, $c$, and $d$ are coefficients.** We don't have real-world data for them. Instead, **we will calculate their values with real-world data and econometric techniques, as discussed later in this chapter.**

It's helpful to interpret these coefficients. I have indicated below whether we expect the coefficients to be positive or negative, but their actual values will depend upon the data.

- The term $a$ is called the intercept. It is a catch-all term that reflects some factors whose values do not change over time. Since it is a catch-all term, we cannot say whether it will be positive or negative.

- The term $b$ measures the effect of changes in the price of bananas on the total demand. Our feeling is that the demand $Q$ will come down as the price $P$ goes up. Hence, we expect the value of $b$ to be negative.

- The term $c$ measures the effect of changes in the price of apples on the demand for bananas. Our intuition is that as the price of apples goes up, the total demand for bananas goes up as people switch, to some extent, to bananas. Hence, we expect the value of $c$ to be positive.

- The term $d$ measures the effect of changes in income on the demand for bananas. Our intuition is that as incomes go up, the total demand for bananas tends to go up. Hence, we would expect the value of $d$ to be positive.

Ok, we now have a good idea of what economic models look like. Let's move on to the core fields of economics.

## LET'S LOOK AT THE CORE FIELDS WITHIN ECONOMICS

Like other disciplines, we have several fields of specialization within economics. The core fields are microeconomics, macroeconomics, international economics, and econometrics.

The word micro means small. That's how we use it in microeconomics to indicate that we are looking at a small picture. In microeconomics, we look at particular markets, such as food, energy, or medical care. In contrast, in macroeconomics, we look at the big picture, as the word macro indicates. In macroeconomics, we look at the economy as a whole. In international economics, as you can expect, we look at global issues. Finally, econometrics is about the statistical techniques that economists use.

## MICROECONOMICS – THE SMALL PICTURE

The core theory is basically the same for all markets. However, when we apply it to a particular market, we adapt it to the market we are looking at. There is a significant amount of consensus among economists about microeconomics.

**Microeconomics is built around the concepts of supply and demand.** The supply comes from producers, and the demand comes from consumers. So, economists look to understand why consumers and producers behave the way they do. It's common to summarize their behavior by demand and supply equations or curves.

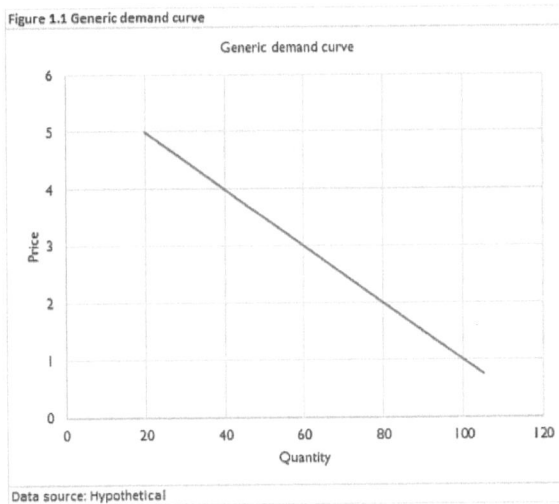

Figure 1.1 Generic demand curve

Data source: Hypothetical

We have already seen a demand equation above. I have shown a generic demand curve in Figure 1.1. It shows that as the price goes up, the quantity demanded comes down. The diagram is much simpler than an equation. But this diagram does not show the other two factors we had discussed above – the price of a substitute, and income. We do have ways to bring in these factors in this diagram. However, this does add some complexity, so let's leave it out from this chapter.

In microeconomics, the key issues are how the price is determined, and how much of the commodity or service will be produced and consumed. **In other words, the price and the quantity bought and sold are the main endogenous variables in microeconomic models.** We have seen above that a demand equation has some exogenous variables. Similarly, a supply equation will also have exogenous variables.

**A noteworthy conclusion from microeconomics is that it makes sense to promote competition among firms.** This has been widely implemented in many countries, which have set up laws and agencies for this purpose. In the US, the Federal Trade Commission works to protect consumers and competition by preventing anticompetitive, deceptive, and unfair business practices without unduly burdening legitimate business activity.

**Economists have extended their analysis to cover issues that were once considered outside the domain of economics.** For example, phenomena such as marriage and family were thought to be outside economics. However, Prof. Gary Becker began to analyze the family as a unit that produces goods and services for itself. He applied the standard economic theory of producers to examine the family's behavior. He got the Economics Nobel Prize in 1992.

We will discuss microeconomics in Volume II of this book.

## MACROECONOMICS – THE BIG PICTURE

Here we look at the big picture for a country. We can narrow it down to a part of a country. Or, we can broaden it to cover several countries. **The core issue is: How is the economy doing? We look at seven endogenous variables to answer this question.**

### Key endogenous variables in macroeconomic models

#### *Total income – GDP*

One of the key endogenous variables is the **total income of the economy**. Is it going up or down? How quickly? There are several ways to measure total income. **A common measure is the Gross Domestic Product (GDP).** There is nothing gross about GDP – it's just a term carried over from accounting. For example, when you calculate your taxable income, you start with your total income – which is called gross income. Then, you take various deductions to determine your taxable income. Similarly, after we make some deductions, we get Net Domestic Product (NDP). In public discussions, the issue is usually the GDP, with the NDP like a footnote, rarely reported or discussed.

The GDP of several countries is shown in Figure 1.2. In 2019, the US GDP of about $ 21 trillion was the highest in the world. It's amazing that if California were a

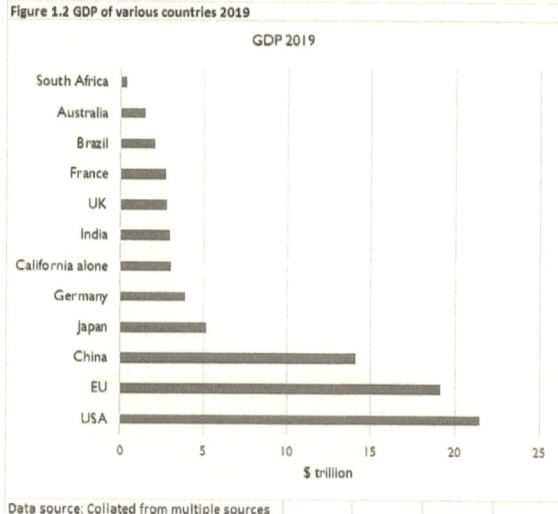

Figure 1.2 GDP of various countries 2019

GDP 2019

South Africa, Australia, Brazil, France, UK, India, California alone, Germany, Japan, China, EU, USA

$ trillion

Data source: Collated from multiple sources

separate country, it would be the fifth-largest economy in the world. China was the second-largest economy at about $ 14 trillion, though there are questions about the reliability of China's GDP numbers. The EU was ahead of China at about $ 19 trillion. Following Brexit, when you take out the UK, which had a GDP of around $ 3 trillion, the EU is still ahead of China.

We will discuss GDP in detail in Chapter 8.

### Income inequality – Gini coefficient

A second endogenous variable is **income inequality**. There are usually differences in the incomes of different people within a country. Rich people have much higher incomes than poor people. How do we summarize these differences? There are several measures available for this purpose. **One widely reported measure of income inequality is the Gini coefficient, which looks at everyone's income.** The Gini coefficient runs from 0 to 1, or 0 to 100. Higher values of the Gini coefficient indicate more inequality, and 0 implies perfect equality.

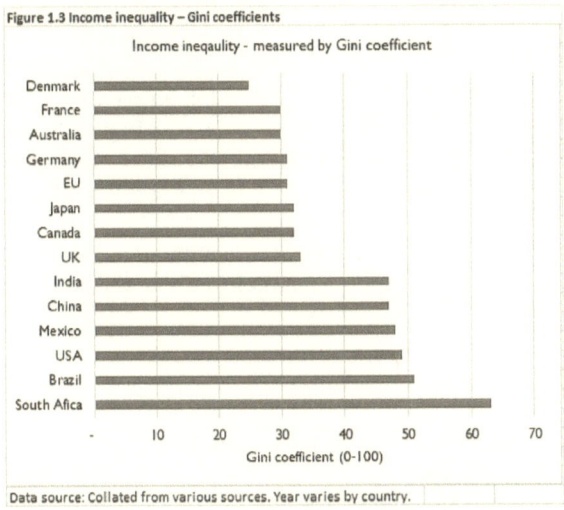

Figure 1.3 Income inequality – Gini coefficients

You can see the Gini coefficients of several countries in Figure 1.3.

In 2019, the US Gini coefficient was about 49, just a bit higher than China. Germany, the fourth-largest economy in the world, had a Gini coefficient of around 30. This indicates that incomes in Germany are less unequal than in the US and China. **The Nordic countries generally have low Gini coefficients. For example, Denmark's Gini coefficient is around 25.**

We will discuss income inequality in Chapter 9.

### Unemployment rate

A third variable is the **unemployment rate**. What is the share of people who are looking for work but cannot get a job? It seems a straightforward question, but there are many real-world complexities. What do you have to do to be counted as looking for work? Further, are you counted as employed if you work part-time – just a few hours a week?

As a result, the US has several measures of unemployment. The most common measures are called U-3 and U-6. U-3 is the official unemployment rate. U-6 is a broader measure of unemployment and is always higher than U-3 because U-6 includes those in U-3 and adds some more.

Note that a low unemployment rate does not always mean that people are well-paid. It's possible that you can be employed at a low wage that makes it hard for you to make ends meet.

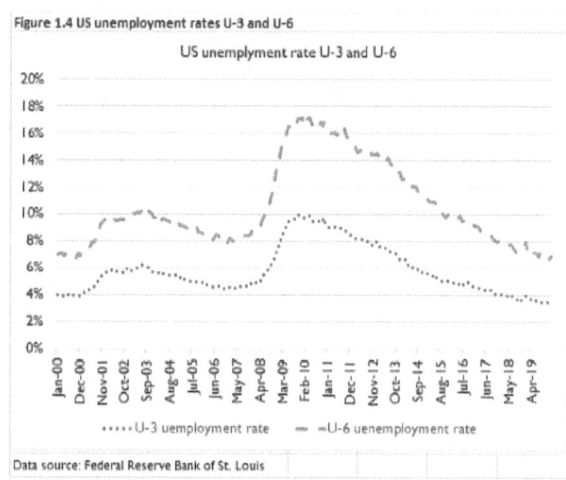

Figure 1.4 US unemployment rates U-3 and U-6

US unemplyment rate U-3 and U-6

Data source: Federal Reserve Bank of St. Louis

In February 2020, U-3 was 3.5%, a historically low value, while U-6 was 7.0%. (The rates shot up after that because of the economic crisis caused by the coronavirus). You can see the historic US employment rates in Figure 1.4. Germany's unemployment rate is around 3%. However, other European countries have higher unemployment rates, such as France at about 8% and Italy at approximately 10%.

## Wage rate

A fourth variable is the **average wage.** This is what people earn before paying taxes. In the US, the Bureau of Labor Statistics publishes the average hourly earnings of all employees on private nonfarm payrolls. The average US wage was around $ 28 per hour in November 2019, which translates to about $ 50,000 per year. In China, the average hourly wage is now around $ 4 per hour, but keep in mind that the cost of living is lower in China than in the US.

**We will discuss the wage rate in Volume II of this book.**

## Inflation rate

A fifth variable is the **average price of the things that people buy.** People are always concerned that the cost of living is going up. This cost of living depends upon the many things that people buy. The prices of some things, such as electronics, tend to go down over time. On the other hand, the prices of other things, such as new cars, tend to increase over time. We need a way to summarize these changes, which means we need to calculate the average change in prices. **The average percentage change in prices is called the inflation rate**. For example, if, on average, across commodities, the price increases by 5%, we say that the inflation rate is 5%.

One question related to this indicator is how we selected the things whose prices we want to track. Some people eat lots of meat. Others are vegetarians. We take account of these differences by averaging out what different people buy.

In the US, the most commonly used measure of inflation is the Consumer Price Index for All Urban Consumer (CPI-U). The US's inflation rate was about 2% in 2019, similar to the rate in Germany. China's inflation rate is higher, at around 4-5%. Japan is one of the few countries where the inflation rate was negative in several recent years, meaning that the average price fell.

**We will discuss inflation in detail in Chapter 7.**

*Interest rates*

A sixth variable is the **interest rate.** In any economy, there are many different interest rates, depending on who is borrowing how much for what period. In general, creditworthy borrowers pay lower rates than borrowers who are seen as risky. In most countries, the government is seen as the most creditworthy borrower. This is the case in the US. Consequently, the US government borrows money at a rate lower than anyone else in the US.

Since the US government borrows at the lowest rates in the US, the rate at which it borrows is taken as a benchmark for other rates. But, the rate for which loan? Most often, it is the rate for 10-year loans taken by the US government. This rate is reported as a yield, which is a measure of what a borrower will actually earn. We will discuss this difference between what the government pays and what a borrower gets in Chapter 5. Here we just note that unlike the interest rate paid by the US government, the yield changes every day.

Further, in general, loans for longer periods have higher rates than loans for shorter periods. For example, the interest rate for a 3-year car loan will be lower than a 7-year car loan. Again, the reason is the difference in the risk. The more distant future is seen as more uncertain and riskier than the immediate future.

In most economies, the market interest rates are affected by the actions of the central bank, such as the US Federal Reserve Bank, which is often called the Fed. The central bank's action place in the bond market, which is somewhat like a share market, but for large-scale loans.

**We will discuss the bond market in Chapter 5.**

*Government budget deficits*

Another endogenous variable is the **government budget deficit**. This measures how much more the government spends than the revenue it collects in a given time period. A government can decide how much it spends. However, the revenues it gets depend upon the economy. Hence, the budget deficit is an endogenous variable.

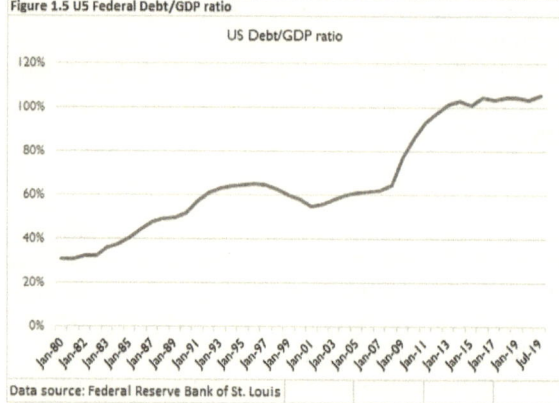

The total amount the government owes from all its borrowings is the government's debt. To put the value of this debt in perspective, we compare the debt to the country's GDP. Thus, apart from the actual deficit in a particular year, **a more useful measure is the debt-to-GDP ratio.** The US total debt in 2019 was about $ 23 trillion, and the debt/GDP ratio was about 105%. The historical values of the US debt/GDP ratio are shown in Figure 1.5.

Germany's debt/GDP rate was around 62%. Here we just note it is not a good idea to have a high debt/GDP ratio. An extreme case is Greece, where this ratio is around 180%, which is a very high value. It is closely related to Greece's ongoing economic crisis, in which the GDP fell for several years, and is now growing slowly.

**We discuss government deficits at various places in the book**.

## Exogenous variables in macroeconomic models

**Apart from endogenous variables, macroeconomic models have exogenous variables. For example, the government sets the tax rates**. Government rules and regulations are also exogenous. For instance, if the government sets a minimum wage rate, that is an exogenous variable.

For a small country, the price of internationally traded commodities is also an exogenous variable. For example, a small country cannot change the international price of crude oil. For this country, the oil price is what it is – take it or leave it.

## Nature of macroeconomic models

**The relationships between the endogenous and exogenous variables are complex. For example, the interest rate affects the GDP, but the GDP itself affects the interest rate.** We can discuss these relationships in qualitative terms, but, in the end, these variables are numbers in the real world. So, we need to know the numerical relationship between them. That's where mathematics comes in. **Economists represent these relationships in mathematical terms in the form of equations.** This specification leads to several equations. This set of equations makes a macroeconomic model.

In the real world, such models have hundreds of equations. For example, as we will see below, **the Congressional Budget Organization's model of the US economy has 900 equations.**

There are considerable disagreements about the nature of these relationships. There are different, competing schools of thought. When people find economists disagreeing with each other, it is mainly in connection with macroeconomic analysis.

**Economists had a challenging time when most of their models failed to predict the economic collapse of 2008.** Further, conventional policies did not bring back economic growth quickly. We still don't know the exact causes of the collapse. However, one common view is that the economic models did not pay enough attention to the financial sector, which was the origin of the recession.

**We will discuss these issues in Volume II of this book.**

## LET'S LOOK AT THE WORLD - INTERNATIONAL ECONOMICS

Here we look at international trade in goods and services, movements of investment money from one country to another, and movement of workers from one country to another. In this section, I have limited the discussion here to international trade.

## Endogenous variables in international trade

### Trade balance

**One endogenous variable that we look at is the trade balance.** The trade account is the difference between the overall value of a country's exports and imports in a specified period. Mathematically,

*International trade balance = value of exports − value of imports*

If the trade balance is positive, then the country has a trade surplus, and if the trade balance is negative, then the country has a trade deficit.

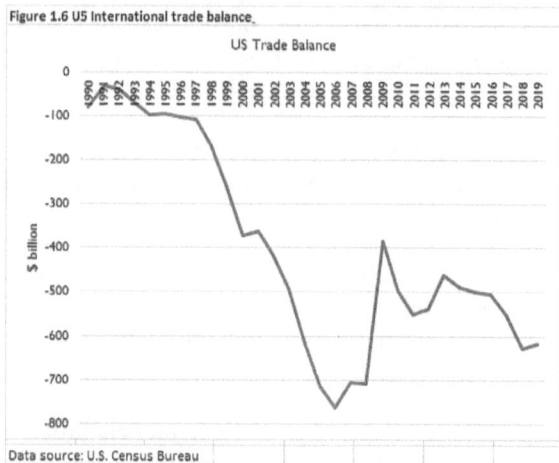

Figure 1.6 US International trade balance.

In 2018, overall US imports were about $ 3,100 billion, and exports were about $ 2,500 billion. This led to a trade deficit of about $ 600 billion. The historical values of the US international trade balance are shown in Figure 1.6.

In contrast to the US, China had a trade surplus of about $ 0.35 trillion, and Germany also had a trade surplus.

### Exchange rate

Another endogenous variable in international economics is the **exchange rate.** This is the rate at which we convert one country's currency into another country's currency. We usually compare a country's currency to the US dollar, as this is the dominant currency worldwide. For example, in February 2020, the US-Euro exchange rate was about $ 1 = € 0.92. This rate means that a person converting US dollars into Euros would get about 0.92 Euros for one US dollar. Sometimes, the exchange rate is written the other way, as in € 1 = $ 1.09, which means that one Euro is worth $ 1.09. Both styles of writing the exchange rate are correct.

**In most industrialized countries, such as the US and the EU, market forces determine the exchange rate of their currency.** The rates are determined by the supply and demand for their currencies. For example, in Germany, there would be a demand for US dollars from those who want to import things from the US. The supply of dollars would come from German exporters who have sold their products in other countries, and have been paid in US dollars.

**In other countries, the governments set the exchange rate, though they may change it frequently. China is one such country**. There have been charges that China has set its exchange rate to promote its exports, which means China would be a currency manipulator. While the US has threatened to label China as a currency manipulator, this has not happened so far.

## Is international trade good or bad?

Most economists think international trade is good for all participants. For many decades, the world's focus was on increasing international trade. The World Trade Organization's mission was to promote international trade.

However, in recent years, international trade has become politically controversial. One reason is that China has become a major exporter, and runs a trade surplus. There are concerns that international trade has led to job losses, particularly in countries like the US, which import a lot from China.

However, China is not the only country of concern. In the 1990s, when the US signed the North American Free Trade Area (NAFTA) agreement with Mexico and Canada, people were worried that manufacturing jobs would shift from the US to Mexico. NAFTA was replaced in 2020 by a new trade agreement called the US-Mexico-Canada Agreement (USMCA.)

The US is not alone in worrying about job losses due to international trade. Many countries look to protect selected groups of producers from foreign competition. Even if imported goods are cheaper, the countries want them to be produced locally for various reasons.

### Protecting your producers from international trade

Countries can protect their local companies from foreign competition in two ways. The first way is to impose tariffs. Tariffs are taxes that importers have to pay when they import something into the country. They are sometimes called import duties or customs duties.

A low level of tariffs indicates that a country is receptive to imports. In contrast, a high level indicates that a country wants to discourage imports by increasing the prices of imported goods. In 2019, the US increased its tariffs significantly, particularly for imports from China. Since the level of tariffs is set by governments, it is an exogenous variable.

The second way is to impose non-tariff barriers on imports. These barriers can take many forms. One way is to limit the total import of a commodity from a particular country. For example, in the 1980s, the US put a limit on how many cars could be imported from Japan. Sometimes, countries impose production conditions that are tough to meet. For example, some European cheeses are not allowed to be imported into the US because they use unpasteurized milk. Since governments impose non-tariff barriers, they are exogenous variables.

**We will discuss these issues in Volume II of this book.**

## LET'S LOOK AT ECONOMETRICS

If we look at it narrowly, econometrics is not a field of economics. The reason is that econometrics does not directly deal with any economy or market. Instead, **econometrics consists of statistical tools that economists use in their analyses.**

However, in a broader sense, econometrics is a critical part of economics. We could not analyze real-world data rigorously without econometrics because it contains the tools that we use to calculate the coefficients of an economic model's equations. For example, let's look at the demand equation we wrote above.

$$Q = a + b*P + c*S + d*I$$ Demand equation, where * indicates multiplication

Here we have to calculate the values of the coefficients $a$, $b$, $c$, and $d$. For this, we collect real-world data related to the observable variables $Q$, $P$, $S$, and $I$. The data could be monthly, quarterly, or annual.

Then, we apply econometric techniques to this data to calculate the value of the coefficients $a$, $b$, $c$, and $d$. The mathematical formulas used to calculate these values give exact answers, running to as many decimal places as you want. However, this precision is not real. We call them estimates of the coefficients, not precise values.

Since the precision of the estimates is illusionary, we want to convert the precise values into ranges within which the true value lies. We do this by bringing in probability theory.

## Bringing in probability theory

Once we bring the tools of probability, we can turn these precise estimates to ranges that include the true values. You know that polling data often shows the margin of error when the results are reported. For example, a poll of a sample of 500 people may state that 43% of them approve a particular policy. The poll will usually indicate that there is a margin of error in the estimate, say +/-3%.

This means that when you consider all the people, not just the sample of people who were questioned, the percentage of people who approve the policy is between 43-3 = 40% and 43+3 = 46%. In other words, the share of people who support the policy is somewhere in the range of 40-46%. This error margin is derived by using probability theory in the analysis.

### *Add a random term to an economic equation*

Economists use similar methods in their analysis. However, there is no place for probability in the above demand equation. How do we bring it in? **To bring in probability, we add a random term to the demand equation.** We modify the demand equation as:

$Q = a + b*P + c*S + d*I + \varepsilon$, where $\varepsilon$ is a random variable with a probability distribution.

I have written the random term as the Greek letter epsilon $\varepsilon$ to signify that it is different from all the other terms in the demand equation. This random term is similar to but different from the intercept term $a$. The term $a$ captures all the fixed factors that have been excluded from the demand equation. By fixed, we mean that their values don't change over time.

The term $\varepsilon$ is also a catch-all term for factors that we have left out. The difference from the term $a$ is that in $\varepsilon$ we consider changeable factors that we have left out from the demand equation. Since we don't know what these factors are and how they change, we just say that $\varepsilon$ is a term that varies in a random manner.

In this way, $\varepsilon$ **is a conceptual variable. There are no real-world data available for this term.** The addition of this random variable means that the demand equation now includes all the factors that have an effect on the value of Q as all the missing effects are subsumed under $\varepsilon$.

### *Random term brings in probability*

The most important benefit of adding the random term is that now we can apply probability theory to our calculated values of *a, b, c,* and *d*. Specifically, when we calculate values for the coefficients *a*, *b*, *c*, and *d*, the statistical formulas also calculate the margin of error for each estimated coefficient.

**Many decades ago, economists mainly used a statistical technique known as Least Squares** to calculate the values of the coefficients in an economic equation. The Least Squares method was formulated long ago by mathematicians, without using probability. **The Least Squares method looks to calculate the coefficients to get the best fit to the data. One example of the Least Squares method is fitting a trend line to a data set.**

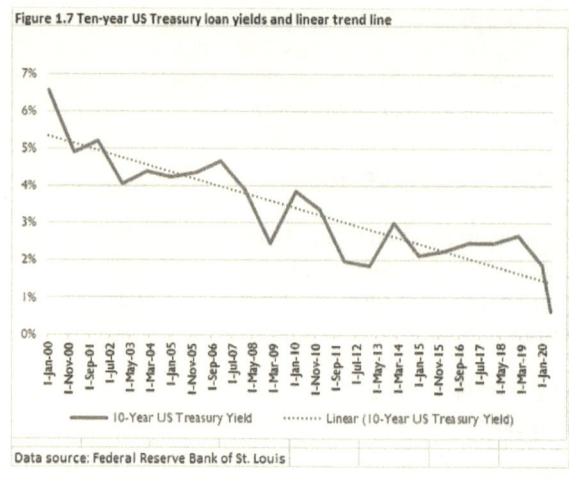

Figure 1.7 Ten-year US Treasury loan yields and linear trend line

Data source: Federal Reserve Bank of St. Louis

In Figure 1.7, you can see the 10-year US loan yield and the trend line for several years.

### Which statistical technique is suitable?

Once you add a random term, probability theory says that one condition for the Least Squares method to give acceptable results is that the right-hand side of the equation has only exogenous variables. There should be no endogenous variables on the right-hand side. **However, in the demand equation, *P* is an endogenous variable on the right-hand side. This means that Least Squares is not a suitable technique for this demand equation.**

**Over time, economists have developed many statistical techniques, all more complex than Least Squares.** So, econometrics has become much more challenging to understand. It seemed worthwhile to accept this additional complexity because it would lead to methodologically superior estimates of the coefficients. **The newer techniques have indeed led to coefficient estimates that are superior in terms of probability theory.**

What is disappointing is that the newer techniques have not given us more definitive values of the coefficients we are interested in. For example, consider this seemingly straightforward issue. Suppose the government raises the minimum wage. Will this reduce the number of workers these restaurants hire? Economic theory says the answer is likely to be Yes. But, by how much? That can be answered only by using real-world data and econometric techniques. After many studies over many years, we still do not have a definitive answer. Some studies find that there is no decline at all, but other studies find a sizable decline. As a result, there is no consensus.

It's not right to fault econometric techniques for this lack of certainty. Different studies have used data from different places. Further, the equations in their models are different. **But what is clear is that more complex econometric techniques will not necessarily give definitive answers, even when the studies are conducted by highly qualified economists.**

## ECONOMIC FORECASTS AND POLICY ANALYSIS

The US has plenty of forecasts for the economy. Some forecasts predict what to expect next month, such as for the unemployment rate or the number of jobs created. Others are for a year or two, and some others for more extended periods.

**In this introduction, we look at the forecasts prepared by the Congressional Budget Office (CBO).** The CBO is a respected nonpartisan agency created by Congress. And, the CBO gives you the details of its analysis, unlike some other groups that consider their detailed work a commercial secret.

### Ten-year CBO forecasts

Among other things, the CBO produces forecasts of the US economy for the next ten years. The CBO provides its forecasts twice a year in January and August. The CBO has described the process in Robert W. Arnold *How CBO Produces Its 10-Year Economic Forecast*, Congressional Budget Office Working Paper 2018-02 February 2018.

The CBO's macroeconomic model is at the heart of its forecasts. This model has about 600 endogenous variables, 300 exogenous variables, and 900 equations. Most of the equations in this model are of the type of the demand equation discussed above. In other words, these equations have an endogenous variable on the left-hand side, and endogenous variables, exogenous variables, and a random term on the right-hand side.

### *Steps to develop forecasts*

The CBO prepares its forecasts in four steps.

The first step is to **forecast the future values of the exogenous variables**. As we have seen above, exogenous variables affect the values of the endogenous variables. So, if we want to know the future values of the endogenous variable such as GDP, then we have to know the future values of the exogenous variables. So, the CBO forecasts of the future values of the exogenous variables in the model.

The second step is to prepare an **initial forecast of the economy**, using CBO's macroeconomic model. In making this forecast, the CBO feeds in the forecasted values of the exogenous variables developed in the first step.

The third step is a **review of the initial forecast.** Various experts review the second step forecast, and give their comments and suggestions for change.

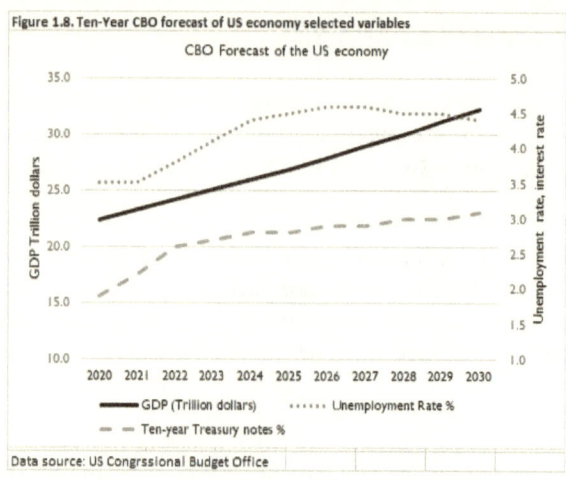

Figure 1.8. Ten-Year CBO forecast of US economy selected variables

The fourth step is the **final forecast.** The initial forecast is adjusted to take account of the comments and suggestions, and any data updates. In Figure 1.8, you can see parts of the CBO forecast released in January 2020.

## Analysis of policy changes

We now look at two separate policy changes. First, we look at the changes in tax rates enacted in 2017 under the Tax Cuts and Jobs (TCJ) Act. For this, we look at the CBO's analysis. Then we look at the increase in US tariffs in recent years. For this, we look at several studies.

### *Impact of Tax Cuts and Jobs (TCJ) Act of 2017 on the economy*

When the CBO analyzes the effect of policy changes, the changes are reflected in the values of one or more exogenous variables in CBO's macroeconomic model. In 2018, the CBO postponed the release of its ten-year forecast from January to April to have the time to analyze the effects of the changes in tax rates enacted in 2017 under the TCJ Act. In brief, the TCJ Act reduced the tax rates for businesses and individuals, though it expanded the definition of taxable income.

**The CBO analysis created two ten-year forecasts of the US economy.** One forecast, called the baseline scenario, did not include the tax changes. The other forecast, called the policy scenario, included the tax changes. Then, the differences between the values of the variables in the two scenarios were due to the tax changes.

The CBO concluded that the TCJ Act would increase the GDP and employment for every year over 2018-2028, with the highest effect in the middle years. Further, the Act would also increase the budget deficit and interest rates.

**The CBO noted that there is considerable uncertainty about these conclusions.** The main reason for this uncertainty is that CBO is not sure how households, businesses, and foreign investors will react to these tax changes. People and companies are always looking for ways to reduce the taxes they pay while obeying the rules. Hence, what exactly they will do in response to changes in tax rates is uncertain.

## Who pays when US tariffs go up?

In 2018, the US increased its tariffs on several imported products, particularly from China. When a tariff is imposed, there is a question about who actually pays the tariff. Does the exporting country pay the tariff, or does the importing country pay it?

Consider a simple case in which the US puts a 25% tariff on imports of toys from China. Suppose there is a toy that China exports for $ 10 per toy. In other words, the US importer pays $ 10 per toy. If there is no change in the import price, then the US importer would pay a duty of $ 2.50 per toy (25% of $ 10). And, the importer's cost would increase to $ 12.50. In this case, the US importer is paying all of the import duty. In turn, the importer may increase the price that the consumers have to pay.

That's not a happy situation. So, the US importer may try to negotiate down the import price. Suppose the exporter agrees to reduce the price to $ 8. Now, the importer would pay a duty of $ 2 per toy (25% of the new price of $ 8). The importer's price remains the same as before: $ 10 = $ 8 import price + $ 2 import duty. In this case, it is the Chinese exporter who is paying all of the import duty by taking a price cut.

**In the real world, we expect that there would be some sharing of the import duty between the exporter and the importer.** In other words, the Chinese exporter would reduce the price to some extent, and pay part of the duty. The remaining portion would be borne by the US importer. The actual sharing of the import duty would depend upon the particular commodity on which the tariff has been imposed.

Hence, **the actual shares can be determined only by real-world data**. However, it is not enough to just look at the import prices before and after the tariffs are imposed. The reason is that import prices change frequently due to several factors. So, just by looking at the import prices, it is not possible to be sure whether the change is due to the tariffs or due to some other factors.

What this means is that it is necessary to have two scenarios: a baseline scenario and a policy scenario, as in the CBO analysis of the TCJ Act. Since the analysis is of historical data, the policy scenario would be based on the actual data. The baseline scenario would be a hypothetical situation of what would have happened if there had been no new tariffs. As in the TCJ Act, the difference between the two scenarios would be the effect of the tariffs.

There have been several studies about who is paying the tariffs. **The conclusion is that so far most of the tariffs are being paid by the US**. One study, led by a staff member of the Federal Reserve Bank of New York, concluded, "US import price data indicate that prices on goods from China have so far not fallen. As a result, US wholesalers, retailers, manufacturers, and consumers are left paying the tax."

Another study, also led by a staff member of the Federal Reserve Bank of New York, found that "US tariffs have caused foreign exporters of steel to substantially lower their prices into the US market. Thus, **foreign countries are bearing close to half the cost of the steel tariffs**. Since China is only the tenth largest steel supplier to the US market, these costs have largely been borne by regions like the EU, South Korea and Japan."

These are the costs in the short term. If tariffs persist, then over time, US importers will look for and find ways to adjust their activities so that they have to buy less of the higher cost imports. Thus, in the longer run, the annual costs will be lower than the short-run costs. By how much? We don't know that from these studies.

## KEY TAKEAWAYS

1. Economists do two broad things. One, they try to understand how the economic world works. Second, economists use this understanding to forecast the economy, and to figure out the impact of policy changes on the economy.

### Prof. Akerlof's Nobel Prize-winning model

2. Markets will work better when buyers and sellers have the same or similar information about the product. Hence, it is worthwhile to reduce information asymmetries.

## Let's look more generally at economic models

3. Economic models have endogenous and exogenous variables. A variable is endogenous if its value is determined by the actions of the economic participants in the economic model. Otherwise, it is an exogenous variable.

4. Economic models have coefficients, which measure the strength of the relationships between the model's variables.

## Let's look at the core fields within economics

5. The core fields of specialization within economics are microeconomics, macroeconomics, international economics, and econometrics.

6. Microeconomics is built around the concepts of supply and demand. The price and the quantity bought and sold of a commodity are the main endogenous variables in microeconomic models. The detailed discussion of microeconomics is in Volume II of this book.

7. In macroeconomics, the main issue is: How is the economy doing? We look at several key endogenous variables to answer this question. These variables are the country's total income (GDP), income inequality, unemployment rate, wage rate, inflation rate, interest rate, and the government budget deficit.

8. In international economics, we look at international trade in goods and services, movements of investment money from one country to another, and movement of workers from one country to another. Two of the endogenous variables we looked at in this chapter are the trade balance and the exchange rate. The detailed discussion of international economics is in Volume II of this book.

9. Econometrics consists of statistical tools that economists use in their analyses. These tools allow economists to estimate the coefficients in an economic model, using real-world data.

## Economic forecasts and policy analysis

10. The US Congressional Budget Office (CBO) uses a macroeconomic model with about 600 endogenous variables, 300 exogenous variables, and 900 equations to produce a 10-year forecast for the key endogenous macroeconomic variables.

11. The CBO used the same model to figure out the impact of Tax Cuts and Jobs (TCJ) Act of 2017 on the US economy.

12. Two studies have found that most of the cost of the import tariffs imposed by the US in 2018 is being borne by the US, not by the exporters.

A natural question that arises in this context is: What are some of the remarkable insights that economists have been able to derive from their models? We will discuss them in the next chapter.

## CHAPTER 2.    GREAT IDEAS IN ECONOMICS

What are the great ideas in economics? **One way to find them is to look at the work of selected winners of the Nobel Prize in Economics**. It was difficult for me to choose a shortlist – I found myself trying to include many more, as all of them have made valuable contributions. Then, I decided to drop the economists whose work is mainly technical, and directly relevant for economists only. That helped a bit. Then, I created a shortlist based on my views and biases. I discussed it with some economists and took account of their comments to come up with the final list.

There's one catch with this approach. **What about all the people who lived before the Nobel Prize in Economics was set up? It makes no sense to ignore them.**

### Chapter flow

We discuss the economists in chronological order, beginning with the early economists, and ending with the Nobel Prize winners in this century.

### EARLY ECONOMISTS

I have selected five people: Kautilya, Adam Smith, David Ricardo, Alfred Marshall, and John Maynard Keynes.

### Kautilya

Hardly anyone outside India has heard of Kautilya. Let me rectify that now. Kautilya was an adviser to an Indian Emperor about 2,300 years ago. He wrote a book with the title *Arthshastra*, a Sanskrit word that loosely translates to *The Art and Science of Money*. **His focus was on how the Emperor should administer financial matters.**

Unfortunately, his book disappeared from public view, and a copy was found only in 1904. The book was translated into English a few years later.

Kautilya recommended that the government should give incentives to develop infrastructure. He wrote, "In the case of construction of new works, such as tanks, lakes, etc., taxes (on the lands below such tanks) shall be remitted for five years."

Kautilya recommended a proportional income tax system, with a rate of about 16% of your income. For people with no income, Kautilya recommended a subsidy.

Kautilya wanted the Emperor to encourage imports, partly to earn some tax revenues from import duties. The imports would also help people by increasing the variety of goods they could buy.

In short, Kautilya had many ideas that are familiar to today's economists.

## Adam Smith

Adam Smith is so famous that it is not necessary to discuss in detail here his landmark book *The Wealth of Nations* (1776). He is famous for his result that when individual producers act in their self-interest in a market system, then they will meet the consumers' needs. In other words, there is no need to tell producers what to make. **The invisible hand of the market place will guide the producers in the right direction.**

Here is one of his famous quotes.

> "It is not from the benevolence of the butcher, the brewer, or the baker, that we expect our dinner, but from their regard to their own interest. We address ourselves, not to their humanity but to their self-love, and never talk to them of our own necessities but of their advantages."

His endorsement of markets still carries considerable weight. However, there remain two significant concerns about the market system. One, the market serves only those who can afford to pay. So, what happens to those who cannot pay? In many countries, governments give some help to low-income people so that they can buy more than what their incomes allow. For example, the US provides food stamps, and other countries give doles. Currently, in the US, there is a raging debate about providing adequate healthcare to poor people.

Second, the market system may lead to local and global pollution. No one owns the air and water, so people are free to dump waste into them. Some countries have rules about what you can dump. However, there are no workable rules for global resources, such as the oceans or the earth's atmosphere.

## David Ricardo

Ricardo was a versatile economist, with many contributions that still stand today. I will discuss only one of them – his support for international trade. **Ricardo developed the concept of comparative advantage** in his analysis of international trade in his book *On the Principles of Political Economy and Taxation* (1817).

Ricardo's comparative advantage shows that international trade will benefit all participants, even if one of the participants has lower productivity across the board.

My experience is most people who use the term comparative advantage use it in its natural, intuitive sense. This is to compare two different countries in the production of the same thing. For example, my country is better than yours at producing steel. But, that's not what Ricardo meant. **Ricardo's comparative advantage concept requires a two-step calculation, not a one-step calculation.**

### *A simple example*

While Ricardo developed his concept in the context of international trade, the idea is more general than that. Here I will demonstrate it in a simple example. Let there be two commodities: food and clothing. And, let there be two people Aay and Bee.

The first step in figuring out Ricardo's comparative advantage is to calculate the cost ratio of the two commodities for each person. In this example, we calculate the ratio of the food cost to the clothing cost for Aay and Bee.

The second step is to compare Aay's cost ratio for food to clothing to Bee's cost ratio.

In other words, we compare cost ratios. We don't compare Aay's cost of producing food to Bee's cost of producing food. We don't compare Aay's cost of producing clothing to Bee's cost of producing clothing. We can write the cost ratio as the cost of food to the cost of clothing, or the way around – both ways give the same result.

Then, this is the result we get. If Aay's cost ratio is the same as Bee's cost ratio, then no one has a comparative advantage, and there will be no benefit from trade. If the cost ratios are different, then Aay will have a comparative advantage in one commodity, Bee will have a comparative advantage in the other commodity, and both will gain from trade.

## Assumptions in the comparative advantage model

To keep it simple, we make some numerical assumptions. But the results are general. Instead of numbers, we could write variables $x$ and $y$, but that would make it harder to follow. The assumptions are:

- The only cost of production is the time it takes to produce one unit of food and one unit of clothing.

- Aay has a lower cost of production for both food and clothing than Bee. Their costs are shown in Table 2.1.

Table 2.1 Food and clothing costs, and comparative advantage

|  | Food costs minutes/unit | Clothing costs minutes/unit | Cost ratio Clothing to Food | Comparison of cost ratios |
|---|---|---|---|---|
| Aay | 0.6 | 1.2 | 1.20/0.60 = 2.00 | Bee has a higher cost ratio, i.e., clothing is relatively more expensive for Bee than for Aay. So, Bee has a comparative disadvantage in clothing and a comparative advantage in food. |
| Bee | 1.0 | 3.0 | 3.00/1.00 = 3.00 | |
| Intuitive comparison | Bee has a higher cost in both food and clothing, so Bee cannot gain from trade with Aay. | | | |
| Comparative Advantage comparison | Our analysis shows that Bee has a comparative advantage in food, and both Bee and Aay will benefit from trade. | | | |

Data Source: Hypothetical

OK – so, where's the benefit of this comparative advantage? To show this, we make two more assumptions.

- Both Aay and Bee work 8 hours per day.

- Both Aay and Bee split their time equally between food and clothing, so both work 4 hours each on food and clothing.

### Pre-trade situation

Since there is no trade, Aay and Bee consume what they produce. The pre-trade production and consumption are shown in Table 2.2.

Table 2.2 Pre-trade production and consumption of food and clothing

|  | Food | Clothing |
|---|---|---|
| Aay | 100 units per hour, so **400** units in 4 hours | 50 units per hour, so **200** units in 4 hours |
| Bee | 60 units per hour, so **240** units in 4 hours | 20 units per hours, so **80** in 4 hours |

Data source: Calculations based on assumptions.

## Trade will help both Aay and Bee

First, Bee quits making clothing, in which Bee has a comparative disadvantage. So, Bee will make 480 units of food and 0 units of clothing.

Second, Bee keeps 250 units of food for own use, which is more than the 240 units Bee had in the pre-trade situation in Table 2.2. That leaves Bee with 230 units of food to trade with Aay for clothing,

Third, Bee offers Aay 230 units of food, and asks Aay to reduce Aay's production of food by 220 units. That leaves Aay with 410 units of food, which is more than what Aay had in Table 2.2. Since Aay makes 100 units of food per hour, cutting back food production by 220 units frees up 2.2 hours of Aay's time.

Fourth, since Aay makes 50 units of clothing per hour, with the freed-up 2.2 hours, Aay makes 110 additional units of clothing. Now, Aay keeps 20 units of this additional clothing units for own use, which puts Aay ahead of the pre-trade situation in Table 2.2. Then, Aay gives the remaining 90 units to Bee. Bee accepts this trade, because Bee now has 90 units of clothing, which is more than in the pre-trade situation in Table 2.2.

Table 2.3 Pre-trade and post-trade production and consumption of food and clothing

|  | Food | | | Clothing | | |
|---|---|---|---|---|---|---|
|  | Pre-trade production & consumption | Post-trade production | Post-trade consumption | Pre-trade production & consumption | Post-trade production | Post-trade consumption |
| Aay | 400 | 180 | 410 | 200 | 310 | 220 |
| Bee | 240 | 480 | 250 | 80 | 0 | 90 |
| Total | 640 | 660 | 660 | 280 | 310 | 310 |

Data source: Calculations based on assumptions

After the trade, both Aay and Bee consume more of both food and clothing, as you can see from Table 2.3 and Figure 2.1. The benefits from trade arise because Aay and Bee have different cost ratios. If their cost ratios were the same, there would be no comparative advantage and no gains from trade.

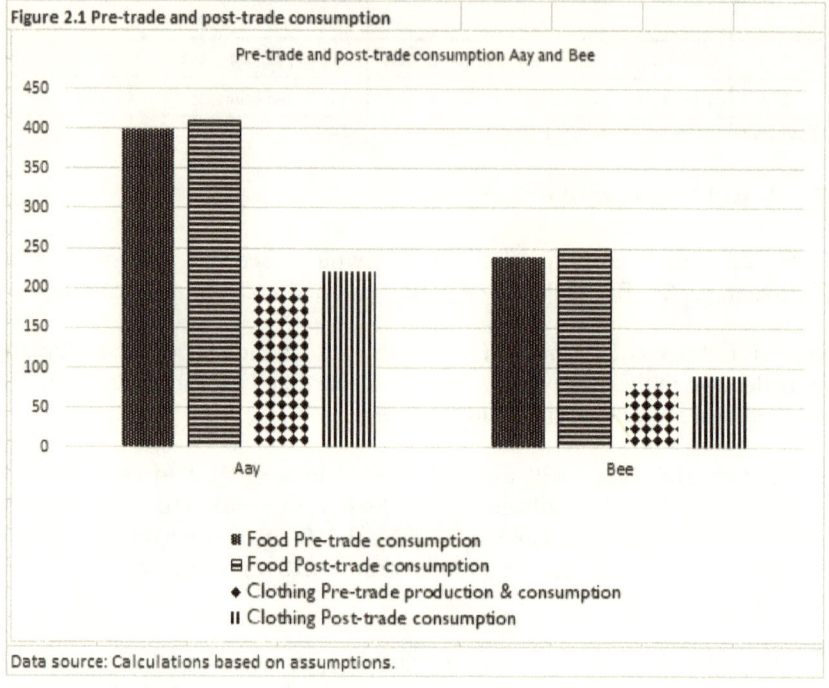

Figure 2.1 Pre-trade and post-trade consumption

Pre-trade and post-trade consumption Aay and Bee

Data source: Calculations based on assumptions.

- ❚ Food Pre-trade consumption
- ⊟ Food Post-trade consumption
- ◆ Clothing Pre-trade production & consumption
- ❙❙ Clothing Post-trade consumption

## Alfred Marshall

Marshall was a Professor of Economics at Cambridge University. He wrote *The Principles of Economics* (1890), a widely-used book. It lays out many of the concepts that economists continue to use today. **One of the concepts that Marshall developed is elasticity, which remains a key element of economic analysis.**

Elasticity is a way to measure how responsive one variable is to a change in another variable. Let's look at the elasticity of demand as an example.

We know that the quantity demanded comes down when the price of a commodity goes up. To what extent? We need to measure this in a way that can be applied to all commodities, and with any currency. The elasticity of demand is such a measure. We define the elasticity as:

*Elasticity of demand = % change in quantity / % change in price*

Let's look at an example. Suppose the owner of a bus system in a city decides to increase the fares by 20%. We know that this will reduce the demand to some extent. But how much? Suppose that demand goes down by 10%. Then, in this case, we get:

*Elasticity of demand = 10%/20% = 0.5*

However, if the demand went down by 30%, then we get:

*Elasticity of demand = 30%/20% = 1.5*

In other words, the elasticity of demand measures how responsive the demand is to price changes. A higher value of elasticity indicates that the demand is more responsive to changes in the price. Conversely, a lower value of elasticity indicates lower responsiveness.

The lowest value of elasticity is zero, which indicates no change in demand when the price goes up.

### Revenue implications of different values of elasticity

If the elasticity of demand is zero, then after the price increase, there will be no change in the number of bus riders. In this case, the bus system's revenues will go up by 20% because all riders will continue, and they will all pay the higher price.

If the elasticity of demand is 0.5%, then after the price increase, the total revenues earned by the bus system will go up but by less than 20%. The reason is that 10% of the riders will drop out, and pay nothing to the bus system.

If the elasticity of demand is 1.5%, then after the price increase, the bus system's total revenues will go down because 30% of the riders drop out and pay nothing to the bus system.

I leave it to you to figure out what happens to the bus system's revenues if the elasticity of demand is 1.0.

### Elasticity comparisons

By now, you may have noticed the elasticity is a unit-free number. This makes it easier to compare elasticities for different commodities. For example, we could compare the responsiveness of the demand for bus rides and taxi rides in a city by calculating the elasticities of demand for both of them.

We could also compare the elasticity of demand for bus rides in two different countries. There would be no issues of converting the currency of one country into the other country's currency because the elasticity is not measured in the currency of either country.

### Generalization of elasticity concept

Our example has been about the elasticity of demand with respect to price changes. However, elasticity is a general concept that works with any two variables. For example, we can calculate the elasticity of labor supply with respect to changes in income tax rates. Or, we can calculate the elasticity of demand with respect to changes in income. Or, we can calculate the elasticity of demand for loans with respect to the interest rate.

More generally, we can calculate the elasticity of variable X with respect to changes in variable Y. This general definition of elasticity is:

*Elasticity of X with respect to Y = % change in X / % change in Y*

## John Maynard Keynes

John Maynard Keynes is one of the most influential economists of recent times. Keynes wrote the ideas he is famous for in *The General Theory of Employment, Interest and Money* (1936).

He is one of the few economists who has a whole field of economics named after them. People talk about Keynesian economics and post-Keynesian economics. And, I can't think of any other economist who has been cited in the way President Nixon mentioned him. Nixon said, "We are all Keynesians now."

**Keynes is famous for the idea that when an economy is down, the government can bring it up by spending money**. Even if the government doesn't have the funds because tax collections are down due to lower incomes. It's OK for the government to borrow and spend the money.

### The Keynesian multiplier

How does Keynes' idea work? The Keynesian multiplier is at the heart of the matter.

Let's say that the economy is down, and the government borrows and spends $ 100 billion. Then, the multiplier says that the GDP will go up by a multiple of $ 100 billion. Say, the multiplier has a value of 3. Then, the GDP will go up by $ 300 billion. Now, it seems worthwhile to borrow and spend the money.

Where does the multiplier come from? It comes from a ripple effect that runs through the economy. When the government spends $ 100 billion, that money goes to some people and some companies. Call them as Group 1. Group 1 increases their consumption because they have just got some extra money.

Say they save 20% and spend the other 80%. That means Group 1, who got the initial $ 100 billion, go out and spend $ 80 billion.

Now, this $ 80 billion goes to some other people and some other companies. Call them Group 2. So far, GDP has gone up by $ 100 billion + $ 80 billion. Next, Group 2 will spend some of the $ 80 billion they earned. To keep it simple, let's say they also save 20% and spend 80%. This means that Group 2 spends $ 64 billion. So far, GDP has gone up by $ 100 billion + $ 80 billion + $ 64 billion = $ 224 billion.

Keep doing this again and again. Each time you do it, you add to the GDP but less than the previous time. We started with $ 100 billion, the next round was $ 80 billion, and then $ 64 billion. See the pattern? The next number is the previous number multiplied by 0.8. So, after $ 64 billion, we will get $ 64*0.8 = $ 51.2 billion, and so on.

Where does the 0.8 come from? It comes from the assumption that people spend 80% of the additional money they get and save 20%.

How do we add it all up? There is a formula in mathematics to add up numbers in such a series. In this case, when you apply the formula, you will get a total increase of $ 500 billion in GDP. **Or, the multiplier's value is 5.0 here.**

### Three practical issues about the multiplier

**First, how long does it take for the government to spend $ 100 billion?** It could take a long time because schemes and projects have to be formulated. And, the government has to spend the money according to rules and regulations.

That's why President Obama was looking for what he called shovel-ready projects when he was trying to boost the US economy after the 2008 economic meltdown. Shovel-ready means projects that were ready to launch right away, and the government could start spending the money quickly.

**Second, how much time do the rounds of spending** take? Does it take months for the Group 1 recipients of government money to increase their expenditure? That depends upon the country. And, it may depend upon which round of spending we are looking at.

**Third, is this multiplier for real?** What is its value in an economy? When the government borrows and spends, does it set in motion a backlash that reduces the multiplier effect? The multiplier's real-world value is a thorny issue. Some economists think that the value is too small for such government expenditures to be a useful policy tool to fight economic slowdowns.

Let's leave the discussion here, and come back to it in Volume II of this book.

## NOBEL PRIZE WINNERS 1969-1985

In 1968, Sweden's Sveriges Riksbank (central bank) announced that it would create a prize in economics. Formally, it is called the Sveriges Riksbank Prize in Economic Sciences in Memory of Alfred Nobel. So, it's different from the original five Nobel Prizes. However, it has become common to call it the Nobel Prize in Economics.

### Paul Samuelson

Many people expected that Paul Samuelson would be the first winner of the Economics prize because he was such a dominant figure. As it happened, he had to wait until the second year.

Samuelson was an all-round economist. His Prize citation says that he "has done more than any other contemporary economist to raise the level of scientific analysis in economic theory." In other words, he taught economists how to do modern economic analysis. This came in his *Foundations of Economic Analysis* (1946).

Even the title boggles my mind – in one book, you lay the foundations for a whole field. The book was based on his doctoral dissertation. So, his thesis was not about any particular topic. It was about economic analysis itself. That made him a star right away.

Economists had used mathematics in their analysis for decades before Samuelsson. **But Samuelson made mathematics an integral part of economics.** At the same time, **for Samuelson, mathematics was a tool, a means, not an end.**

He went on to write another book, *Economics: An Introductory Analysis* (1948). This was a textbook with no algebra. Just text and charts. It's probably the best-selling economics textbook ever. It was translated into multiple languages. In the 1950s and 1960s, many college economics courses used this book.

**Samuelson's textbook's influence continues even today, when there are so many other college textbooks**. For example, I learned introductory economics from this book when I was a college student. Forty years later, when I taught introductory economics, I used a different textbook. However, I could see that Samuelson's book was the base of this book, and also of most introductory economics textbooks.

So, Samuelson not only taught economists how to do economic analysis, he also taught them how to teach economics. That's not all. He wrote many path-breaking academic articles!

## Simon Kuznets

People had long been interested in looking at the economy as a whole, not sector by sector. For this, there had to be a systematic way to add up all the components. And, when you added it all up, you had to be sure that you were getting an estimate of the country's national income.

In 1934, the US Commerce Department prepared a report with the title *National Income 1929-32.* Kuznets led the preparation of this report. This report laid out two ways, still used today, to calculate national income.

The first way is to add up the incomes of the participants in the economy. The report had three broad categories of income: Labor incomes, Property incomes, and Entrepreneurial income. Add them up, and you get national income.

The second way is to add up the incomes in various sectors, such as agriculture, manufacturing, transportation, and services. Add them up, and what you get is the total income by the source of production. **It is this method that led to the commonly used term GDP, which we discussed briefly in Chapter 1.**

The two methods should give the same answer. The reason is that the value of the output in the different sectors becomes some one's income. In effect, the two ways look at the same income streams in different ways. However, to get the same answer, the data must be collected in a prescribed, systematic manner.

In short, Kuznets set in motion the idea that the US government would collect national income data, and other countries followed soon after.

## Friedrich Hayek

**If you are looking for a leading anti-Keynesian economist, you have come to the right place.** Hayek had a raging academic debate with Keynes about what causes the economy to slow down. Keynes's final shot in this debate was his famous book *The General Theory of Employment, Interest and Money.* Keynes won the debate in the mind of most economists and people interested in public policy.

**Hayek said that economic slowdowns happen when interest rates are set too low by central banks.** These low rates would lead to excessive investments and investments of the wrong type, i.e., which would not have been undertaken with correct, higher interest rates. Then, inevitably, there would be a slowdown to correct this over-spending spree. Hence, the way out was to ensure that interest rates were not distorted by wrong policies. **There was no place for Keynesian spending in this view of economic slowdowns.**

**While Keynes eclipsed Hayek, Hayek did not fade away.** His ideas influenced many economists. One of them was Milton Friedman, who also won an Economics Nobel Prize. And, Prime Minister Thatcher and President Reagan found comfort in Hayek's views in support of free markets and his writing against socialism.

Hayek's ideas continue to resonate with several groups that want to popularize Hayek's views on slowdowns, free markets, and socialism.

## Milton Friedman

**Milton Friedman, a dominant figure in economics, promoted free markets.** He was a professor at the University of Chicago. Several of the students who got their doctoral degrees from Chicago were known as the Chicago Boys. They were from Latin American countries, and went home to implement the ideas they learned at Chicago. One of the most prominent examples is the transformation of Chile from a left-leaning country to a fast-growing market-oriented economy in the later 1970s and early 1980s.

**There's no such thing as a free lunch.** Friedman used this phrase as the title of a book he wrote in 1975. He did not come up with the phrase, but he made it popular. **His point was to stress that everything has a cost that someone has to pay.** It may be free to you, but someone is bearing the cost. Economists call this opportunity cost, and we will discuss it in the next chapter.

**One of Friedman's major contributions was the concept of monetarism.** The core idea here is that the economy's growth is heavily influenced by the actions of the central bank, such as the US Federal Reserve Bank. And the primary recommendation is that the central bank should not try to increase or reduce interest rates in response to what is happening in the economy. Instead, **the central bank should focus on what economists call as money supply** and increase it in response to what is expected to occur in the economy. **Suppose the economy is expected to grow at 3%. Then, the central bank should let the money supply increase by 3%.**

We will discuss in detail what economists mean by money supply in Chapter 4. But it's worth pointing out here that major central banks have not followed this advice in recent years. Instead of looking at the money supply, most central banks have focused on keeping the inflation rate in check. Many central banks have formal or informal targets for the inflation rate. For example, the US, the EU, and the UK have a target inflation rate of around 2%, Australia 2-3%, China 3%, India 4%, and South Africa 4.5%.

## Sir W. Arthur Lewis

**Arthur Lewis was one of the first economists to focus on the growth of low-income countries.** In 1954, he wrote that these countries had two distinct sectors, or parts. One part was traditional agriculture, where most of the people worked. The other part was modern manufacturing, which had fewer workers.

**This gave rise to the term dual economy**. Meaning that these countries did not have a single, unified economy; instead, they had two separate, barely connected parts. The agricultural sector had low productivity and too many workers. Economic growth would come from some of these workers moving out every year into the modern manufacturing sector.

The wages in the manufacturing sector would stay low because there would be, as Prof. Lewis put it, an unlimited supply of labor available to manufacturing as people moved out of agriculture.

He was knighted by the Queen of England in 1963. He also became a professor at Princeton University in the same year.

# NOBEL PRIZE WINNERS 1986-1999

## Gary Becker

Becker applied standard microeconomic theory to several areas that had previously been seen as out of bounds for economists. One of these areas is the behavior of families. Becker looked at families as production units, producing goods and services for their consumption. How do families decide what they should produce, and what they should buy? And, who should do what within the family? A critical factor in this production is time. Becker developed a general theory for how a household allocates its time.

Some of the main goods and services produced in a household are cooking, cleaning, and caring for family members – all of which are time-consuming. It follows that if the market wages are high enough for the family members who would normally do these things, then they will consider working outside, and paying someone else to do this work. Or look for a machine to do some of the work. Or, buy pre-cut meat and vegetables, or ready-to-eat microwaveable food.

In fact, as women's wages and work opportunities have increased, the demand for babysitting, prepared foods, home delivery, and other such activities has increased.

Suppose family incomes rise because the income of one member, often the husband, rises. Then, family members may switch part of their time from producing goods to leisure activities. The work at home would then be done by hired workers, or by eating out. Or going on a vacation, staying in a hotel, and letting the hotel take care of all your daily needs.

**Another area that Becker worked in is wage discrimination.** Becker argued that wage discrimination based on irrelevant personal characteristics is economically inefficient. It hurts both the workers and the employer. Suppose you are a firm that uses steel as an input. Two steel plants offer the same quality of steel. One plant wants a higher price than the other one. Would you buy some of the steel from the higher price plant and some of it from the lower price plant? Usually not. You would buy all of it from the lower price plant.

If this is the right choice, why would you buy some labor at a higher price from some suppliers who have a particular personal characteristic, such as the color of their skin, or their gender? **In practical terms, what sense does it make to pay higher wages to, say, white men if their productivity is the same as, say, African-American women?** It doesn't make economic sense.

But we know that there is wage discrimination in the real world. Economists do study it. We will look at these analyses in Volume II of this book.

## Myron Scholes and Robert Merton

Fischer Black and Myron Scholes were collaborators, but Black passed away just two years before the Nobel Prize was given for their work. Robert Merton did his work separately, but it was closely related to what Black and Scholes did.

Their work is related to financial markets - Wall Street for short. By now, we know that what happens on Wall Street does affect the economy. For example, Wall Street had a role to play in the 2008 economic meltdown. **At that time, many news agencies told the public that Wall Street was slicing, dicing, and collating risky home loans in ways that made no sense and nobody could understand.**

**"That made no sense and nobody could understand." That was the wrong message**. It was difficult to understand what Wall Street was doing because most people were never taught those things. And, Wall Street uses opaque jargon, using words to mean something that has no intuitive meaning in everyday language.

From my perspective, the right message is, **"Try to understand what Wall Street does. It's no harder than learning other difficult things."** With this message, let me begin by talking about financial transactions in general, and then move to this Nobel prize.

### *Financial transactions and risk*

**Most financial transactions have an element of risk.** When you buy a home, you expect to make a profit when its value goes up in the future. So, your home is not just a place to live in. It's a risky investment. Just ask the people whose homes fell in value after the 2008 economic slowdown. They found that their loans were more than the reduced values of their homes. Some of them just stopped paying, walked out, and told their lenders to take over their homes. In 2020, there are many unfinished apartment buildings in India because home prices have declined. It's no longer worth completing the building.

**When you buy car insurance, there is a risk that you will suffer a loss**. The insurance company is betting that you will not suffer a loss, and you want to be covered in case you do suffer a loss. So, you are willing to pay a small amount every month to keep the bet going. This small amount is your insurance premium.

When you take a loan to attend college, the risk is that you will find it difficult to repay because your job will not pay enough. That makes some people scared to take a loan, and they go to a cheaper college. Now, some lenders are offering Income Sharing Agreements. Under these, you do not repay a fixed amount. Instead, you agree to pay some part, say 7-10%, of your income for several years, say ten years. You will pay less if you get a low-income job, and you will pay more if you get a high-income job. The lender is betting you will get a high-income job, and you are covered just in case you get a low-income job, or no job at all.

**In short, our everyday financial transactions have risks**. In effect, we want to shift our risks to someone else, and pay them something to do so. Simple and straightforward.

**But it does not stop there. It happens that the person taking the risk from you thinks of passing on the risk to someone else.** For example, insurance companies cover their risks by buying insurance themselves. From whom? From reinsurance companies. Lloyd's of London is one such famous company.

How does it work? Say a hurricane damages many homes in a region. The insurance company has to pay the insured people for their loss. In turn, the insurance company takes money from a reinsurance company. The insurance companies have been paying a premium to the reinsurance company. **In effect, the insurance companies have sold their bet to someone else.**

## *A simple analogy of selling a bet*

Consider a bar or a pub in which people are discussing politics. One of them, called Rum, says, "I am sure that Polix is an up and coming politician. Polix's approval rating will increase from 10% now to 40% in three months. I am willing to take a bet."

Another patron, called Wine, hears this. Wine is financially savvy. So, Wine offers this bet. "If Polix's approval rating rises, I will pay you in this way. Up to 25%, I will pay you nothing. After that, I will pay you one dollar for every point increase. For example, if Polix's rating is 37%, I will pay you $ 12 = 37-25."

Rum is happy to hear this. Wine continues, "You will have to pay me something today for me to make this bet with you. How much will you pay?"

Rum adds a complication. Make this bet in writing, and payable to whoever who has the loan paper. We will get the Bartender to sign it, which will make it official. That's fine with Wine. Then they agree that Rum will seal the deal by paying one dollar to Wine. Rum pays up.

One month later, Polix's ratings have increased to 15%. That's good news for Rum. Now, Rum goes to Gin and says, "Look at this bet. It looks like a winner to me. But I need some money today. I want to sell this bet to you."

Gin says, "I don't get it. Explain." Rum says, "Give me $ 2 today. I will transfer this paper to you. Chances are you will collect $ 12-15 from Wine in two months because Polix's approval ratings will continue to rise."

Gin is wary. "How can I be sure that Wine will pay me?" Rum says, "The Bartender has signed it. No one crosses the Bartender." Gin is satisfied.

Gin and Rum haggle. Gin and Rum agree to sell and buy the bet for $ 1.80.

In turn, Gin can sell it again later.

How does it end? I leave it to you to finish it the way you want.

What we have seen here is that bets and risk can be sold and bought.

### *Black, Scholes, and Merton*

In the Nobel Prize winners' work, the bet is about the future price of a share in a company. In the above example, replace the percent signs with dollar signs.

A share in a company called Polix sells for $ 10 today. Rum is confident that it will rise to $ 40 in three months. Wine takes the bet, and will pay $ 1.0 for every dollar the share is over $ 25. Rum pays $ 1.0 for the bet, and sells the bet later to Gin for $ 1.80.

Now for some financial jargon.

- The shares in the Polix company are called underlying assets.

- The bet described above is a call option.

- This type of a bet is also called a derivative, meaning that the bet is derived from an underlying asset. Note that this derivative is different from the derivative in calculus.

- **The opposite of a call option is a put option.** In brief, when you think that the price of a share will fall in the future, you buy a put option. If the share price does fall, you will make a profit.

**The Nobel Prize winners developed formulas for the pricing of call and put options**. In the above example, I arbitrarily set the price at $ 1.0, and the later sale price at $ 1.80. In the real world, these options are bought and sold not by one person to another person. In the US, they are bought and sold on the Chicago Board Options Exchange, just as shares are traded on the New York Stock Exchange.

Since these formulas are highly mathematical, I will not discuss them here. I just want to note that they have been adopted by financial markets and still widely used.

**All of this seems like pure speculation. Does it serve any purpose? Yes, it does.** The market price of a call option represents a balance of the opinion of many interested participants about a company's future. And, they are backing up their opinions with their money. This summary opinion could be wrong, but it still sends a clear message to the company.

## Amartya Sen

**An economist with a philosophical bent, Sen's work has focused on social welfare.** This term is economists' jargon for looking at society's well-being. The term welfare here is not related to people who are said to be on welfare when they receive payments from the government because they are poor.

**One of Sen's lasting contributions is related to the measurement of poverty.** You have probably heard of the poverty rate. This rate measures the percent of people below some poverty line, measured in terms of income or expenditures. In India, these people are called as BPL, which stands for Below Poverty Line. If you have BPL status, you are eligible for various government subsidies.

Economists call this measure as the headcount rate. You are above, or you are below the poverty line. Count the number of people below the poverty line, and calculate the percentage. Clean and simple.
**Not so fast, said Sen. Using the poverty rate ignores the depth of poverty.** A person with near-zero income is no different from a person who is just below the poverty line. That's not right because there is a huge difference in how they live.

Worse, governments who want to say that they have reduced the poverty rate may focus on people just below the poverty line. Move them above the poverty line, leaving the very poor still down in the dumps. Nevertheless, you can claim that you have successfully reduced poverty.

Sen's work inspired Foster, Green, and Thorbecke (FGT) to propose two alternative measures of poverty. They take account of how poor the poor people are. One of them, called the squared poverty gap index, gives high importance to the very poor. **The FGT squared gap measure has become widely used in the economics literature.** However, most countries do not calculate it routinely.

Sen also said that money is not the only way to look at the status of the poor. We must also look at how healthy and educated they are. Sen's views inspired the United Nations to calculate the Human Development Index, which takes account of health and education, and the Multidimensional Poverty Index, which we will discuss in Chapter 9.

# NOBEL PRIZE WINNERS 2000 ONWARDS

## Joseph Stiglitz

Stiglitz shared the Prize with George Akerlof, whose model we saw in Chapter 1, and Michael Spence. Stiglitz focused on information asymmetry in financial markets.

For example, consider the market for car insurance. The insurance company does not have full information about the drivers who are looking to buy insurance. In other words, individual drivers know their driving style and habit better than the insurance company. The insurance companies would like to get more information about the driver, but there are practical limits to what they can ask for and expect to get.

In this situation, it makes financial sense for insurance companies to set up a system in which the drivers find it worth their while to reveal more information about themselves. **Suppose you think you are a very safe driver, and there's very little chance that you will get into an accident. Then, you would prefer a policy that combines a low monthly premium and a high deductible.** Here, the deductible is the amount you have to pay before the insurance payments kick in when you have an accident.

Why is a high deductible OK for you? Why are you willing to pay a high amount before the insurance company starts to pay? Because you are confident that the chances are low that you will have an accident, and then be forced to pay the high deductible.

By choosing a low-premium high-deductible insurance policy, you have reduced some of the information asymmetries between the insurance company and yourself.

In recent years, Professor Stiglitz has focused on issues related to developing countries. He was the World Bank's Chief Economist in 1997-2000, and urged the Bank to rethink its development model. In particular, he argued that it was not enough to promote well-functioning markets in developing countries.

According to Stiglitz, the development model should recognize that governments have a major role to play in economic development. For example, governments have a key role in creating physical infrastructure, ensuring that all people have access to quality education and finance, and in supporting technology and innovation.

## Muhammad Yunus

Yunus is the only economist to have won the Nobel Peace Prize, not the Economics Prize. And, perhaps the one whose ideas have directly helped millions of poor people. His main idea was to give small loans to poor people in villages to finance their micro-projects to increase their incomes. Then, make sure they pay back the loans. It's called micro-finance because the loans are so small.

Before Yunus, it was tough to give loans to poor villagers, particularly women. Usually, they had no collateral, which most lenders want. Given the small size of the loan, it was too costly to evaluate the borrowers and their projects. But, Yunus found ways to overcome these problems, and micro-finance has spread to many countries.

Micro-finance has increased the incomes of most of its borrowers, even if it has not pushed them above the poverty line. Some people complain that the micro-finance interest rates are too high – they can be as high as 20-30% per year. However, these are realistic rates in the areas for these microloans. Anyhow, for these borrowers, it is the ability to get a loan that is more important than the interest rate itself.

In some instances, the borrowers have taken more loans than they can repay. This has created difficulties for the borrowers, who are trapped in debt, and the lenders, who run the risk of not getting their money back.

In some countries, such as India, micro-finance has given way to a system of providing a variety of financial services, not just loans, to low-income people. This development makes it clear that poor people need modern financial services just as much as well-off people.

## Paul Krugman

Before Krugman, the most recent version of the economic theory of international trade dated to 1933, with an update from Samuelson in the early 1950s. It was showing signs of being outdated. For example, it could not explain why Japan would export certain types of cars to the US, and import different types of cars from the US. How could this fit with the notion of comparative advantage?

**Krugman updated and expanded the conventional theory of international trade.** One part of his theory was to give up the assumption that 'cars are cars.' Instead, there are different types of cars. Another part of his approach was that it pays to specialize in the type of cars that you produce. In particular, assume that the average cost of production falls as the scale of production increases.

American companies might choose to focus on large cars, which they would sell in the US. If they export some of their cars to Japan, this will increase their scale of production. In turn, this would reduce the average cost of production of American cars. And suppose that some Japanese consumers want large cars, not the small cars typically made by Japanese car companies. Now, there will be good chances of exporting large American cars to Japan.

Japanese companies might choose to focus on smaller cars, which they would sell in Japan. If they export some of their cars to the US, this will increase their scale of production. In turn, this would reduce the average cost of production of Japanese cars. And, suppose that some American consumers want small cars, not the large cars typically made by US car companies. Now, there will be good chances of exporting small Japanese cars to the US.

Thus, two different countries would export cars to each other but of different types. The driving forces would be a diversity of consumer tastes and cost reductions arising from increases in the scale of production.

## Richard Thaler

**Richard Thaler is one of the pioneers of behavioral economics, which introduces some psychological factors in explaining people's behavior.** Thaler brought in three psychological factors.

**The first new factor is called limited rationality.** This is different from conventional economic theory, which assumes that people are fully rational in making their decisions. Full rationality means you look at everything carefully, and then choose what is best for you from all available options. **Limited rationality implies that people don't consider everything – they make their decisions in a simplified way.**

How do people limit what they consider in making limited rationality decisions? There does not seem to be a simple, general theory about it.

**The second new factor is that our sense of fairness affects our decisions.** For example, tourists often tip taxi drivers and restaurant waiters. Since the tippers are unlikely to meet the same servers again, the tippers are not expecting better service from these people in the future. Yet, they tip even though it costs them some money because tipping is the norm, and they want to be fair to the servers.

**The third new factor is a lack of self-control.** Oscar Wilde said, "The only way to get rid of temptation is to yield to it ... I can resist everything but temptation." Most of us are like this to some extent. We overeat even though we know that this is a bad idea. We find it hard to give up cigarettes or drugs though we know they are unhealthy. We delay doing our work even though we know it will cause problems later on. In other words, we focus on consumption now, not its longer-run effects. We cannot help ourselves.

*A practical example*

Let's look at a practical example. Suppose you want to increase the number of people who will donate their organs in case of accidental death. You could offer people a chance to enroll in this program, at a suitable time, such as when they meet a doctor.

The doctor asks you, "Do you want to take part in this program?" **We call this the opt-in method**. No one has made a decision on your behalf. **You are free to get into the program if you want to,**

Or, the doctor could first enroll you, and then ask, "Do you want to not take part in this program?" **We call this the opt-out method**. Someone has made a decision on your behalf. **You are free to get out of the program if you want to.**

If there is full rationality, the results should be the same with these two methods. People who want to participate will do so, and those who don't want to participate will not do so. There is no compulsion. However, **in practice, the participation rates are higher with opt-out than with opt-in. It seems that the opt-out approach nudges people to make a particular choice, without any compulsion.**

This finding has led some people to suggest that governments or companies should use nudges to promote the choices that they favor. For example, some US companies have enrolled their employees in a savings plan, and then let them opt out of it. The companies found that this led to higher participation rates than with an opt-in method. However, some people do complain that this approach smacks of paternalism or Big Brother, and reject the opt-out plan.

## William Nordhaus

Nordhaus created a Dynamic Integrated Model of Climate Change and Economy (DICE) designed to figure out the suitable economic policies to fight climate change. In effect, it is a macroeconomic model for the world as a whole with forecasts for many decades in the future. **The specific new feature of DICE is that climate change is an intrinsic part of the model.**

The model works in this way.

**Step 1.** Economic production is associated with greenhouse gas emissions.

**Step 2.** Greenhouse gas emissions bring about future changes in the climate.

**Step 3.** The future changes in the climate reduce the world's future output, based on the relationships between the climate variables and economic variables.

### The discount rate is a key feature

Now, compare the current gain in production with future losses in production. To do so, we use a discount rate.

The discount rate is conceptually similar to the interest rate in the compound interest formula. In compounding interest, we usually calculate how much an amount of money will grow into in the future. For example, we start with $ 100 today with an interest rate of 5%. We let it grow for years.

What do we have 50 years later? The answer is that the money will grow to about $ 1,146.

When we discount, we run the compound interest formula in reverse. Suppose we want $ 1,000 in our account fifty years in the future. The interest rate is still 5%.

How much do we have put in today to get to $ 1,000 fifty years into the future? The answer is about $ 88. That will grow into $ 1,000.

Formally, in this example, we would say that the discounted value of $ 1,000 fifty years in the future (with no inflation) with a discount rate of 5% is $ 88 today.

The discount rate can be interpreted as a way of quantifying how concerned we are about the future. If the discount rate is zero, then we are very concerned about the future. Specifically, we say that $ 1,000 today is the same as $ 1,000 in the future, no matter how far into the future we look. When you use a zero interest rate in a compound interest rate formula, there is no growth.

Or, if the world is going to lose $ 1,000 in output (with no inflation) fifty years from now, then that future $ 1,000 is as important or valuable as an output of $ 1,000 today.

**However, if the discount rate is higher, then we care more about today than the future**. For example, if the discount rate is 5%, then $ 1,000 in output fifty years in the future is worth only about $ 88 today.

What's the right discount rate? That's a contentious issue, which we will discuss in Volume II. Once we have set the discount rate, we are in a position to determine how much climate change to avoid in the future.

### What does the model do for us?

The model determines how much climate change to avoid or accept in the future. No doubt, this is a subjective outcome, but the underlying assumptions and processes are clear and transparent.

Once we know how much climate change to avoid in the future, DICE can determine the policy measures to be implemented now and over time that will mitigate the greenhouse gas emissions by the required amount.

## KEY TAKEAWAYS

I set out to describe some of the great ideas that economists have developed over the years. We saw that these ideas cover a wide variety of topics. I think there is no need to summarize the ideas here, and I have not done this.

We also saw that there are some differences among economists. Some of the differences are intrinsic, and cannot be resolved by compromise.

The first and second chapters have focused on a broad range of economic ideas and concepts. In the next chapter, we move to a more detailed look at a core concept in economics: scarcity.

## Chapter 3.   Economics of Scarcity

We are all familiar with scarcity. We don't have enough time to do everything we want to do. And we don't have enough money to buy everything we want to buy. So, we end up juggling time and money until we come up with an allocation of time and money that's the best option for us.

**For economists, scarcity is a key, persistent feature of economic life.** Even though we have had economic growth for centuries, most countries are still faced with a scarcity of goods and services. There just does not seem to be enough for all.

So, countries have to make decisions about how they allocate their scarce resources. And, the world as a whole has to make decisions about scarce global resources – whether in coordination or haphazardly.

### Chapter flow

This chapter has six main parts. We begin by looking at opportunity costs, which are the relevant costs in economic decisions related to scarcity. In the second part, we look at the nature of decision-making with scarcity. We show that the decisions to allocate scarce resources follow the marginal principle. In the third section, we show that markets allocate scarce resources properly, with a major exception called externalities.

We discuss the concept of externalities in the fourth part, with some real-world examples in the fifth part. Finally, in the sixth part, we discuss the parts of the economy where most countries don't use markets to allocate resources.

### TRUE COSTS ARE MEASURED BY OPPORTUNITY COST

When we consider how to allocate resources or money, we have to look at the costs and benefits of our decisions. In this section, we discuss how to measure costs.

**Economists use the term opportunity cost to define and measure costs in the context of scarcity.** The idea behind this term is simple. When you choose something over other options, you give up other options or other opportunities. Say you choose Option A, and Option B is the next best option for you. **Then, the opportunity cost of choosing Option A is the value of Option B.**

Let's look at a simple example. Say, you get a full scholarship to attend a college. No tuition fees, and a stipend to cover your textbooks, living costs, etc. So, in this case, what is your cost of attending college? Zero because you are not paying anything.

That's the wrong answer. Your financial costs are indeed zero. But you are giving up the opportunity to work and make some money. That's part of your costs.

In short, your true cost of going to college is not just your financial expenditure of attending college. It's your financial expenditure plus the value of what you don't do because you go to college.

As an economist, I knew this, but it came home to me when I was about 40 years old. I thought it would be a good idea for me to get a law degree – have always been fascinated by the law. I figured that I could manage to pay for law school for three years. But I would also have to give up most of my earnings for those years. Together, it was too costly. I never got a law degree.

## International dumping

**There is a real-world application of the opportunity cost concept in international trade.** This is called dumping, where the term dumping does not have its usual meaning. Instead, it's a jargon term with a special meaning, which is easier to understand with an example.

China sells shoes in the European Union (EU). The EU thinks that the price of Chinese shoes is too low. What does too low mean? It means that the selling price is below China's opportunity cost of production. As we saw above, the opportunity costs are not necessarily the same as the financial cost. **So, dumping means selling a product abroad at a price that is below your opportunity cost.**

Why is dumping a problem? How can you lose if someone wants to sell you things at low prices? The answer is that consumers don't lose. However, the low prices do hurt local producers in what is seen as unfair competition. So, **the purpose of preventing dumping is to protect domestic producers in the importing country.**

Note that the price could be above the exporter's financial cost. If the price is above the financial cost, there will be a financial profit, not a financial loss. Say a government gives an exporting company some inputs, such as electricity or land for its factories, at a subsidized price. That reduces the exporting company's financial costs. So, the exporter can sell abroad at a low price, and make a financial profit.

However, the subsidy from the government does not change the opportunity cost. The subsidy means that the government is bearing part of the opportunity cost. So, an exporter could be making a financial profit but still be selling below the opportunity cost.

In 2005, the EU began a formal investigation of a complaint that China and Vietnam were dumping leather shoes in Europe.

The EU declared China and Vietnam as nonmarket economies, meaning economies in which prices were not determined by market forces. The implication was that the actual costs of producing shoes in these countries were not acceptable, as they were not opportunity costs.

So, the EU set out to calculate the economic costs of producing the shoe. For this, the EU looked for a country that made shoes, with the prices of the inputs determined by markets. The EU decided that Brazil was a suitable country for this purpose.

Next, the EU found out the costs of producing shoes in Brazil. Brazil's costs were higher than the price of shoes from China and Vietnam. The EU took the Brazilian costs to be the true costs of shoe production in China. **As a result, while the exporters in China and Vietnam were making financial profits, they were still judged to be dumping, in the jargon sense, shoes because the selling price was below the opportunity costs, as measured in Brazil.**

Based on this finding, the EU imposed import duties on shoes from China and Vietnam. These duties would raise the prices of the shoes in the EU, with the result that the selling price would be above the opportunity cost.

## Difference between private costs and social costs

Consider again the example in which you get a full scholarship to cover all your college financial costs. However, there are still some costs of your attending college. You are not paying these costs. **Your private costs are zero.** However, whoever gave you the scholarship is paying these costs. **We call the actual costs that occur when you attend college as social costs.**

In many situations, there is no difference between private and social costs. However, as we will see below, **there are several significant situations where there is a difference between private and social costs.** In these situations, resources may be wrongly allocated, as we will discuss later in this chapter.

## UNDER SCARCITY, RESOURCE ALLOCATION DECISIONS TAKE PLACE AT THE MARGIN

Now that we have the economic definition of costs, we can look at how to compare costs and benefits in making a decision. We don't have a special definition of benefits. For individuals, we do know that the benefits of the same action can vary from person to person. And, when we are looking at a group level, we have to find some way of aggregating the benefits. This aggregation can be subjective. For the moment, let's assume that we have some way of quantifying the benefits.

**Often, a key choice that we have to make is not whether to do something but how much of it.** For example, if you have a car, one of your decisions is how many miles to drive each month. Let's say you are driving a gasoline car. Suppose the price of gasoline goes up. What's your response to this change, given that you have a limited budget? You may decide to drive less. For example, you may not be able to change your commute, but you may decide it's no longer worth it to drive to that far-away store.

In other words, you would be comparing the benefits of driving to that store to the cost of driving to that store. And you may conclude that you would not do it any longer. This would not be a significant change in your total miles per month because you would still have your commute miles. It's a small, marginal change.

### Equality between marginal benefit and marginal cost

Let's put this in a formal context, and define what we call marginal benefit (MB) and marginal cost (MC). Here, the word marginal refers to a small change. And note that we use the term change, which allows for a small increase and a small decrease.

*An example*

Consider a small change in the miles you drive. It could be an increase of one mile in the total miles you drive. Then, the benefit you get from driving that extra mile is your additional benefit (MB). The benefits are real – we call them marginal because they are coming from a change in what you do.
What about a decrease of one mile in your driving? Now, you will lose some benefits. The benefits you lose by driving one mile less are also your MB. In other words, MB is a number by which your benefits change. The change can be positive – which means you get some more benefits. Or, the change can be negative, which means that you lose some benefits,

Thus, the MB of driving is measured by the change (increase or decrease) in your total benefits of driving from a change (increase or decrease) of one mile in the total miles you drive.

Similarly, **we can define marginal cost (MC) as the extra cost of driving that additional mile**. Again, the costs are real – we call them marginal because they are linked to a marginal change in what you do.

To repeat, MB and MC are the benefit and cost associated with a marginal change in your activity, which, in this case, is the miles you drive.

### Decision rule MB = MC

One mile? Who even looks at one mile when you are driving more than a thousand miles a month? True. In our simplified analysis, we are assuming that you spend your money very carefully, in a calculated manner, down to the last mile. This allows us to derive insights that are generally applicable.

In fact, in real life, we do make some decisions in such marginal terms. How much sugar do you want to add to your coffee? How much salt do you want to add? Your answer may be, "Just a bit more." And, when you are walking, that extra mile may indeed be a critical decision point.

In short, people consider their MB and their MC when they think about the extent of their activity. How much to eat? How much to drive? How much to work? How much TV time? When people say, "No more," economists say that at this point, the MC is more than their MB. Or, it's not worth doing it. On the other hand, when people say, "Let's do more," economists say that the MB is more than the MC.

**It turns out that the final stopping point comes when the marginal benefit is equal to the marginal cost, i.e., MB = MC**. At this point, you don't want to do more because it's not worth it. And you don't want to do less because doing more is still good.

### Mathematical foundations of decision rule

**The MB = MC result is consistent with what mathematics teaches us.** You can read it or just jump ahead to the conclusion if you find even the mention of calculus intimidating. To start, define

*Net Benefits = Total Benefits – Total Costs*

In the above example, the benefits and costs depend upon the miles you drive. Then, calculus tells us how to find the value of miles that will maximize Net

Benefits. In other words, calculus tells us how many miles you should drive to get the maximum net benefits from driving.

Calculus requires us to take the first derivative of Net Benefits with respect to miles. Then, as required by calculus, set the first derivative equal to zero, and solve the equation for the miles to be driven. In turn, taking the derivative of Net Benefits implies that you have to take the first derivatives of Total Benefits and Total Costs.

From calculus, the first derivative of Total Benefits with respect to miles driven is the change in Total Benefits when the distance driven changes by a minimal (minuscule/infinitesimal) amount in the miles driven. Just above, we had defined this term as MB. In other words, **MB is the first derivative of Total Benefits.**

Similarly, from calculus, the first derivative of Total Costs with respect to miles driven is the change in Total Costs when the distance driven changes by a minimal distance (minuscule/infinitesimal) amount in the miles driven. Earlier, we had defined as MC. In other words, **MC is the first derivative of Total Costs.**

To maximize Net Benefits, we need the first derivative of Net Benefits to be equal to zero. We can write this as:

$$MB - MC = 0$$
Or

$$MB = MC.$$

So, calculus teaches us that MB = MC is the condition for maximizing your net benefits, taking account of benefits and costs. **In short, optimal decision making occurs at the margin, and, in the end, we should have MB = MC.**

Note that in getting to this result, we did not put any constraints on what you consider as benefits. That's why the result is so general. The benefits are what the decision-makers think they are, and they act according to their own sense of the benefits. **Hence, this result applies not only to the decisions of individuals but also to national and international decisions.**

## MARKETS NORMALLY ALLOCATE RESOURCES PROPERLY

How are a country's resources allocated? Who decides what is to be produced, and with which resources?

In market economies, these decisions are heavily influenced by people's willingness and ability to spend their money. Private firms are in the market to make a profit for themselves and their shareholders. So, they produce what sells and gives them a profit. This is what Adam Smith taught us – how the invisible hand of the market place guides firms to meet the consumers' needs.

In looking to make good profits, private firms seek to keep their costs low. Their costs depend upon the prices of the inputs they use, including workers. This brings us to the markets for inputs, which are different from the markets for the goods and services consumers want to buy. For example, none of us wants to buy stainless steel. But firms that make forks, spoons, refrigerators, cars, and many other things have to buy steel from steel producers. So, there is a market for stainless steel. And, then firms that make stainless steel have to buy iron, coal or some other fuel, and various other things to make stainless steel. Next, think about the markets for iron and coal.

In short, there are markets for what consumers buy and markets for what producers buy. Together, the markets for consumer goods and production inputs allocate resources in a country. Markets also determine the prices of all these things, including the earnings of people in the workforce.

## Apply the MB = MC rule to resource allocation

In the end, for resources to be properly allocated, the result MB = MC should hold throughout the economy. If it does, then resources are allocated properly.

It's a core result in economics that markets generally allocate resources efficiently. However, this result does not hold when there is a difference between social costs and private costs. The reason is that markets operate according to private costs. In contrast, resources should be allocated according to social costs, as these are the true costs.

We will discuss this result in detail below. But before we do this, let's look at one significant condition that must be met for markets to work properly.

### *Role of governments*

For markets to work properly, governments need to protect the property rights of the market participants, and provide ways to settle commercial disputes. Among the properties to be protected are intellectual properties, which include patents, copyrights, trademarks, trade secrets, and even seeds, plants, fish, and food items created in labs. Without the protection of property rights, the incentive to invest in any business would be limited. The reason is that you would not be sure of getting or keeping your earnings.

And, the government must set up a legal system that settles commercial disputes quickly and fairly. Without this system, there would be limited faith in commercial agreements and transactions.

## MARKETS DON'T ALLOCATE RESOURCES PROPERLY WHEN THERE ARE EXTERNALITIES

Sometimes economists adopt awful words as their jargon for significant concepts. One of these words is externality. Let's ignore the unappealing aspects of the term, and focus on what it means.

### Externality rule

What's an externality? It's easiest to understand it from an example. Suppose you play your guitar or your music system loudly at night, and disturb my sleep. The fact that you bother me without compensating me at all means that my well-being depends upon an external source. **Formally, there is an externality when there is a negative impact on one person (me) from the actions of another person (you).**

Another way to look at this situation is to note that there is a difference between the private cost of the responsible person and social costs. In this case, you are the responsible person. When you play loud music, your private cost is zero. However, this leads to some cost for me. So, the social cost is greater than zero, while your private cost is zero.

This externality leads to a misallocation of resources. In particular, you produce more loud music than you should be creating.

This leads us to a general rule: markets don't allocate resources properly when there are externalities.

### *Positive externalities*

So far, we have looked at externalities that have a negative impact. However, **we can also have positive externalities.** Assume that I have an attractive garden in my front yard. (Not much of an assumption. It's pretty accurate.) People who are walking by enjoy it, and sometimes stop to tell me that they enjoy it. But they don't pay me for this benefit that they get.

That leads to a positive externality. The reason is that there is a difference between my private benefit and social benefits. If I took account of the social benefits, I would devote even more resources to create a better garden than I have.

So, more generally, we can think of an externality as a situation in which one person's actions have a negative or positive impact on someone else. Or, there is a difference between private and social costs, or between private and social benefits.

We will see below some real-world situations in which negative externalities have a substantial negative impact. But externalities can be tackled and mitigated.

## Ways to tackle externalities

There are three common ways of tackling externalities, particularly negative externalities.

**One way is to issue rules and regulations**. We call this the command-and-control approach. For instance, in the above case of loud music, the authorities can ban loud music or all loud activities at night. In effect, there is a rule about how loud your music can be at night.

**A second way is to create a market** in which the right to engage in the externality activity is bought and sold. For example, in the above case of loud music, I could offer you this deal. For every hour of loud music that you play between 10 pm and 1 am, you pay me 100 pesos per hour. After that, the rate goes up to 200 pesos per hour. You agree. You play loud music, and you compensate me.

There's a controversial theoretical flip possible here. In theory, but perhaps not a probable real-world occurrence, we could reverse the payment system. In this flip, I would pay you not to play loud music when I don't want to be disturbed. In other words, I buy my peace and quiet.

Let's go back to the case where you pay me. Now your private cost has gone up from zero to what you pay me. So, you will balance your benefit from playing loud music against the cost. At the same time, my negative benefit from your music has now been removed.

**A third way is to levy a tax.** The tax would be paid by the person creating the externality. In the above example, the person playing loud music at night would pay the tax to the government. Such a tax is often called a Pigouvian tax, in honor of Professor Pigou, who put forward the idea in 1920.

**Economists call the second and third ways as internalizing the externality.** (Yes, they do, even though it an awful choice of words.) Let's call the loud music as a form of noise pollution. Then, what we are doing is asking the polluter – the person creating the loud music – to pay. When we apply it more generally to other forms of pollution, we call it the **polluter pays principle.** In other words, increase the costs of the polluter.

## SOME REAL-WORLD EXAMPLES OF EXTERNALITIES

Let's look at several examples of negative externalities, and how they have been tackled.

One common feature in many negative externalities is a lack of private ownership of a resource. Instead, the resource is said to be common property. In this case, there is no market for the resource, and people and companies can use it without any payment. **When a resource is commonly owned, it tends to be over-exploited. This phenomenon is called the Tragedy of the Commons.**

However, it is not necessary that commonly-owned resources will always suffer from the Tragedy of the Commons. Elinor Ostrom got an Economics Nobel Prize for showing how common property can be successfully managed by local people without any regulation by central authorities or privatization.

Let's look at the origin of the term Tragedy of the Commons.
In 1832, an English economist named Lloyd pointed out that the pasture on the common lands in England was in bad shape. He wrote, "Why is the common itself so bare-worn, and cropped so differently from the adjoining inclosures (sic)?" The difference was not due to some inherent quality of the pasture. Instead, it was due to the difference in how common and enclosed pastures were managed.

The enclosed pastures were privately owned. An owner had an incentive to maintain a private pasture so that the owner's cattle could continue to graze on the land into the future. However, this incentive was missing for common pastures. In fact, there was an incentive to let your cattle graze on the common pasture before other people's cattle grazed it down. Once the land became bare-worn, it could not provide enough sustenance to the cattle, and its use would end or at least slow down. But the land could never recover fully.

In 1968, a biologist named Hardin coined the term Tragedy of the Commons to describe this situation.

This over-exploitation is a case of a negative externality. My cattle grazing on the commons leaves less grass for your cattle, and for all cattle in the future. **Thus, a negative externality can hurt not only other people now but also people in the future.**

## Examples of command-and-control policies

**Under the command-and-control approach, the government sets rules on what is permitted, and everyone has to follow the rules.** We will look at two examples here. The first one is about emissions from cars. The second example is about pollution in a major water body in the US.

### Emissions from cars

**Most countries have restrictions on emissions from automobiles.** One of the earliest controls was to remove lead from gasoline. The use of leaded gasoline increased the public's exposure to lead, which has adverse health effects. In other words, there was a difference between the private cost and social cost of using leaded gasoline. Thus, there was an externality. This externality was tackled by requiring all cars to use unleaded gasoline. Similarly, in many countries, all cars must have catalytic converters, which reduce the cars' emissions of some gases that harm the public.

This command-and-control has been successful, and there is no major debate now about it.

### Pollution in the Chesapeake Bay

Figure 3.1 Chesapeake Bay watershed

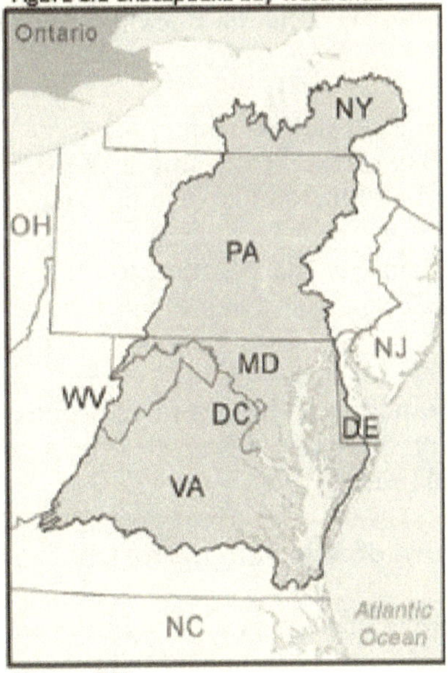

Source: EPA

**The Chesapeake Bay, the largest estuary in the US, is polluted.** The Bay's watershed covers six States (New York, Pennsylvania, West Virginia, Virginia, Maryland, and Delaware) and the District of Columbia, as shown in Figure 3.1.

According to a report by the US Environmental Protection Agency (EPA) published in 2010,

63

"The Bay and its rivers are overweight with nitrogen, phosphorus and sediment from agricultural operations, urban and suburban runoff, wastewater, airborne contaminants and other sources. The excess nutrients and sediment lead to murky water and algae blooms, which block sunlight from reaching and sustaining underwater Bay grasses. Murky water and algae blooms also create low levels of oxygen for aquatic life, such as fish, crabs and oysters."

In 2010, the EPA decided to set a Total Maximum Daily Load (TMDL), which set limits on how much pollutants could flow into the Bay every day. The TMDL reduced the nitrogen and phosphorus flowing into the Bay by about 25% each, and sediment by about 20%. The reductions were to be achieved in full by 2025. The EPA allocated cutbacks to the various States, after discussions with the States. It was up to each State to figure out how it would achieve its cutbacks.

Several groups filed a legal challenge to the EPA plan soon after it was announced. The argument was that the EPA did not have the legal authority to implement such a plan. The case took time to make its way through the legal system. Finally, in 2016, the US Supreme Court ruled in favor of the EPA.

In December 2019, the EPA released its assessment of the implementation plans submitted by the six States and the District of Columbia. **The EPA concluded that five of the seven jurisdictions were not on track to achieve their goals.**

Further, there have been concerns that under President Trump, the EPA is not really committed to the Chesapeake Bay cleanup plan. In March 2020, Maryland and the non-profit Chesapeake Bay Foundation were thinking of suing the EPA because the EPA did not appear to them to be serious about forcing Pennsylvania to meet its targets. Pennsylvania is critical to meeting the TMDL goals because it is the most significant contributor to the nutrients flowing into the Bay.

In the case of the Chesapeake Bay cleanup, the command-and-control approach has run into legal and political problems. At this time, there is no assurance that the 2025 TMDL targets will be met.

## Example of creating a market: Control of acid rain in the US

In the US in the 1980s, there was a concern that the rain falling from the clouds was not pure water. The rain contained a small amount of sulfuric acid in it. Acid? In the rain? How come?

It came from coal-burning power plants that generated electricity. The coal was not pure. It had some amounts of sulfur mixed in it. Burn the coal, burn the sulfur. That led to emissions of sulfur dioxide gas into the atmosphere. The gas mixed with moisture in the clouds, and became sulfuric acid.

So, the need was to cut back on sulfur emissions from several power plants. There was a scientific consensus that cutting back the gas emissions by half would be enough. The command-and-control way would be to force each power plant to cut back its emissions by 50%.

Forcing each power plant to cut back would be costly because some plants were too old to be easily retrofitted with pollution-reducing equipment. However, **economists had a cheaper way to cut back gas emissions. It's called cap-and-trade.**

The US EPA identified all the responsible power plants, and their sulfur dioxide emissions. In the first phase (1995-1999), the EPA included 263 highly polluting power plants. In 2000, the EPA extended the program to more than 3,200 power plants.

**Then, the EPA created emission permits equal to half of the total 1980 emissions. This was the cap in the cap-and-trade program.** The power plants got these permits for free – no payment. The catch was that for each power plant, the permits were less than its current emissions.

Now, **each power plant had two choices**. One choice was to cut back its emissions to the allowed limit. The other option was to not cut back and compensate by buying permits, or offsets as they are now called, from other power plants. In effect, there would be a market in which power plants would buy and sell permits. **This was the trade part of the cap-and-trade.**

Who were the sellers? Some power plants would cut back even more than the allowed limit. They would sell this extra cutback to another power plant. The buyers would be power plants that found it expensive to cut back. They would buy offsets instead of cutting back.

How did this help? Some power plants found it costly to cut back. So, they limited the amount of their cutback. Other power plants could cut back cheaply. They saw it as a way to make some money by cutting back, and selling the permits. **So, the cutbacks would come from the power plants that found it the cheapest to cut back.**

In 1990, the average cost of the cutback was estimated to be $550 per ton of sulfur dioxide, with a range of $370-$800. The actual costs were around $ 200-250 per ton. However, a part of the lower costs was due to factors other than the cap-and-trade program, such as lower costs for low-sulfur coal.

Overall, the cap-and-trade program curbed sulfur dioxide emissions as required. Those power plants that found it expensive to cut back - they chose to buy permits, instead of cutting back. On the other hand, power plants that found it cheap to cut back - they cut back more than they needed to. Hence, the program ensured that the cutbacks would come from power plants with lower costs of cutting back. This was cheaper than asking all the power plants to cut back.

*Look at the acid rain outcome in terms of the marginal principle.*

Let's look at the acid rain program in terms of the marginal principle. **Consider first a power plant that has low costs of cutting back**. The cost of cutting back one ton of sulfur dioxide is the plant's marginal cost MC. The benefit of selling this ton of permit is the price of cutbacks in the market. This is the MB. If the MB is greater than the MC, the manager of this power plant will cut back. However, if the MB is less than the MC, the plant's manager will say, "Don't cut back." In effect, **the manager will stop when MB = MC**.

Now, **look at a power plant that has high costs of cutting back**. The benefits for this plant's manager are the cost savings from not cutting back emissions. So, for this manager, the MB is the cost savings from not cutting back one ton of emissions. The MC is the cost of buying a permit for one ton of emissions in the market. Again, so long as the MB is more than the MC, the manager will say, "Buy some more." However, if the MB is less than the MC, the manager will say, "Don't buy more." In effect, **the manager will stop when MB = MC.**

Thus, the overall process will stop when MB = MC for all the plants. The required cutback would be achieved because that's the cap already imposed at the outset. And, we can go beyond this result.

## A powerful general rule from the acid rain program Price = Marginal Cost

Now we derive the result that P = MC, or the price is equal to the marginal cost when the market settles down.

From the viewpoint of the sellers of cutbacks, the MB is the price that they get when they sell permits. So, we get the result:

$$P = MB$$

We already know that

$$MB = MC$$

Let's put them together. This gets us

$$P = MB = MC$$

Or, we can write:

$$P = MC.$$

This is the result we are looking for.

We derived this result by looking at the market from the sellers' viewpoint. Does it hold up from the buyers' perspective? The buyers are not producing cutbacks – they are buying cutbacks. As we noted above, the MC is the cost of buying a permit for one ton of emissions. Hence, here we get the same result:

$$P = MC$$

Hence, it's confirmed that P = MC from the viewpoint of both sellers and buyers in this market.

This result is broader than in just this example. The more general result is that markets allocate resources properly when they follow this result, i.e., the price is equal to the marginal cost. In the above example, the allocation we are looking for is which firms should devote resources to cut back sulfur dioxide emissions,

Formally, we get this result for competitive markets, with several assumptions that are not always valid in the real world. For this reason, **P = MC is taken as a kind of ideal outcome that we should aim for.** We will see a significant real-world example below when we look at the economics of climate change.

## Example of creating a market: Preventing overfishing

In the US and some other countries, the danger of overfishing has been recognized for many decades. The initial response was to put in place programs that limited the total amount of fish, by species, that could be caught in a particular fishing season. However, there were no restrictions on how much fish an individual could catch. It was a variant of the command-and-control approach. Call it the limited catch method.

However, there were concerns that the programs were not working well. One problem was what came to be called the "race to fish." In other words, catch the fish as soon as possible because the allowed quota would be exhausted

67

soon by other people catching the fish. And, this led to increased investment in larger fishing vessels so that you could catch more fish quickly.

### Catch shares approach

The limited catch method has been replaced by programs whose umbrella name is catch share. These programs create individual fishers as owners of part of the allowed catch. These shares are in the fish that can be caught now and in the future. Most importantly, these shares can be sold. Figure 3.2 shows how the program works in New Zealand, a pioneer in implementing these programs.

Figure 3.2 How the catch share program works in New Zealand.

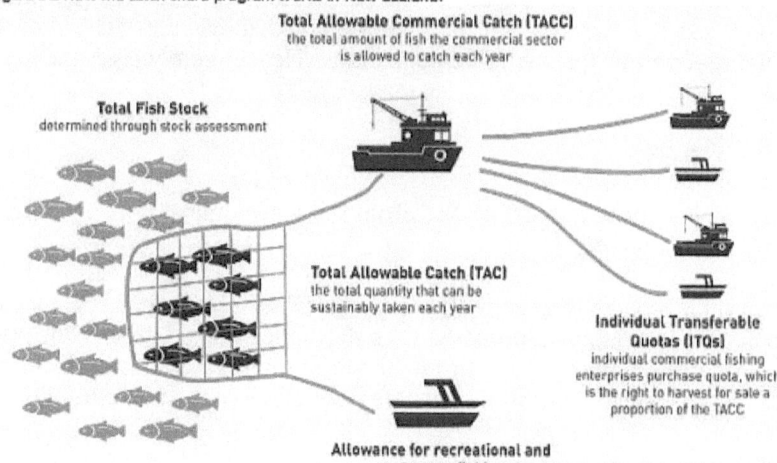

Source: Fisheries New Zealand.

Thus, if the stock of fish increases over time, the total allowable catch increases over time, and the amount of fish each person or group can catch increases over time. So, **the fishers have a financial stake in sustainable fishing**. Since the shares can be sold at any time, sustainable fishing has a direct monetary value.

In effect, the government has created a market in not just current fish but also in future fish. So far, overall, these programs have been judged to be successful. These programs are now in use in nearly 40 countries. In the US, the first program was implemented in 1990 in one area. Now, there are programs in several areas for different species of fish, as shown in Figure 3.3.

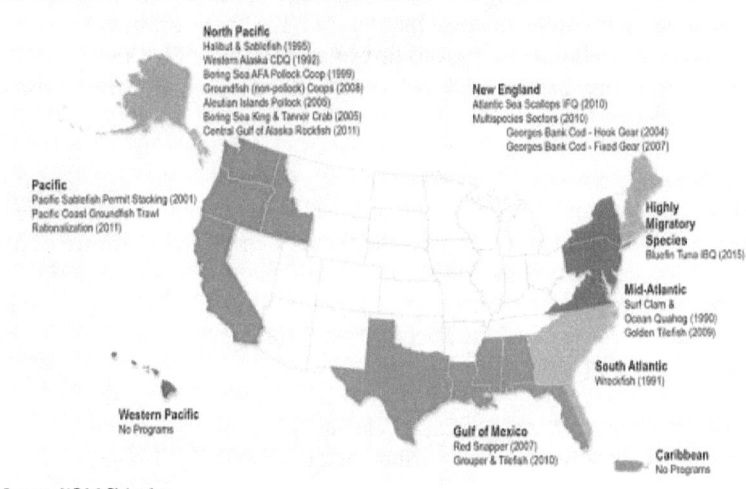

Figure 3.3 Catch share programs in the US (March 2020)

Source: NOAA Fisheries.

## Example of setting taxes: climate change

Climate change is the most critical externality facing the world. The scarce resource that is being overexploited is the carrying capacity of the atmosphere. Scientists tell us that there was some noticeable climate change when the level of carbon dioxide $CO_2$ in the atmosphere reached 300 parts per million (ppm). At 350 ppm, there is a threat of more significant climate change.

In March 2020, the $CO_2$ level was more than 410 ppm. Hence, the issue is how much climate change we will experience, and when, not whether we will experience any climate change. But this is a matter of scientists, not economists.

From an economist's viewpoint, it's the future generations who will suffer the most because of the actions of the past and current generations. Economists quantify this loss in terms of the reduction in future output because of climate change. In short, we emit $CO_2$ today, and future generations suffer a GDP loss. Or, we cut back carbon dioxide emissions today, reduce the impact of climate change, and reduce future loss of GDP.

### *Social cost of carbon (SCC)*

How much loss? For this calculation, we use models such as the Dynamic Integrated Model of Climate Change and Economy (DICE) we discussed in Chapter 2. **One significant number that we calculate from these models is called the social cost of carbon (SCC)**. It should actually be called the social cost of $CO_2$, because that's how it is calculated - as dollars per ton of $CO_2$.

What is the SCC? It's the additional loss of future GDP when current $CO_2$ carbon dioxide emissions increase by one ton. The loss of future benefits due to our emissions today is the cost to future generations. **This means that the SCC measures the future cost of an additional ton of carbon dioxide emissions.**

Now, let's turn this around. Let's ask: What's the additional benefit to future generations of cutting back $CO_2$ emissions? This additional benefit is the cost they will not incur. **In formal terms, the future benefit is the future avoided cost.** Avoided cost is a technical term that we use to measure benefits. It is sometimes a bit confusing to use a cost estimate to measure benefits. Just keep in mind that we are talking about costs that future generations will not have to incur – so that becomes their benefit.

In the terminology that we developed earlier, we can say that the SCC is the future marginal benefit (MB) of cutting back current $CO_2$ emissions.

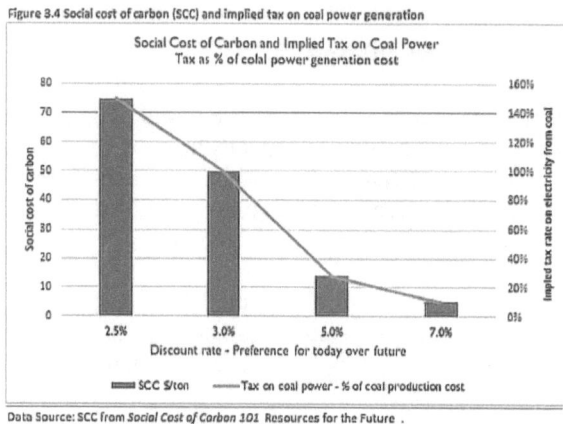

Figure 3.4 Social cost of carbon (SCC) and implied tax on coal power generation

Data Source: SCC from *Social Cost of Carbon 101* Resources for the Future .

What's the value of SCC? There is much uncertainty about this number because it depends on the current and future values of many variables, which are uncertain. However, we do know that **the SCC depends crucially on the discount rate** (Chapter 2). The relationship is inverse (see Figure 3.4). **The higher is the discount rate, the lower is the SCC.** In simpler terms, a lower discount rate means we care more about the future. **So, the more we care about the future, the higher is the SCC.**

The values of the discount rate in Figure 3.4 reflect an ongoing controversy in the US. The Obama Administration preferred to use discount rate values of 2.5%, 3%, and 5% in its analysis. However, the Trump Administration shifted to using the discount rate values of 3% and 7%. As you can see, with a discount rate of 7%, the SCC is very low.

*Impact of SCC-based tax on coal power generation*

**We need some context to interpret the values of SCC in policy terms.** As we will see below, the SCC can be used to put a tax on economic activities that generate $CO_2$. Let's look here at the generation of electricity on coal, which produces carbon dioxide. For discussion purposes, we take the current cost of generation from coal as 5 ¢/ kWh as a reasonable round number estimate. In technical terms, one unit of electricity is one kilowatt-hour (kWh) of electricity. Then, levy a tax per kilogram of $CO_2$ emitted. A reasonable round number estimate of the carbon dioxide emitted from coal power is 1 kilogram per unit of electricity produced.

In short, our reasonable round number assumptions are:

- 1 kWh of electricity generated from coal costs 5 ¢/ to produce.

- 1 kWh of electricity from coal emits 1 kilogram of $CO_2$.

With these assumptions, we can calculate the tax on coal electricity for different levels of SCC.

- As shown in Figure 3.4, with a discount rate of 2.5%, the SCC will be $ 75/ton of $CO_2$.

- We impose a tax of $75/ton on the $CO_2$ emissions from power plants.

- This tax works out to 7.5 ¢/kWh of electricity produced.

- With a coal power generation cost of 5 ¢/kWh, the tax is 150% of the production cost.

The implication is that with a tax of $ 75/ton of $CO_2$, coal power generation would no longer be financially viable. On the other hand, with a discount rate of 7% and SCC = $ 5/ton, the tax on coal electricity generation would be only 10% of the production cost. **In short, a discount rate of 2.5% and SCC = $ 75/ton would likely wipe out power generation from coal. In comparison, a discount rate of 7% and SCC = $ 5/ton would have a small financial impact on coal power generation.**

### Why should the carbon tax be equal to SCC?

Now let's ask: Why do we use the values of SCC in calculating the tax on coal power generation? The answer is that it is appropriate to use the SCC as the tax on all activities that generate $CO_2$.

In other words, we are talking about putting a tax on all activities worldwide that generate carbon dioxide. Everyone would have to pay. So far, no one has found a way to make this happen, but here we are looking at the theory. So, hold on. Since the current price on $CO_2$ emissions is zero, the tax would be the price of carbon dioxide. Let's see what happens when we set the price as the value of the SCC. We get:

71

$P = SCC$, i.e., the price paid to emit 1 ton of CO2 is set equal to SCC.

We have already determined that:

$SCC = MB$, i.e., SCC measures the marginal benefits of cutting back 1 ton of $CO_2$ emissions

This gives us:

$P = SCC = MB$, i.e., the price set by SCC is equal to the marginal benefits of cutting back 1 ton of $CO_2$ emissions.

Note that this the same result we had derived in the acid rain example. Now, let's look at the marginal costs of cutting back $CO_2$ emissions. For example, consider power utilities around the world that are generating power from coal. They have to decide whether to cut back $CO_2$ emissions to pay the price.

Or, from the manager's perspective: Do I cut back one more ton $CO_2$, or do I pay the tax? It's similar to the question in the acid rain example. In short, the manager will stop cutting back when the price to be paid is just equal to the marginal cost of cutting back. In symbols,

$P = MC$, i.e., the price will be equal to the marginal cost of cutting back $CO_2$ emissions.

Hence, we get the same result as in the acid rain example.

$P = SCC = MB = MC$, i.e., the price set by SCC is equal to the marginal benefits and the marginal costs.

Note that since the price is the same worldwide, MC will be the same worldwide for all activities that emit $CO_2$. **This means that we have achieved the global cutback at the lowest cost on a worldwide basis.**

This is the reason why there is a consensus among economists that the best way to fight climate change is a worldwide price on $CO_2$ emissions, with the price based on the SCC.

**The hitch with this plan is the difficulty in getting international agreement to implement it.** When you think of imposing a tax on $CO_2$, you run into all the issues associated with any tax. Is it fair to force everyone – rich and poor – to pay the same tax? What will you do to tax cheats and tax evaders? Will all countries participate? Who will enforce that participating counties comply?

## Example of setting taxes: congestion pricing

Many roads and commercial areas are congested- there's are so many automobiles that there is a traffic jam that reduces the average speed of travel. This is an externality. My driving on the road hurts others by slowing them down.

**The common resource that is being overused is the carrying capacity of the road.** Everyone is free to use it - there's no charge. However, in a limited number of places, governments have begun to set a price to ease congestion. Note these congestion fees are different from the tolls that are usually charged on certain roads, bridges, and tunnels. Those charges are designed to raise revenues, and those roads, etc. are often congested.

### Area entry fee

**One example is a fee for an automobile to enter a designated area at selected times.** For instance, in Singapore, Stockholm, London, and some other cities, private cars have to pay a fee to enter designated parts of the city at certain times. New York City has developed a congestion pricing plan for parts of Manhattan, but it has not yet (May 2020) become effective. In some cities, the fee is adjusted to keep the traffic flowing smoothly, while in other places, the charge is pre-set, though it may vary by the time of the day.

### Toll lanes

Another example of congestion pricing is to designate selected lanes of a road as express lanes or some such name, and charge people a toll to use them. In some cases, the charge varies according to the traffic conditions. For example, in San Diego, California, since 1998, autos with just the driver pay a fee when they use designated lanes on Highway I-15. The price varies with the level of traffic, and can change every six minutes. The minimum charge is $ 0.50, and the maximum charge is $ 8.00. Cars with two or people don't have to pay the toll.

**There is clear evidence that congestion charges do reduce congestion. However, they have not become widely used.** One reason is that congestion fees are like taxes, and hence they are subject to the usual issues and concerns about taxes.

## MOST COUNTRIES DON'T USE MARKETS FOR SOME PARTS OF THE ECONOMY

In most countries, there are some parts of the economy where governments, not markets, provide goods and services. Or, governments ban the consumption of some goods that people want to buy. There is no consensus or hard-and-fast rule about these commodities, and the affected goods and services vary from country to country, or even within large countries.

We will not discuss in detail the affected goods and commodities. This is a brief discussion just to introduce the idea that even though markets work well in general, in some cases, societies don't let market forces work on their own for certain goods and services.

## Banned or discouraged goods and services

**Some goods and services are banned or strongly discouraged in many countries.** The usual suspects here are alcohol, drugs, cigarettes, gambling, and prostitution. Even where they are not banned, there are often restrictions as to who can buy or sell them. Note that buyers and sellers often find ways to circumvent these limitations to some extent.

## Required goods or services

**Some goods and services are required by law.** These requirements are usually for physical safety or financial protection. For example, automobiles are required to have certain safety features, such as seat belts and airbags. In some countries, people on two-wheelers such as motorcycles are required to wear helmets.

Some countries want to protect their people in financial transactions. Sometimes, there are limits on interest rates in consumer loans. Or, there may be a requirement that consumers can cancel a financial transaction. For example, in the US, you can cancel the transaction within three days of completing all the formalities when you refinance a home loan.

## Health and education are often government provided or supported

**Most countries don't rely only on for-profit companies for education and health services.** Schools, colleges, and universities are mostly owned by governments or non-profit entities. In the US, most students attend local schools that are owned and financed by local governments with taxpayers' money. As for colleges, look at any worldwide list of top-ranked universities. You won't find any for-profit university.

One reason that societies don't rely on for-profit firms and markets for education is that education is seen as an investment in the future for society as a whole, not just for individual firms or people. Further, equal access to education is a way to increase equality of opportunity, which is a social objective, not an objective of for-profit firms.

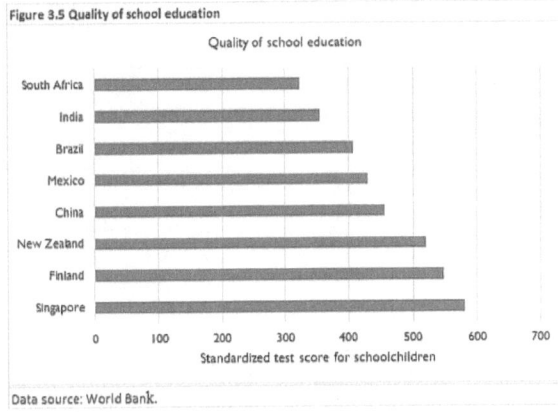

Figure 3.5 Quality of school education

However, there's no assurance that taxpayer-funded institutions will provide a good education. See Figure 3.5. In fact, in many Asian and African countries, the quality of education in government schools is poor. One measure of the quality of education is the World Bank's Human Capital index. For example, India and South Africa scored poorly on a standardized test scale for school children.

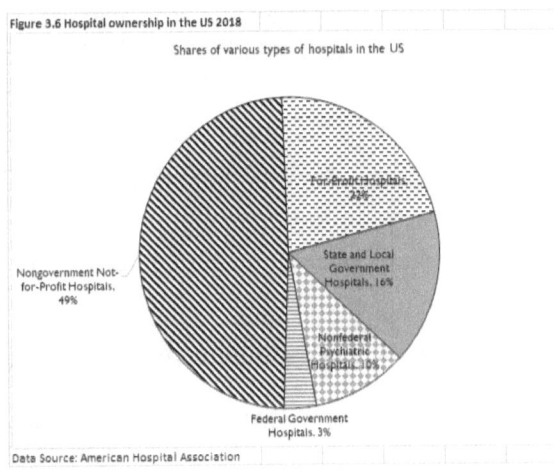

Figure 3.6 Hospital ownership in the US 2018

**There are similar arguments for health services in many countries.** Even in the US, which has not adopted government-provided medical services, most hospitals are run by not-for-profit companies. See Figure 3.6.

## Infrastructure

**Infrastructure is often owned by governments.** Most roads in the world are owned by governments, though some ways have been found to get private firms to invest in building roads. Railway tracks are also often owned by governments, as in India and China, which have extensive rail networks. However, in 2020, the Indian railway system has allowed private firms to run their trains on selected routes. Ports and airports are also often owned by governments. Electricity supply is another commodity that has some government involvement in many countries.

## Emergency services

**Emergency services are often provided by governments or non-profit groups.** These services range from everyday emergency phone numbers such as 112, 999, and 911 to rescue operations for people who are hurt or stranded for a variety of reasons. Even roadside assistance for drivers is often provided by non-profit entities, such as AAA in the US, though AAA usually sends for-profit firms to help drivers in need.

## KEY TAKEAWAYS

### True costs are measured by opportunity cost

1. Economists use the term opportunity cost to define and measure true economic cost. When you have two options, the opportunity cost of choosing Option A is the value of Option B.

2. There is a real-world application of the opportunity cost concept in international trade. This is called dumping, where dumping means selling a product abroad at a price that is below your opportunity cost.

3. There can be a difference between private costs, which is what a person or group incurs, and social costs, which is what the society as a whole incurs.

### Under scarcity, resource allocation decisions take place at the margin

4. We define marginal cost (MC) as the change in total costs when you increase/decrease the production of a commodity by one unit. Correspondingly, we define marginal benefit (MB) as the change in total benefits when you increase/decrease the consumption of a commodity by one unit.

5. Net benefits (Total Benefits − Total Costs) are maximized at the amount of the commodity where the marginal benefit is equal to the marginal cost, i.e., $MB = MC$.

### Markets normally allocate resources properly

6. It's a core result in economics that markets generally allocate resources properly. However, this result does not hold when there is a difference between social costs and private costs.

7.  For markets to work properly, governments need to protect the property rights of the market participants, and provide ways to settle commercial disputes.

## Markets don't allocate resources properly when there are externalities

8.  An externality occurs when one person's actions have a negative or positive impact on someone else. Or, there is a difference between private and social costs, or between private and social benefits.

9.  There are three ways to tackling externalities, particularly negative externalities. One way is to issue rules and regulations. We call this as the command-and-control approach. The other two ways internalize the externality. One way is to create a market in which the right to engage in the externality activity is bought and sold. Another way is to levy a tax. In both of these cases, the aim is to reach a situation where the price becomes equal to marginal cost, i.e., we get to $P = MC$.

## Example of setting taxes: climate change

10. The social cost of carbon (SCC) is the future marginal benefit (MB) of cutting back current $CO_2$ emissions. Since it is the cost that future generations will avoid due to actions to limit climate change, these avoided costs count as benefits.

11. There is a consensus among economists that the best way to fight climate change is a worldwide price on $CO_2$ emissions, with the price based on the SCC.

## Most countries don't use markets for some parts of the economy

12. Most governments play a key role in the provision of health, education, infrastructure, and emergency services to markets.

With this chapter, we come to the end of Section I of this book. Now, we move to Section II, a detailed look at the financial sector of an economy.

## SECTION II.    FINANCIAL MARKETS

This section, consisting of Chapters 4-5, is related to financial markets. In this section, I have occasionally mentioned the changes in these markets brought about by the coronavirus-induced economic crisis that started in March 2020.

In Chapter 4, our focus is on understanding what economists mean by the money supply. This is a jargon term, which has a formal, specific meaning. We discuss the role of central banks, currencies, commercial banks, and investment banks in this context.

**This sets the stage for Chapter 5, where we focus on a particular financial market: the bond market.** We focus on the bond market because what happens in this market has a close relationship with what happens in the economy.

## Chapter 4. Money Matters

Money. It makes the world go around. But financial markets can also create economic problems. Many economists and other observers think that the US financial markets were partly responsible for the 2008 economic crisis. Before this crisis, many people ignored the financial sector. A common attitude was to leave the financial sector to the specialists. That changed quickly soon after the crisis began to hurt economic growth and create unemployment in the US and many other countries.

### Chapter flow

This chapter has six parts. To begin with, we define the term money as economists use it in their analysis. In the second part, we look at central banks, which control money in modern economies. Next, we look at how the money supply is measured. In the fourth part, we look at currencies, followed by commercial banks. Finally, in the sixth part, we look at one fund offered by investment banks.

### Money is not what you think it is

We all know what money is. We have several nicknames for it. We call it bread, dough, moolah, bucks, dinero, and perhaps some more. However, **if we want to understand how the economy's financial markets work, we have to define money more formally**.

### Core role of money

In economic analysis, the core function of money is to facilitate buying and selling without bartering. In barter, you exchange two things or services. I will cut your lawn if you repair my bathroom leak. No money exchanged. In modern times, there are very few barter transactions. **When you sell a commodity or a service, you want to be paid by something that you can later use to buy goods or services from someone else. This something is what we call money.**

In the past, people have used all kinds of things as money. Historically, people have used precious metals such as gold and silver, shells, and minerals as money. The main reason sellers accepted these things as payment was a reasonable belief that they could use them to pay for what they wanted to buy.

In other words, **it's not money unless people believe that other people will accept it in payment**. People across the world – even crooks – take US dollars in payment because they know that they can pay someone else with them. On the other hand, people in Zimbabwe lost trust in their currency. They began to use first the South African rand, and then the US dollar for their transactions.

## Money vs. wealth

We can now differentiate between money and wealth. Your wealth consists of all the valuable things you have, such as your motorcycle, your diamonds, the money in your retirement plan, the cash in your pocket, and the cash you have hidden under your mattress. All of these are your financial assets.

All these assets are not equally spendable. If you take your precious diamond to a car dealer to buy a car, chances are the shop will not accept the diamond in payment. Your diamond will not be accepted in payment even if it is worth much more than the car you want to buy. In economic jargon, a diamond is not a liquid asset, meaning you cannot use it to buy something. On the other hand, the cash under your mattress is a liquid asset. You can pull it out and go buy something with it.

In short, in economic jargon, money is the readily spendable part of financial assets.

## Money supply

**The amount of money in an economy is called as the money supply**. This term can be misleading. The correct term is money stock, not the money supply. (Let me differentiate between a stock and a flow here. For example, the amount of pollution in a lake at any time is the stock of pollutants. The amount of pollutants that come into the lake in a year is the flow of pollutants.)

The reason we should not call it money supply is that it also reflects the demand for money. Wait a minute. How can we even talk about the demand for money? Doesn't everyone want more money? Yes, in the casual sense of money, most people want more money. But, let's use the term money as defined above. In this sense, most people want more wealth, not necessarily more money!

Suppose you get a windfall of € 2,000. You go out and buy a smartphone that costs € 1,000, and deposit € 1,000 in your retirement plan. You have no more money, though you do have more financial assets! Your demand for money from the windfall is zero.

Nevertheless, we will continue to use the term money supply, and not money stock, because it is deeply entrenched in public discussions.

## CENTRAL BANKS ARE MAJOR PLAYERS IN THE ECONOMY

**With some exceptions, every country has a central bank.** For example, the US has the Federal Reserve System, often just called the Fed. All the euro countries together have the European Central Bank. China has the People's Bank of China. Mexico's central bank is the Bank of Mexico.

Central banks control a country's monetary policy. Monetary policy is about manipulating the money supply and interest rates with the ultimate aim of influencing key economic variables such as unemployment, inflation and GDP.

**A systematic effort to increase the money supply and reduce interest rates is called a loose monetary policy.** The ultimate aim is to boost GDP and reduce unemployment when the economy is down. However, a reduction in interest rates does hurt savers, who earn less interest at lower rates.

In contrast, a tight monetary policy aims to reduce the money supply and raise interest rates. The ultimate aim is to keep inflation in check when the economy is doing well.

In market-based economies, central banks don't set interest rates or determine the money supply. Instead, central banks intervene in financial markets to move interest rates and the money supply in the desired direction, with the ultimate aim of moving key macroeconomic variables in the desired direction. The interventions of the central banks in financial markets take place through a complex set of transactions, which we will discuss in Chapter 5.

### Many central banks have adopted inflation targets

In recent decades, **central banks have come to think of themselves as the agencies that keep inflation in check.** For example, the Bank of England has set a target for inflation of around 2% every year. South Africa's central bank wants to keep inflation within the 3-6% range. India's target range is 4-6%. The Fed is said to have an implicit inflation target of around 2%.

### Central banks also focus on economic growth

However, **central banks have not forgotten economic growth. Their interventions do support economic growth.** Consider what happened in the US when it suffered an economic meltdown in 2008. Let's use September 15, 2008, as a marker because this was the day when Lehman Brothers, a large, well-established Wall Street firm, declared bankruptcy and shook financial markets worldwide.

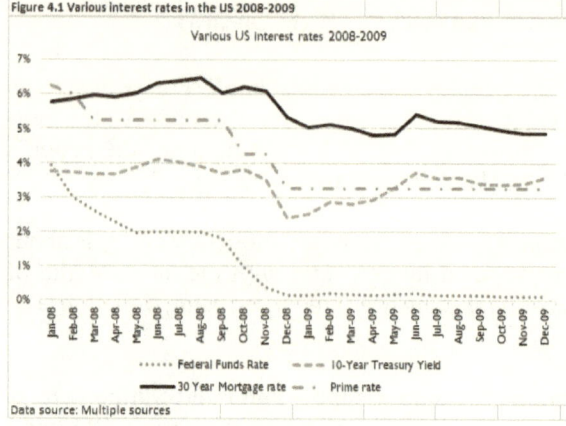

Figure 4.1 Various interest rates in the US 2008-2009

Data source: Multiple sources

The Fed was able to reduce interest rates within a few days of September 15, 2008, as shown in Figure 4.1. The Fed most directly manipulated the Federal Funds rate. This is the interest rate on an overnight loan from one bank to another bank. We will see in Chapter 5 how the Fed influenced this rate. Here, we just note briefly that the Fed's method was to increase the money supply.

First, let's look at the impact on the US government. The yield (interest rate) on 10-year US Treasury bonds declined soon after the Fed's intervention. In effect, the Federal government would have to pay a lower interest rate on fresh loans, which it needed to finance the stimulus expenditures. However, the rate did rise later, which indicates that it is the financial markets, not the Fed, that ultimately determine interest rates.

Next, look at private firms. The Prime rate is the interest rate banks charge for loans to large, creditworthy companies. This rate declined soon after the Fed intervened, which reduced the borrowing costs of large companies. The idea was that firms would look to increase their investments, which would ultimately increase output and employment.

Finally, look at households. The interest rate on 30-year fixed-rate mortgages also declined, though a meaningful decline occurred only in December 2008. This reduced the monthly payments on home loans, which would leave people with more money to spend. If they spent some of this extra money, the increase in demand would ultimately have a positive effect on economic growth and unemployment.

## Comparison of monetary and fiscal policies

The government controls fiscal policy, which is about government expenditures, taxes, and subsidies. In response to the 2008 economic meltdown, President Obama decided to launch a stimulus program of the type recommended by Keynes. For this, Mr. Obama needed the support of the US Congress, which had to approve the budget request. President Obama signed the American Recovery and Reinvestment Act (ARRA), which authorized the stimulus package on February 17, 2009.

It took the Federal government five months to even begin to boost the economy. Further, the ARRA funds were to be spent over three years. **Thus, monetary policy began to work more quickly than fiscal policy.**

### Impact of fiscal and monetary policies was slow in coming in 2008

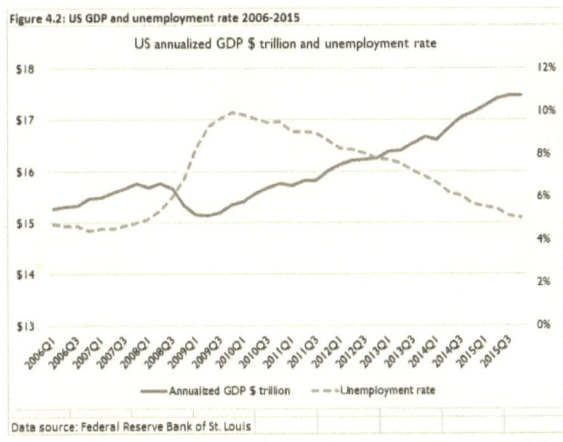

Figure 4.2: US GDP and unemployment rate 2006-2015

In this case, the aim of both fiscal and monetary policy was to boost GDP and reduce unemployment. They worked together. However, it still took time for the US economy to recover, as shown in Figure 4.2. At the end of 2010, the GDP had recovered to the level in mid-2008. However, the unemployment rate took nearly seven years to fall back to its mid-2008 rate.

## Central banks should be independent of governments

As seen above, central banks have a major role in determining what happens in an economy. In addition, in many countries, central banks supervise and regulate commercial banks. In the US, the regulatory system for commercial banks is complex. It includes institutions other than the Fed, but the Fed still has significant control over commercial banks. For example, for large banks, the Fed runs the so-called stress tests designed to determine whether the banks will be able to handle shocks such as the 2008 economic meltdown. **In short, the managers of the central banks are quite powerful in financial markets.**

### *Central bank independence*

How should central bank managers conduct their operations? Under the control of the government? In coordination with the government? Or, independently of the government?

**The consensus among economists is that the central bank should be independent of the government**. This consensus does not come from economic theory. Instead, it comes from the fear that the government will push the central bank to reduce interest rates, which would mean increasing the money supply. In turn, this would increase the inflation rate.

For example, in Zimbabwe in 2008, the money supply increased so much that the government stopped keeping track of inflation. Prices in the evening could be higher than the prices in the morning! The country's currency, the Zimbabwe dollar, became worthless, and people refused to use it. Ultimately, the government had to accept the people's shift to the South African rand and the US dollar.

Even the US has felt this tension. In September 2019, President Trump criticized the Fed Chair, Jay Powell, for not reducing interest rates enough. In a tweet, Trump wrote, "Jay Powell and the Federal Reserve Fail Again. No 'guts,' no sense, no vision!" Similarly, there were reports of behind-the-scenes tension between India's Prime Minister and a Governor of the Reserve Bank of India. This tension ultimately led the Governor to quit before his term ended.

In China, the central bank reports to the Chinese government, which means the bank is not independent. However, the bank does try to base its decisions on its technical judgment, to the extent possible.

Thus, while economists continue to ask for central banks to be independent of the governments, there are signs that central banks are under pressure from governments to adopt looser monetary policies.

## HOW DO WE MEASURE THE MONEY SUPPLY?

The central bank is responsible for measuring the money supply. The measurement takes place at a point of time – on a particular day. The value changes every day in response to changes in demand and supply.

There are several measures of the money supply, labeled as M0, M1, M2, etc. They are defined in such a way that each measure is larger than the previous one. Most countries use only M1 and M2.

## M1 measure of money supply

M1 is the first commonly used method of measuring the money supply.

M1 has two components. The first component is the currency in the hands of the public, meaning the value of the currency in circulation. The second component is selected bank deposits at commercial banks and other places similar to commercial banks, such as savings and loan associations, savings banks, and credit unions.

Note the term commercial banks. These are the usual, familiar places where we keep our money. People's deposits in these places are usually insured by some government agencies, such as the Federal Deposit Insurance Corporation in the US, often with a cap on the insured amount.

In the US, there are other large financial institutions, such as Goldman Sachs and JP Morgan Chase, which are often called investment banks. They do accept money from ordinary people, but these funds are not insured by any government agency. Lehman Brothers, which failed spectacularly in 2008, was one such investment bank. Any deposits with investment banks are not part of M1.

**The selected deposits in M1 are the accounts from which you can withdraw or spend your money without any restrictions**. In the US, the Fed calls these accounts as transaction accounts. This name reflects the idea that the funds in these accounts are used to finance transactions, i.e., to pay for what you want to buy. These accounts are commonly known as demand deposits and checking accounts. Thus, **M1 measures the most easily spendable - most liquid – financial assets.**

The transaction deposits in M1 also reflect the loans that the banks make, in addition to deposits by people and firms. For example, when a business takes a bank loan, the bank just adds that money to the firm's account at the bank. We will take a deeper look at these loans/deposits later in this chapter.

## M2 measure of money supply

M2 is the second method to measure the money supply. M2 consists of M1 plus some forms of money that are less easily spendable than the elements of M1. In the US, these additional elements are savings accounts, time deposits of under $100,000, and money in retail money market mutual funds. These funds are less easily spendable because there are some restrictions on their use. For example, you cannot withdraw funds from time deposits until they mature. Note that money market retail funds offered by investment banks, not by commercial banks, are part of M2. Commercial banks do offer similar a sounding account called money market deposit account, which is counted as part of savings accounts.

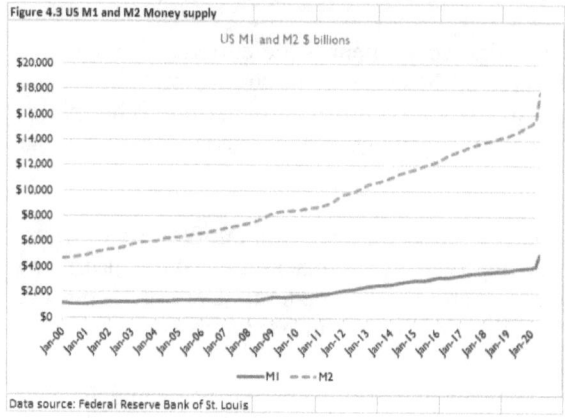

Figure 4.3 US M1 and M2 Money supply

US M1 and M2 $ billions

Data source: Federal Reserve Bank of St. Louis

In the US, M1 and M2 have increased every year, as you can see in Figure 4.3. **The Fed looks at M2 in making its policy decisions.**

**Most countries use similar definitions of money supply, with some changes to reflect local circumstances.** Some also define broader measures such as M3 and M4, which include more and more financial assets that less easily spendable.

We have seen that the money supply has two broad components. The first component is currency, and the second component is various types of deposits in banks and other financial institutions. Let's look at these components, and after that, we will look briefly at the deposits held by investment banks.

## LET'S LOOK AT CURRENCIES

### Are currencies backed by gold?

The US dollar is the world's dominant currency. What is its backing? Is it backed by gold or some other precious commodity? No. The dollar has no such backing. It is money simply because people accept it as money. The US government accepts only dollars in payments of taxes and other fees. That's all the dollar is backed by. It's all about trust. People trust that they will be able to pay for their purchases in US dollars, or convert their dollars into a local currency as needed.

It wasn't always like this. In 1934, US President Roosevelt set the official price of gold as $ 35/troy ounce. There was an implicit promise that the US would give you an ounce of gold if you showed up with $ 35 to exchange. However, this exchange privilege was not available to people - only to the central banks of other countries. The US would convert their dollars into gold.

This promise made the dollar as good as gold for practical purposes. In 1944, several major governments agreed to implement what came to be called the Bretton Woods system. In this system, the values of all major currencies were tied to the dollar. In effect, all major currencies were indirectly tied to gold *via* the dollar.

This system worked for several years. However, as the number of dollars in circulation increased over time, it became clear that the US did not have enough gold to back up all the dollars in circulation. When some foreign banks converted some of their dollars into gold, this led to a decline in US gold reserves.

Finally, in 1971, the US abandoned this system. Since 1971, gold's price in the US and worldwide is set by market forces, and the dollar is not backed by any precious commodity. Other currencies are no longer tied to the dollar, and their exchange rates change every day.

## Moving to cashless economies

As an economy grows, the number of financial transactions increases as people and companies buy and sell an increasing number of goods and services. This implies that the money supply will increase. On the other hand, **in recent years, cash is not used in an increasing number of transactions.** Checks became common many years ago, and digital payments are now increasing.

**Using cash for transactions creates many problems**. There are dangers of theft and embezzlement. For each sale, the cash offered has to be counted carefully, and change returned. Then, at the day's end, the store has to count the total cash in the tills, and deposit some of it deposited in a bank. On the other hand, stores do have to pay a small fee to an operator who processes digital transactions. For example, when you pay by a debit card, the store pays a fee to the operator who takes out the funds from your bank account to pay the store.

This implies that the need for the currency may not increase quickly, i.e., there will be a gradual move to a cashless economy.

### M-Pesa in Africa

M-Pesa, which originated in Kenya in 2007, is a digital payment system that has dramatically changed how people make payments in several African countries. The system is now in use in Kenya, the Democratic Republic of Congo, Egypt, Ghana, Lesotho, Mozambique, and Tanzania, with about 37 million users. And there are other competing systems in some of the countries.

M-Pesa was launched by Safaricom, a company linked to Vodafone, the cell phone company. M-Pesa was designed to be used by people with a Vodafone phone. There is no need for a user to have a bank account. This is a huge advantage in countries where most people don't have bank accounts. When M-Pesa was launched in Kenya, less than 15% of the people in Kenya had bank accounts. Though the number of bank accounts has increased over time, many people in Kenya and other African countries still don't have bank accounts.

Instead of depositing their money in a bank, they hand it over to a local authorized agent. The agent loads the deposit into an account that can be accessed by a basic phone that can send text messages (called SMS). Payments are made from the buyer's phone to the receiver's phone, which also has an M-Pesa account. And, it's not just for transactions. You can transfer money to anyone through the recipient's phone number. Recently, M-Pesa allowed people to scan a merchant's QR code and pay that way.

### Other countries moving to cashless payments

**Sweden is increasingly cashless**. More and more people pay with a debit card or a mobile payment app. **In China, the use of cash has come down as people shift to paying with mobile apps**. In 2016, the Indian government declared that currency notes in the denomination of 1,000 (about $ 15) and 500 rupees were no longer valid in a policy that came to be called demonetization. These notes would have to be deposited in banks, which would issue new, valid notes. One of the ideas behind this change, which hurt the economy in the short-run, was to promote digital payments.

### The US exception

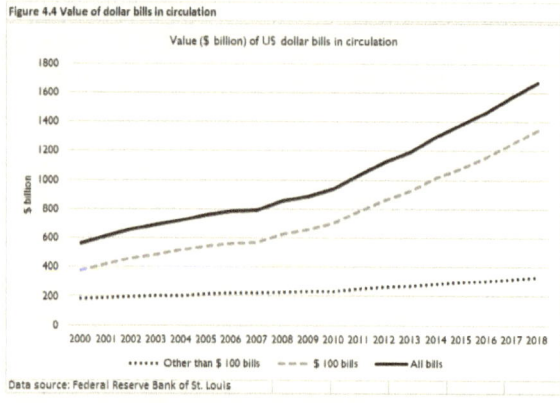

Figure 4.4 Value of dollar bills in circulation

Value ($ billion) of US dollar bills in circulation

Data source: Federal Reserve Bank of St. Louis

The US is an exception because the total value of the dollar bills in circulation has risen every year. See Figure 4.4. Over time, in the US, more people and stores have started using electronic payments. Fast food stores will let you pay for even a single cup of coffee electronically. **So, you would expect the amount of cash in circulation to decline. But that's not what has happened.**

One reason for the continued use of dollar bills in the US is that several million people don't have bank accounts. Some don't use banks because they are poor and not a part of the formal workforce. Others don't have valid work permits

90

and may also be poor. For these people, cash is perhaps the only realistic option for making payments.

Another reason is that some people want to be paid in cash even though they have bank accounts. They probably want to avoid paying income tax on these earnings. Or, it could be that they are making some money on the side, which they don't want anyone else to come to know officially.

However, these off-the-books transactions are usually small in value. They cannot explain the increase in the value of $ 100 bills. **In Figure 4.4, we see that the increase in the value of the dollar bills in circulation is mainly due to the rise in $ 100 bills.** Why this increase in the $ 100 bills? Who needs $ 100 bills for buying and selling anything? It's a lot of money for everyday transactions - which anyhow are increasingly electronic. And most people and companies make large payments electronically or by check – not in $ 100 bills.

**One possible reason is that some foreign countries use the US dollar as their currency**. This is called dollarization. Panama has used the US dollar as its currency for more than a hundred years. In recent decades, Ecuador and El Salvador have given up their currencies and shifted to the dollar. As the economies of these countries expanded, they would absorb additional US dollar bills.

Another significant reason for the increase in $ 100 bills is that they are used in large-scale illegal or shady transactions in the US and abroad. For example, illicit drugs flow into the US from various countries. How do the drug exporters get paid? It's mainly a cash business, though their funds do often end up in banks that tend to be secretive about their customers and transactions.

And the cash they would use is $ 100 bills. You can stuff $1 million in $ 100 bills into a typical briefcase. And the weight would be around 20 pounds (about 9 kilos). A bit heavy for a briefcase, but still manageable. But, if you have more money, you can use suitcases. Some years ago, the widow of an African dictator was arrested at an airport as she was trying to leave the country. She had many suitcases – not briefcases – full of dollar bills. No one knows for sure, but, very likely, they were $ 100 bills.

The US $ 100 bill had some competition from the € 500 bill, equivalent to about $ 550. However, over time, it became clear that a significant number of € 500 bills were being used in shady transactions. Hence, no new € 500 bills have been issued after April 2019, though the existing bills remain legal and can be used for purchases.

## LET'S LOOK AT COMMERCIAL BANKS

Commercial banks don't set out to influence the money supply. But their actions do have a major impact on the money supply. Specifically, their loans affect the money supply. The reason is that the loans they make often show up a deposit in your account. For example, if a firm wants to borrow $ 1 million from a bank, then the loan will show up as a deposit in the firm's accounts with the bank.

This new deposit is an increase in the money supply. To understand why this is the case, we have to look at how banks take deposits and make loans. In general, banks don't make loans from their own funds. Instead, the banks lend the money they have taken as deposits.

Look at it in another way. When you make a deposit in your bank, this deposit becomes a part of the money supply. Then, your bank lends this money out at a higher interest rate to a borrower. And the amount of the loan is also a deposit, which makes it a part of the money supply. However, your deposit is still a part of the money supply.

Let's look at an example. Suppose you deposit $ 15,000 in your savings account. That $ 15,000 deposit is part of M2 that day – and every day until you take out some of your funds. The next day, the bank lends $ 12,000 of your money to a firm, and deposits this amount in the firm's checking account. Now this $ 12,000 deposit has become part of M2 that day. At the same time, your savings account is still showing that you have $ 15,000. So, that is still part of M2.

In other words, by making a loan, the bank has increased the money supply.

How can this be? Isn't something fishy going on here? The bank is showing your $ 15,000 in your account, even though it has lent $ 12,000 to a firm. And, the firm's account at the bank has gone up by $ 12,000. It seems like a case of somehow eating your cake and having it too. **Nothing fishy is going on here. This is conventional, modern banking.**

How much of my deposit can the bank lend out? Are there some limits on how much money banks can lend?

. There are two types of limits on how much banks can lend out. The first limit is called the deposit reserve ratio and the second limit is called the capital adequacy ratio. The capital adequacy ratio is more important than the deposit reserve ratio.

## Deposit reserve ratio

In many countries, regulators require the banks to limit the amount of their deposits they can lend out. In other words, the banks are required to keep a fraction of their deposits with them. **The funds the banks keep with them are called reserves, and this fraction is called the deposit reserve ratio.**

In the US, the Fed's rule (but see below) is that banks must keep 10% of the deposits as reserves, which means that the deposit reserve ratio is 10$. Or, a bank can lend out 90% of its deposits. In the example of a deposit of $ 15,000, the bank would have to keep with it 10%, or $ 1,500. So, the bank could lend out a maximum of $ 13,500.

Then, in that example, why did I set 12,000 as the loan amount? This shows that the banks have some discretion in how much they lend out. They may not be able to find suitable, creditworthy borrowers for the maximum allowed amount. Or, the potential borrowers may not want to borrow as much the banks are allowed to lend. Thus, **the amount of a bank's loans is determined by the allowed amount, the bank's willingness to make loans, and the demand for loans**. Thus, these same factors determine, in part, the money supply, which means that the Fed does not have direct control over the money supply.

I wrote above that the Fed requires banks to hold 10% of their deposits as reserves. That's no longer correct. In March 2020, in response to the economic crisis caused by the coronavirus, the Fed reduced the deposit reserve ratio from 10% to 0%. The purpose of this change was to allow banks to increase their loans. Hence, the change was a part of a looser monetary policy to increase the money supply and reduce interest rates.

How could the Fed feel confident that the banking system would be financially sound with a 0% deposit reserve ration? One factor in this confidence was that several countries have had a 0% rule for many years. This includes Canada, the UK, New Zealand, Australia, and Sweden.

**Other countries, such as China and India, still have deposit reserve requirements**. China reduced its deposit reserve ratio in January 2020, and then again in March 2020 for the same reasons as the Fed. While India's central bank did not change the reserve requirement, it took other steps toward a looser monetary policy.

## Capital requirements

**When a bank makes loans, there is always the risk that some of the loans may not be repaid, or only partially repaid**. For example, suppose a borrower cannot repay a car loan, and the bank repossesses the car. When the bank sells the repossessed car, the sale price may be less than the remaining loan amount. How does the bank absorb this loss?

The bank needs its own funds to absorb losses from loans that are not repaid – it cannot use the depositors' money for this purpose. These funds are called the bank's capital. They are essentially the bank's equity – the money put in by the bank's owners, which include all shareholders.

The US has a complex set of rules related to capital requirements, many of which were put in place after the 2008 economic crisis. There is another set of regulations called Basel III, which stands for the third agreement reached in Basel, Switzerland, in 2010, by an international committee. **The purpose of the Basel III rules related to capital requirements is to ensure that banks have enough capital to absorb losses arising from loan defaults.**

In deciding how much capital a bank should have to absorb losses, we cannot look only at the total loans made by a bank. It is also necessary to consider the riskiness of the loans that the bank has made. For example, suppose that a US bank has bought 2-year Treasury notes worth $ 1 million. In effect, it's a $ 1 million loan to the US government. We can be confident that the US government will repay the loan, so there is no need to hold any capital to absorb any losses from this loan.

However, if the bank had made car loans worth $ 1 million to several individuals, there is a risk that some of the loans would not be repaid. The bank would repossess the cars, and sell them, but it would not get the full value of the remaining loans. So, the bank must have some capital to absorb this loss.

The general principle is that a bank must have different amounts of capital to absorb losses from loans with varying degrees of riskiness, with more capital needed for riskier loans.

Let's look at a simple example that illustrates this principle. Let me say that the example is truly illustrative – it leaves out all the real-world complexities.

Suppose you have a two-part rule requirement. For loans of type A, which are less risky, you have a capital requirement of 5%. Meaning that if you make a type A loan of $ 100, you should have $ 5 of capital with you.

For loans of type B, which are riskier, you have a capital requirement of 8%. Meaning that if you make a type B loan of $ 100, you should have $ 8 of capital with you. The reason that the capital requirement is higher type B loans is that you expect higher losses with this type of loan.

## Risk-Weighted Assets (RWA) - another way of taking account of the riskiness of loans

In the real-world regulations, the calculation of capital requirements is based on a different mathematical calculation that gives the same result. In this alternative method, the percentage requirement is kept constant, but the loan amount is adjusted to reflect its riskiness.

In the above example, keep the capital requirement as 5% for all types of loans. If you applied this 5% to the actual value of the loans, you would not take into account the differences in the riskiness of different loans. The solution is to adjust the loan amount. In the above example, we do it this way.

- Count a type B loan of $ 100 as a loan of $ 160.

- Then, apply a capital requirement of 5% to this amount of $ 160.

- We get $ 160 x 5% = $ 8.

- This is the same result as applying a requirement of 8% to a $ 100 loan.

- Call this $ 160 as the risk-weighted value of a type B $ 100 loan.

So, if we want to keep the percentage requirement the same for loans with different levels of risk, we must suitably adjust the loan value to reflect its riskiness.

**In bank accounting jargon, the loans that a bank makes are called its assets.** Using this term, what we need to do is calculate the value of a bank's assets (loans), taking account of the different levels of the riskiness of each type of loan.

Let's look at an example in which a bank has made a type A loan of $ 100 plus a type B loan of $ 100. Thus, the total loans are $ 200. Or, **using the jargon, this bank's assets are $ 200.**

In the conventional way, we know that the bank needs capital of $ 5 (against the $ 100 type A loan, which has a 5% requirement) plus $ 8 (against the $ 100 type B loan, which has an 8% requirement), for a total capital requirement of $ 13.

Now, let's do the calculation in the alternative way, in which the capital requirement is set at 5% for both type A and type B loans.

- Type A asset (loan) value = $ 100

- Type B adjusted asset (loan) value = $ 160

- Total risk-adjusted asset (loan) value = $ 100 + $ 160 = $ 260

- Capital requirement at 5% = $ 260 x 5% = $ 13.

In this example, the bank's assets adjusted for risk are $ 260, as calculated above. This is called the bank's risk-weighted assets.

Thus, in calculating the value of the loans made by a bank, in the alternative method, we don't just add up all the loans. Instead, **we take account of the riskiness of various loans and calculate a number called a bank's Risk-Weighted Assets (RWA).** In short, the value of RWA downplays safer loans and gives more weight to riskier loans.

### Capital requirement ratio

In the above example, we used a capital requirement ratio of 5%. More formally, this ratio is called the capital adequacy ratio (CAR) and defined as the ratio of the bank's capital to the bank's RWA.

Capital Adequacy Ratio (CAR) = Bank's Capital/Risk-Weighted Assets

Bank regulators divide a bank's capital into Tier 1 capital and Tier 2 capital. **Tier 1 capital is the bank's core capital.** While the details of what is counted as Tier 1 capital are complex, the purpose of Tier 1 capital is straightforward. These are the financial assets that are used to absorb losses from loan defaults. The Basel III accord specifies that Tier 1 capital should be at least 6% of the RWA.

**Tier 2 capital is the bank's secondary capital.** It consists of financial assets that are less liquid than Tier 1 capital, Under Basel III, Tier 2 capital should be at least 2% of RWA.

## Economic downturns increase a bank's RWA and can make it insolvent.

**When there is a major economic downturn, the risk associated with many loans tends to increase**. For example, when people lose their jobs and incomes, they find it difficult to repay their loans. And, if they tighten their belts by cutting back on eating out or vacations, then the financial situation of some restaurants and travel-related businesses becomes shakier. In turn, the loans to these businesses become riskier.

**How do we handle the increased risk?** The capital requirement ratio is fixed, and we don't want to change it. But we still want the bank to have more reserves, so that it can absorb the likely higher losses.

Suppose the capital requirement ratio is set at 5%. What is this ratio applied to? It is applied to the risk-weighted assets (RWA). (Remember, here an asset means is what we call as a loan in everyday language). So, the only we can increase the capital requirements is to increase the RWA. If RWA increases, then 5% of RWA will increase, and the capital requirement amount will increase.

But, how can an economic downturn increase the asset value? It cannot do this. The value of the assets we own tends to go down in a downturn. And, even when you think of a loan as an asset, how can a downturn increase the value of a loan? It cannot.

However, a downturn increases the risk, which in turn increases the RWA because, as discussed above, the RWA depends on the risk. It's a bit counterintuitive, but it becomes clear when you keep in mind that increased risk means increased RWA.

Thus, a major economic downturn tends to increase the value of a bank's RWA, even if its loans remain unchanged. In turn, this increases the bank's need for capital to guard against losses.

A bank that already has enough capital would not be in financial trouble. However, if a bank does not have the additional capital, then it must get it from somewhere. This additional capital could come from the bank's promoters, or it could come from a fresh sale of shares, which increases the bank's equity. **However, if a bank cannot get the additional capital needed in an economic downturn, then the bank faces financial insolvency**. This means that the bank is no longer financially viable.

Consider what happened in the 2008 economic crisis. At that time, the RWAs of many banks increased as their loans became riskier. However, the banks were facing difficulties in raising their Tier 1 and Tier 2 capital. Hence, they were in danger of becoming insolvent. The US government stepped in to help out so that the banks would not fail, with most of the Treasury funds going to big banks such as Citigroup and Bank of America. Some of the funds were loans, while others were used to buy shares in the companies.

The Treasury did get its loan money back and was able to sell its shares later. So, **the Treasury did not lose any money.** However, there is no doubt that the Treasury did support the bank's shareholders because there was no other source of capital for the banks at that time.

## Some of China's and India's banks are in trouble

In China, large banks are financially sound. However, the smaller, local banks are in financial difficulties because a significant portion of their loans may not be fully repaid. Many of these loans were given without regard for the risk because of pressure by local government officials. While this has not yet become a financial crisis in China, it is difficult for these banks to issue new loans, which leads to local credit shortages. In turn, this crimps local investment and economic growth.

In India, several government-owned banks have many loans where the borrowers have not been able to make their installment payments on time. If the due payment is not made for 90 days, a loan is called as a non-performing asset (NPA). For government-owned banks, the share of NPAs in total loans is about 12-13%, which is much higher than the value of around 4% for private banks. While the government-owned banks still meet the capital adequacy requirements, these banks find it increasingly difficult to make fresh loans. As a result, India's central bank's efforts to boost the economy via loose monetary policy may be less effective as major banks don't ramp up their loans adequately in response to changes in monetary policy.

## LET'S LOOK AT MONEY MARKET RETAIL FUNDS

We noted above that one component of M2 are the funds held in money market retail funds, and that these funds are held by investment banks, not commercial banks. These funds are often called money market mutual (MMM) funds.

### MMM funds have some risk

It's useful to look at MMM funds in some detail because they are a simple way to look at financial schemes that allow you and me to earn a higher return than with commercial banks but at higher risk. In other words, **MMM funds illustrate the general financial concept that higher returns are usually associated with higher risk.**

Suppose you put in $ 1,000 in an MMM fund. Then, this deposit will not be recorded as $ 1,000. Instead, your account will show that you now own 1,000 shares in a fund, and the current value of each share as $ 1.00. This value of a share is called Net Asset Value (NAV). While the firm operating the MMM funds tries to ensure that the NAV always stays $ 1.00, there is no assurance that the NAV will actually be $ 1.00. If the NAV falls below $ 1.00, the value of your shares in the fund will fall below $ 1,000.

In short, your deposit in an MMM fund runs the risk of losing value, and you may get back less than what you had put in. In this way, it is similar to buying shares in a company where the value of your shares can come down.

Why would you take this risk of losing your money? Because you are looking for a higher return than the interest rate offered by commercial banks on safe savings accounts. At the same time, you are not taking a big risk because it has been a rare event for the NAV of any MMM fund to go below $ 1.00. And, even there the reduction was limited to a few cents, meaning the NAV did not fall to zero or close to it. So, **experience suggests that your loss, if at all it takes place, will be limited.** At the same time, your return will also not be high.

## Some general financial principles from the workings of MMM funds

An understanding of how MMM funds operate will be useful for the discussion in next chapter. To begin, the MMM fund manager takes money from a large number of people and pools their money together. Once the money is pooled, there is no difference between your money and someone else's money. It's all been pooled together, and you have your share of the pooled funds.

The MMM manager lends this pooled money to relatively safe borrowers such as the government, government-backed entities, well-established large companies, and other such borrowers. Apart from the government, to which the MMM manager can lend any amount of money, all other borrowers from the MMM fund must borrow only limited amounts. This diversification of MMM borrowers means that if one borrower fails to repay, the MMM fund loses only a limited amount of funds. This is an example of the general financial principle that diversification is a traditional way to reduce overall financial risk.

Further, the loans from the MMM fund are for short periods. The maximum allowed length of the loan is just over one year, but the average length has to be only 90 days or less. **This is an example of the general financial principle that shorter-term loans are less risky than longer-term loans, but shorter-term loans offer lower returns.**

In short, MMM funds offer you higher returns than a savings account, but without an assurance that your money will not go down in value. In practice, the risk of loss is small because the MMM funds lend the pooled funds from a large number of people to relatively safe borrowers.

## KEY TAKEAWAYS

### Money is not what you think it is

1. In economic analysis, the word money has a special meaning. Money is the readily spendable part of financial assets. When you sell a commodity or a service, you want to be paid by something that you can later use to buy goods or services from someone else. This something is what we call money.

2. The amount of money in an economy is called the money supply. Technically, we should call it the money stock, but money supply is the well-established term.

### Central banks are major players in the economy

3. Central banks control a country's monetary policy. Monetary policy is about manipulating the money supply and interest rates with the ultimate aim of influencing key economic variables such as inflation, unemployment, and GDP.

4. A systematic effort to increase the money supply and reduce interest rates is called a loose monetary policy. In contrast, a tight monetary policy aims to reduce the money supply and raise interest rates.

5. Monetary policy often begins to work more quickly than fiscal policy, which is related to taxes and government expenditures.

6. Central banks have come to think of themselves as the agencies that keep inflation in check, but they do not ignore economic growth.

7. The consensus among economists is that the central bank should be independent of the government.

### How do we measure the money supply?

8. There are several measures of the money supply, labeled as M0, M1, M2, etc. They are defined in such a way that each measure is larger than the previous one. Most countries use only M1 and M2 to measure the money supply, and M2 is usually the measure the central banks focus on.

9. M1 consists of (i) the currency in the hands of the public, meaning the value of the currency in circulation, and (ii) selected bank deposits at commercial banks and other similar places. M2 consists of M1 plus some forms of money that are less easily spendable than the elements of M1.

## Let's look at currencies

10. The US dollar is the world's dominant currency. The dollar is not backed by gold or anything else. It is money simply because people accept it as money.

11. It's a matter of trust that your seller will accept your currency as payment for what you want to buy. Without this trust, a currency loses it meaning.

12. In modern times, cash is not used in an increasing number of transactions, as people move to digital payments.

## Let's look at commercial banks

13. Commercial banks don't set out to influence the money supply. But their actions do have a major impact on the money supply. Specifically, their loans affect the money supply.

14. There are two types of limits on how much banks can lend out. The first limit is called reserve requirements, and the second limit is called capital adequacy. The capital adequacy requirement is much more critical than the reserve deposit requirement.

## Let's look at money market retail funds

15. Investment banks take deposits into held in money market retail funds, often called money market mutual (MMM) funds. Your deposit in an MMM fund runs the risk of losing value, and you may get back less than what you put in,

16. There is a general financial principle that diversification is a traditional way to reduce overall financial risk.

17. There is a general financial principle that shorter-term loans are less risky than longer-term loans, but shorter-term loans offer lower returns.

In this chapter, we have developed a basic understanding of some aspects of financial markets. In the next chapter, we take a detailed look at one specific financial market, the bond market.

## CHAPTER 5.    THE BOND MARKET

**The bond market is the place where loans are bought and sold**. It functions in complex ways that are often not intuitive, and its jargon can be daunting. When I taught economics in universities, I found that most of my students had hardly any understanding of the bond market, even when they had some sense of the stock market.

Why should we look at this market? Let's look at what James Carville, one of President Clinton's political advisers, said about the bond market. He said, "I used to think that if there was reincarnation, I wanted to come back as the President or the Pope or as a 400 baseball hitter. But now **I would like to come back as the bond market. You can intimidate everybody**."

The bond market intimidates borrowers by collectively changing one of their key financial parameters. This parameter is called their loans' yield, which we will discuss in detail in this chapter. An increase in a borrower's yield is often interpreted as a judgment that the borrower's financial standing is worsening. The result is that the next time a borrower takes out a loan, the interest rate is likely to be higher.

That's bad news for governments that borrow money regularly to finance their budget deficits. In 2010, the yields on Greece's loans went up so much that Greece was forced to ask for a financial bailout, as we discuss later in this chapter.

**In the bond market, loans are bought and sold not just as loans but also as shares that are linked to loans**. These shares are usually called mortgage-based securities (MBS) when they are linked to mortgage loans, and asset-based securities when they are linked to other loans. (Remember that in Chapter 4 that loans are called assets in financial jargon.) Many analysts say that problems with MBS were partly responsible for the 2008 economic crisis.

In short, it's worth making an effort to understand the functioning of the bond market.

## Chapter flow

The chapter has three main parts. In the first part, we discuss the basics of the bond market. In the second part, we discuss the fundamental concepts of a bond's price, and a bond's yield. In the third part, we look at the bond market's functioning in Greece and Germany. In the fourth part, we discuss some of the major details of the bond market. In the fifth part, we discuss how central banks affect interest rates, which includes intervening in the bond market. Finally, in the sixth part, we discuss mortgage-based securities.

## BASICS OF THE BOND MARKET

### What is a bond?

A bond is just a loan. However, there are some important differences between the loans you and I take to buy homes and cars, and the loans underlying bonds.

**First, bonds represent loans taken by agencies, not individuals or households**. The borrowers could be national, state or city governments, large companies, international agencies such as the World Bank, and other such entities. The jargon for the two types of loans is different.

You and I borrow money or take out a loan. The big borrowers are said to issue bonds. The bond issuers are borrowing money from those who buy the bonds.

Second, **these entities borrow much more money at a time than individuals and households**. For example, a single home loan in the US is usually under $ 1 million. However, the US government borrows billions of dollars at a time.

**Third, for most bonds, there is no collateral for the loan.** When you take a car loan, the car is the collateral for the loan. If you don't repay the loan, the lender can repossess your vehicle. When the US government issues a bond, i.e., borrows money, it does not pledge anything as collateral. It's the same for other countries.

When a country fails to make its due payments, it is said to be in default. However, in some cases, before the default actually occurs, the country and its lenders agree to recast the debt. Such agreements are detailed and complex, but the core idea is simple. The lenders agree to take sizeable financial losses, and accept that the country them owes them less than the original debt. However, official international lenders such as the International Monetary Fund and the World Bank don't do such deals. They insist on keeping the old loan amounts, though they do discuss with the borrower ways to clear arrears on past loans.

**Fourth, the repayment schedule for bonds is quite different from the repayment schedule for personal loans.** For personal loans, we typically make a payment every month. The payment includes the interest payment plus repayment of part of the loan. Thus, when the loan period ends, we don't owe anything to the lender.

It's different for bonds. For example, on a 10-year bond, the US government will pay interest twice every six months. There's no repayment of the loan amount until the end of the loan period. At that time, you will get the full amount of the loan back. For example, for a loan of $ 100 for 10 years, you may get $ 2.50 every six months for 10 years, and then repayment of $ 100 at the end of 10 years.

## Some bond market jargon

Like many other fields, the bond market has its own jargon. Some of this jargon came up in the old days of paper but has continued into the electronic age.

Each bond represents a loan amount, for which the jargon term is **face value**. Thus, if the bond is a loan of $ 100, then the bond's face value is $ 100.

Each bond has a **coupon rate,** which is the interest paid by the bond. For example, a bond with a face value of $ 100 that pays $ 2.50 every six months has a coupon rate of 5%. The term coupon comes from the old days when bonds came with paper coupons that were used to redeem the interest payment.

Each bond has a **maturity** and a **tenor.** Maturity is the length of the loan. For example, a 10-year bond has a maturity of 10 years. Tenor is the remaining period of a bond to maturity. For example, four years after being issued, a 10-year bond has a tenor of six years.

**Today, most bonds have a maturity of 30 years or less.** However, in 1993, Disney issued a 100-year bond. Several US universities have also recently issued 100-year bonds. In the past, some countries issued bonds that had no maturity date. Meaning, you could never get your money back. On the other hand, you would get your interest payment forever. For this reason, they are sometimes called perpetuities.

For example, the British government first issued perpetuities called consols in 1751 with an interest rate of 3%. And, they also issued more consols in later years. However, in 2015, the government bought back all the outstanding consols.

How could it work if the British never gave you your money back? How can you wait so long to get your money back from Disney? What if you happen to need your money? Your only option is to sell the bond to someone else.

What's the price you would sell your bond for? We look at this next.

## BOND PRICES AND YIELD TO MATURITY

The only way you can get your money back before a bond reaches the time of its maturity is to sell it to someone else on the bond market. Like shares in companies, bonds are bought and sold every day in the bond market. And, like share prices, the prices of bonds change every day.

Actually, like share prices, bond prices change with every trade, not just every day. Like everything else, the price of a bond is determined by demand and supply of bonds.

A bond's price is closely linked to the bond's yield to maturity (YTM). The YTM is a measure of the expected return on the bond if it is held to maturity. This is a complex concept with quite a bit of abstract arithmetic. It's enough for us to look at a simple example that brings out the key principles.

### A simple example of the sale of a bond

Suppose Aay has lent $ 100 at 6% for seven years to Bee. The repayment schedule is set up as in a bond. Suppose that the repayment schedule is that Bee will pay Aay $ 6 every year at the end of the year, and then pay $ 100 at the end of seven years.

Two years have passed. Bee has been making the interest payments as scheduled. For some personal reasons, Aay wants their $ 100 back. If Aay asks Bee to return the borrowed $ 100, Bee will not do it, as Bee is required to pay this amount only after seven years.

Aay's only choice at this time is to ask someone else to take over the loan. So, Aay asks Cee to take over the loan. Aay offers this deal to Cee.

Cee will pay $100 to Aay, and take over the loan. Taking over the loan means Cee will get from Bee $ 6 each year for the next five years, and then another $ 100 at the end of five years. Aay will get nothing more as Aay will be out of the deal.

Cee rejects this offer. Cee says that the current interest rate is 10%. Why should I settle for only a 5% interest rate? With their $ 100, Cee can get $ 10 every year, instead of $ 6 every year. So, Cee counters with this offer.

Cee will pay Aay $ 60 and take over the loan. This way, Cee get $ 6 every year from Bee, which will be equivalent to earning 10% on $ 60. Cee claims that is a fair price for the loan.

We call the proposed payments of $ 100 or $ 60 from Cee to Aay as the loan's proposed price of the loan. So far, there's no agreement on the price.

Aay says, "Wait a minute. Your proposed price of $ 60 is too low. You will get $ 100 at the end of the loan, even though you would have put in only $ 60. That's a huge bonus of $ 40 on top of all the interest payments! We need to take account of that big bonus."

How do we take account of this big bonus? Aay and Cee turn to Moneysmart for help.

Moneysmart says, "It's a complicated calculation. Cee's proposed price is giving them too good a deal. In effect, Cee's return is more than 10% because the proposed price of $ 60 is too low. So, you must increase the price. This will have two effects that both reduce Cee's return."

"Let me show these two effects with an example. Suppose you raise the price to $ 70. Then, the bonus at the end becomes $ 100 - $ 70 = $ 30. That itself reduces Cee's return on their money. Second, the coupon payment of $ 6 on a $ 70 price is a return of about 8.5%, which is lower than the return of 10% with a $ 60 price. So, raising the bond price from $ 60 to $ 70 will reduce Aay's return."

Whew, that's complicated. So many numbers are flying around. Moneysmart knew this, and summarizes the scenarios in this way.

**A proposed price of $ 60 is very good for Cee but too low for Aay**. With a price of $ 60, and a coupon payment of $ 6 every year, Cee would earn 6/60 = 10% interest ever year. This calculated interest rate is called the **current yield**, which is the interest rate based on the coupon payment and the bond prices. So, Cee would earn 10% every year plus a big bonus at the end. An excellent deal for Cee but a terrible deal for Aay.

**The proposed price of $ 70 is worse than $ 60 for Cee but still low for Aay**. With a price of $ 70, and a coupon payment of $ 6 every year, the current yield would be 6/70 = 8.5% interest. Plus, Cee would get a bonus of $ 30 at the end. The current yield of 8.5% is below the current interest rate of 10%, but the significant bonus payment at the end adds enough to Cee's overall return. Now it like a good deal for Cee but a bad deal for Aay.

And, Moneysmart describes the situation with a price of $ 90.

**A proposed price of $ 90 would likely be too high for Cee but a good deal for Aay**. With a price of $ 90, and a coupon payment of $ 6 every year, the current yield would be 6/90 = 6.7%. That's significantly below the current interest rate of 10%. The small bonus of $ 10 will add something to Cee's return but is unlikely to be enough. Now, it does not look like a good deal for Cee, but it seems to be good for Aay.

We see that increasing the price $ 70 to $ 90 flips the advantage from Cee to Aay. So, there must be some price between $ 70 and $ 90 that is the tipping point. The tipping point is the price that would be OK for both Aay and Cee. How do we find this right price?

## Using YTM to find the right price for the bond

By the right price, we mean that Cee should find it as good as investing their money elsewhere, where they can earn the current market interest rate of 10%.

How do we find this price? By calculating the yield to maturity at each different price for the bond, and settling for the price where the YTM = 10%. Why is this the right way?

What we need is to do is to find a mathematical way of converting that bonus at the end of the loan into an average percent return per year. And, then add this to the current yield. This will give us the loan's total annual return.

For example, in our example, with a price of $ 70, the current yield is 8.5%. We need to convert the bonus of $ 30 into an annual percentage return over the remaining five years. Then, we add this bonus return to the current yield to get the total annual percentage yield.

**Formally, the total annual percentage yield is called the yield to maturity (YTM).** YTM is a percentage return that takes account of all the relevant factors in the deal. They are the face value ($ 100 in the above example), the coupon rate (6% in the above example), the number of remaining years (5 in the above example), and the price of the loan (which is variable).

The formula for calculating YTM is complicated. Let's avoid this complexity here because many calculators are readily available on the internet and spreadsheet software that will do the calculation for you. Let's look at the results in Figure 5.1.

From Figure 5.1, we see that for this example, the YTM is equal to 10% at a bond price of about $ 85. At this price, the current yield is 6/85 = 7.1%. And, the bonus of about $ 15 at the end of five years adds a bit under 3% per year to the current yield. On adding them up, **we get the desired YTM of 10% at a bond price of about $ 85, which is the right price for Cee to pay Aay.**

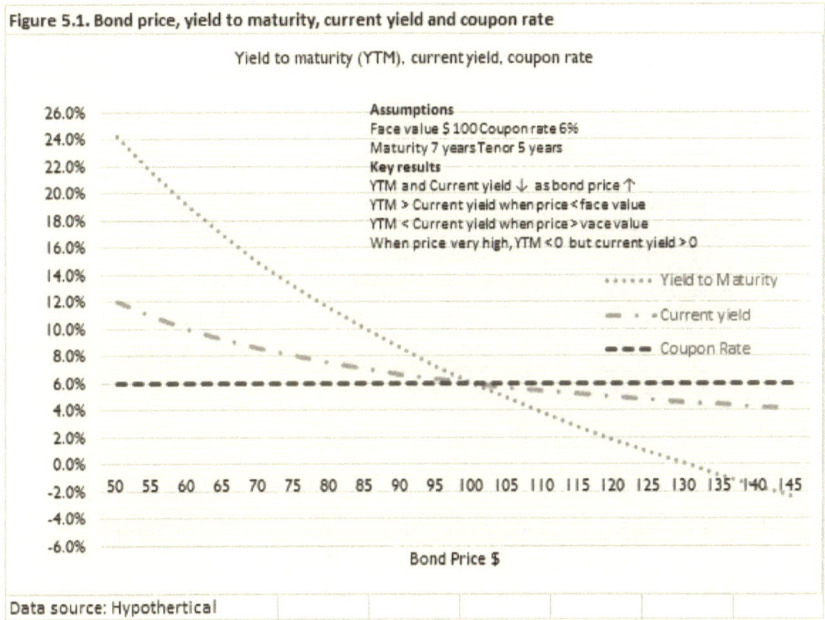

Figure 5.1. Bond price, yield to maturity, current yield and coupon rate

## Rule related to bond prices and YTM

In Figure 5.1, we can see the fundamental results related to bond prices and YTM.

**The rule is that the price of a bond and its YTM are inversely related.** When a bond's price goes up, the yield goes down, and when a bond's price goes down, the yield goes up. For example, in Figure 5.1, we see that when the bond price is $ 50, the YTM is very high at close to 25%. Then, as the price goes up, the YTM comes down.

Thus, if you see news reports that the bond market has rallied, it means that the bond prices have gone up, which implies that the YTMs have gone down. Let's look at two real-world examples of bond prices and YTMs changing.

## BOND MARKET EXPERIENCE IN GREECE AND GERMANY

### Bond market pressurized Greece in 2010

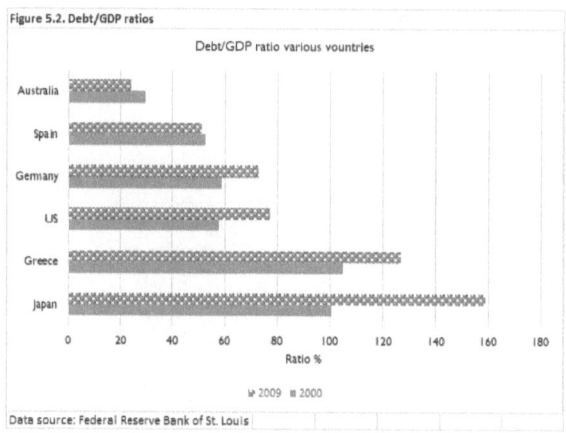

Figure 5.2. Debt/GDP ratios

By the year 2000, the Government of Greece had already accumulated a lot of debt. Greece's debt/GDP ratio was over 100%, much higher than in other countries, as shown in Figure 5.2. And Greece continued to accumulate more debt. By the beginning of 2009, Greece's debt/GDP ratio was more than 125%., which was considered very high at that time.

Note that Japan had a higher debt/GDP ratio than Greece in 2009. However, Japan did not suffer the same fate as Greece. Thus, the debt/GDP ratio is not the only factor that determines the yield.

Like other governments, the Greek government had to borrow money to finance its deficits. Greece's need for additional loans was coming on top of an already heavy debt burden. Hence, there were concerns that the Greek government may not be able to repay its debt. This meant that the additional loans were seen as increasingly riskier. So, potential lenders wanted higher interest rates.

The yield on the Greek government's 10-year bonds had started rising in 2008, as you can see in Figure 5.3. The yield went up from 4.4% in January 2008 to 5.6% in January 2009. That was a clear signal that the government would likely have to pay a higher interest rate the next time it wanted to borrow some money. In January 2010, the yield was about 6.0%, and by April 2010, the yield had risen to about 7.8%.

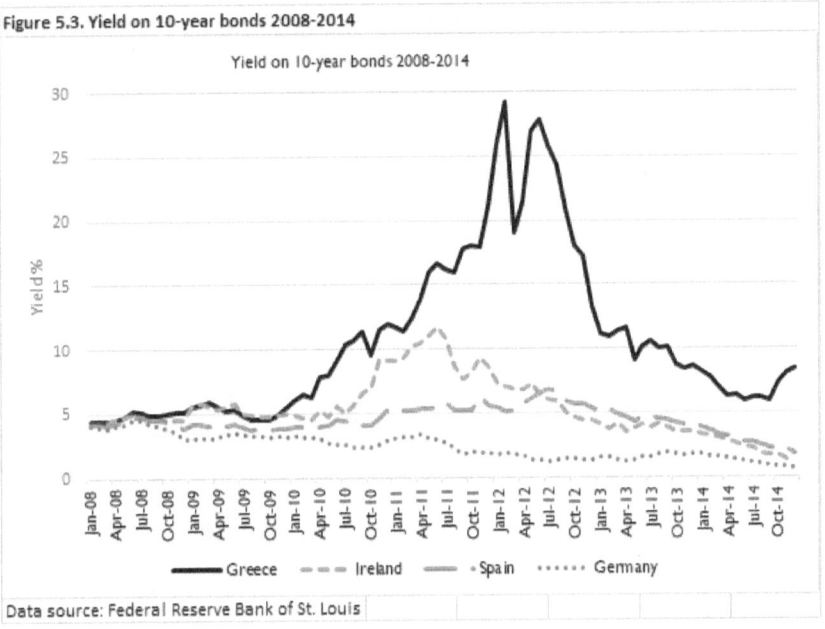

Figure 5.3. Yield on 10-year bonds 2008-2014

Data source: Federal Reserve Bank of St. Louis

This was not the trend in other European countries, as shown in Figure 5.3. Greece's high and rising yields were a clear signal that the Greek government would have to pay a much higher interest rate on future loans than in the past. This higher interest rate would impose a substantial financial burden on the Greek government. **In effect, the bond market had collectively voted against the Greek government's management of the economy.**

For some time, Greece had been repaying old loans that were due by taking out new loans. For example, if Greece had to repay € 1 billion to group A, Greece borrowed € 1 billion from group B, and paid off group A. This way, Greece's debt would remain unchanged. This is what many countries and other people in debt do.

The real potential problem with this type of money shuffle is the interest rate on the new loan. Would group B charge a higher interest rate than group A had charged Greece? If yes, then the debt burden would increase even though the total amount of the debt had not gone up.

The bond market had sent a clear signal to the Greek government that it would have to pay a much higher interest rate for any new loan. The specific problem for Greece was that it had to repay a loan of € 8.5 billion in the third week of May 2010. If the interest rate on this new loan were 8% or higher, that would create a major financial problem for Greece.

**With this assessment from the bond market, the Greek government had no choice but to seek a bailout.** This meant borrowing funds from international and European official agencies. They would charge a reasonable interest rate, but would require changes in economic policies.

In early May 2010, Greece borrowed € 110 billion from the EU and the International Monetary Fund. The loan was to be disbursed over three years. The first installment of this package was € 20 billion. Greece got this installment in the third week of May 2010, just in time to repay its old due loan of € 8.5 billion.

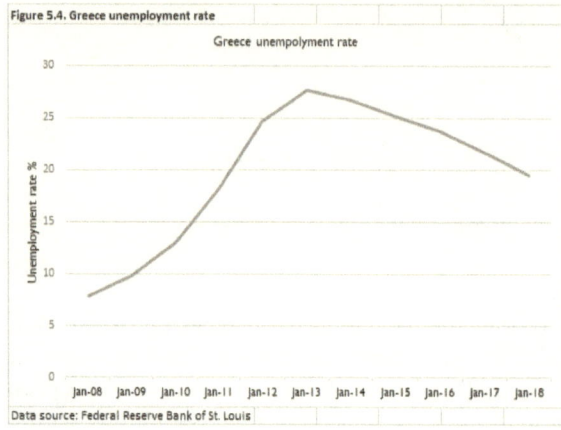

Figure 5.4. Greece unemployment rate

Greece unempolyment rate

Data source: Federal Reserve Bank of St. Louis

**In return, the Greek government agreed to implement a program of austerity, meaning reduced consumption.** Austerity was very painful, with Greece's GDP declining for several years. Greece's unemployment rate zoomed up and stayed high for years to come, as you can see in Figure 5.4.

Further, many young professionals left Greece after 2010, because there seemed to be no hope that the economy would recover soon, or that jobs would come back. This brain drain may have become permanent by now, as Greek emigrants settled down in other countries.

**The lesson is clear. If a government is looking to borrow large amounts of money, it's best to listen to the bond market's message. If the yields on government bonds are rising, there's likely to be trouble ahead. Take quick steps to get your house in order.**

### Greece – falling prices, rising YTM

In Greece's case, some financial investors began to worry that the Greek government would not be able to make its due payment on time. This meant that the risk associated with Greek bonds had increased. So, some investors wanted to sell their Greek bonds. Their feeling was that it was better to take your loss now, and get at least some of your money back. But, how do you sell your bonds when the potential buyers also know the risk associated with the bonds?

One simple way is to reduce the price of the bonds, and hope you can attract some buyers who are willing to take more risk. By lowering the price, you increase the bond's YTM. So, **by a process of interaction between the demand for and supply of bonds, the bond market arrives at a price for the bonds that is acceptable to both buyers and sellers. In Greece's case, the price was coming down over time, and yields were rising**.

Note that the Greek government did not sell bonds every day. Instead, these were investors who had bought the bonds sometime back, either directly from the government or from others, who had become owners of the bonds. In other words, it was the price of already-issued bonds that was falling, which meant that the yields on the existing bonds were rising.

## Germany – rising prices, falling YTM

**What happens if the price of the bond goes above the face value?** Then, there is a loss at the end of the loan. Suppose the bond price is $ 115 in the example shown in Figure 5-1. This means you will face a loss of $ 15 at the end because you will get back only $ 100 even though you bought the bond for $ 115. In Figure 5.1, we see that if the bond price is $ 115, the YTM is about 2.75%, which is below the coupon rate of 6%.

This means that if the bond price is more (less) than the face value, then the YTM is less (more) than the coupon rate. In particular, **if a bond's price rises high enough, then the bond's YTM can become negative, though the current yield remains positive.** In Figure 5.1, we see that if the bond's price is more than $ 130, then the YTM is negative, but the current yield is positive. For example, if the bond's price is $ 140, the YTM is -1.6%, while the current yield is 4.3%.

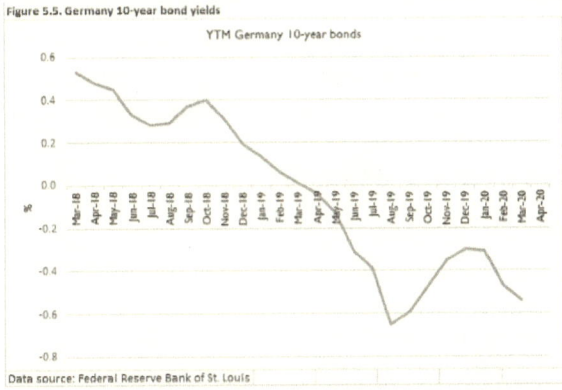

Figure 5.5. Germany 10-year bond yields

YTM Germany 10-year bonds

Data source: Federal Reserve Bank of St. Louis

It's hard to believe, but the YTM of Germany's 10-year bonds has been negative since April 2019! See Figure 5.5. While the YTM has been negative since then, the lowest value came in August 2019. After that, the YTM rose until January 2020, and began to fall after that. Note that the coupon rate on the German bonds is zero – no interest payment at all. The YTM is negative because the sale price is more than the face value.

The German government is getting an unbelievably good deal. It pays no interest on the money it borrows. On top of it, the government can get investors to pay more than the bond's face value. For example, the investors pay € 105 now, earn no interest, and get back € 100 several years later.

Why do investors do this? **What financial sense does it make to buy a bond with a negative YTM, especially when there is no interest payment at all?** These negative yields are not the norm, and have appeared only in recent years. There are no well-established reasons why these negative rates would make sense for many investors. **Yet, this reality of negative yields cannot be denied.**

There is one well-established idea that may help explain the appearance and persistence of negative yields. This idea is that bonds are generally considered a less risky investment than alternatives such as the stock market. In the case of governments of countries such as Germany, there is a belief that your money is safe. The government will almost surely repay the loan. In the case of large firms, their debt payments are their costs, and have to be paid before the firm can pay any dividends from their profits. In this sense, bonds rank ahead of stocks, which means that bonds are safer than stocks.

And we do see a rush to buy bonds when investors think that the economy will have a problem, and the profits of firms will fall. In investment circles, this is referred to as a flight to quality. In this scenario, some investors shift some of their funds to bonds. This increases the bonds' prices, and correspondingly the YTMs fall. This is what happened to US government bonds in mid-March 2020, when it became clear that the coronavirus would hurt the economy, and reduce profits. The YTMs on US government bonds fell sharply within a few days.

So, it is possible that the negative YTMs represent a shift of funds to safe financial investments. Still, these negative rates remain a phenomenon for which there is no well-established explanatory theory or alternative theories.

## DETAILS OF THE WORKING OF BOND MARKETS

### Auctioning bonds

How do governments and companies determine the interest rate they will pay when they issue bonds? Or, do they set the YTM? Or, do they set the coupon rate? How does it work?

When you want to take a loan, you shop around for the lowest interest rate that you have to pay. The bond issuers use the same approach but with a difference. **They set three parameters and let the lenders determine the fourth parameter, which is the price.**

The first parameter is the maturity period, i.e., the length of the loan. This could as little as four weeks. For example, US T-bills run from four weeks to one year. Or, it could be as long as 100 years, as in the case of the Disney bonds.

The second parameter is the coupon rate. We saw above that the German government set the coupon rate at 0%. In early 2020, the US government set a coupon rate of 1.5% on a 10-year bond. And, in April 2020, Ford set a coupon rate of 9.625% on a 10-year bond. These rates are set subjectively but not arbitrarily. The borrowers do have a good sense of the interest rate that lenders will accept.

The third parameter is the total amount the bond issuer wants to borrow. For example, Ford wanted to borrow $ 1 billion for 10 years.

With these parameters, **the bond issuer sets up an auction in which the potential lenders bid on the price they are willing to pay for the bond**. For example, a lender who submits a bid of $ 101 for a bond with a face value of $ 100 and a coupon rate of 3% is effectively saying that I am bidding an interest rate lower than 3%. The reason is that a bid of $ 101 implies a YTM less than 3%.

Thus, in an auction, bidders indicate that they will accept a lower interest rate than the coupon rate by bidding a price higher than the face value. Similarly, they show they want a higher interest rate than the coupon rate by bidding a price lower than the bond's face value.

Then, the bond issuer accepts the bids with the highest prices. Keep in mind that all of them could be less than the face value.

### Risk ratings

We have seen that risk is a major determinant of the price and YTM of a bond. **There are three private firms that assess and rate borrowers. They are S&P, Moody's, and Fitch.** The highest rating, indicating the least risk, is AAA in the S&P and Fitch rating scales, and Aaa in the Moody's scale. The lowest rating is D in the S&P and Fitch scales, and C in the Moody's scale. There are many grades in between these two extremes.

| Table 5.1 Risk rating of various countries April 2020 | | | |
|---|---|---|---|
| | Rating | | Interpretation |
| | Moody's | S&P | |
| Germany | Aaa | AAA | Prime |
| Australia | Aaa | AAA | Prime |
| USA | Aaa | AA+ | Prime/High grade |
| China | A1 | A+ | Upper medium grade |
| Japan | A1 | A | Upper medium grade |
| Mexico | Baa1 | BBB | Lower medium grade |
| India | Baa2 | BBB- | Lower medium grade |
| South Africa | Ba1 | BB | Speculative |
| Greece | B1 | BB- | Speculative |
| Cuba | Caa2 | N/A | Substantial risk |

Data source: Multiple sources

For example, the current ratings for several countries are shown in Table 5.1. I have listed them in order of risk, with the least risky/highest rated countries at the top, and lower-rated countries listed below.

It's not always the case that the different rating agencies have the same assessment. For example, the US has the highest rating from Moody's but not from S&P, where the US rating is one level below the highest level.

Keep in mind that these ratings are, in the end, subjective. And, in 2008, they turned out to be inaccurate because they rated some companies highly, but they proved to be risky. Regardless, these ratings do have a significant effect on the YTM that borrowers must pay when they issue bonds. For example, in January 2020, Mexico issued 10-year bonds worth $ 1.75 billion with a coupon rate of 3.25%. The sale price was just below the face value, and the YTM was 3.31, slightly higher than the coupon rate.

Some countries don't even have a rating from these agencies, which makes it virtually impossible for these countries to borrow money from private international sources.

**The ratings also affect the rate that companies must pay for their loans.** The ratings change as the financial outlook of a company changes. For example, in late March 2020, following the downturn caused by the coronavirus, both S&P and Moody's cut Ford's rating. S&P reduced Ford's rating from BBB- to BB+. This is quite significant because bonds rated BB+ are often called junk bonds, meaning that they are high-risk bonds. Ford's prior rating was BBB-, which is at the bottom border of the non-speculative bonds. No surprise that Ford had to set a high coupon rate of 9.625% in its bond issue in April 2020.

## US Treasury daily yield curve

The US Treasury borrows money with maturity as low as one month, rising to 30 years. Normally, we expect that the YTMs on the shorter-term loans are lower than the yields on the longer-term loans, because they are seen as riskier. We saw this principle in Chapter 4.

If you plot the yields on a particular day for loans of different durations, you get the daily yield curve.

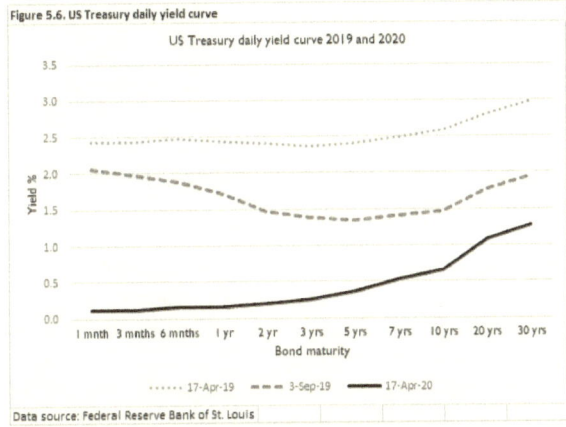

Figure 5.6. US Treasury daily yield curve

In Figure 5.6, you will see the daily yield curve for three different days, i.e., April 17, 2019, April 17, 2020, and September 3, 2019. There's no particular significance to the date April 17. Instead, April 17, 2020, was the most recent day for which data was available when I wrote this section. Then, I chose a date one year earlier for comparison. There is also no special significance for the date September 3, 2019. I picked it for this graph because the data for this date have an unusual characteristic, which we discuss below.

Start by looking at the daily yield curve for April 17, 2019. The curve conforms to the expectation that rates are higher for longer-term loans. Compare this to the curve for April 17, 2020. **All the rates in 2020 are lower than in 2019. This decline comes from a looser monetary policy designed to boost the economy.**

**The decline is the greatest in shorter-term rates, with the 3-month rate falling from about 2.4% to about 0.1%.** On the other end, the drop is the smallest for the 30-year rate, which fell from about 3% to 1.3%. This differential decline shows that **the Fed has a much higher ability to change short-term rates than to change long-term rates.**

How does the Fed influence these rates, which are ultimately set by market forces? We will discuss this next – after we look at the daily yield curve for September 3, 2019.

The yield curve for September 3, 2019, is called an inverted yield curve. In such a curve, long-term rates are lower than short-term rates. It's common to use the 10-year rate to represent the long-term, and the 3-month rate to represent the short-term. Thus, a common comparison is between 3-month and 10-year rates. In this case, the 3-month rate is about 2%, and the 10-year rate is about 1.5%. That's a significant difference because the norm is for the 10-year rate to be higher than the 3-month rate.

What's the significance of an inverted yield curve? Many analysts believe it is an indicator of a future recession or a major economic slowdown. How soon into the future? There is no clear answer to that. Nevertheless, it's worth understanding the reasons behind the inversion.

In some ways, the inversion is like the negative yields seen on German bonds. The similarity is that while the US 10-year yield was not negative, it was much below what would be the norm at that time. In other words, the inversion can be interpreted as a 10-year yield that is lower than expected, based on the prevailing short-term rates.

Just as we interpreted the negative yield on German bonds as a shift to safety, we can interpret the lower US 10-year yield as a shift to safety. Then, the question is: safety against what? Against a likely recession or slowdown. If this happens, then all rates will tend to come down. In particular, short-term rates will come down if the Fed pushes down interest rates, by adopting a loose monetary policy.

What happens to you if you have a 3-month bond? You will get your money back soon, and then you will have to re-invest it. By then, if the Fed has intervened to reduce rates, short-term rates will be way down. And even 10-year rates may have come down. **So, what do you do in anticipation of falling future rates?**

It makes sense to lock in 10-year bonds today. As more people look to buy 10-year bonds, their price goes up. As the prices of these bonds rise, this reduces the YTM on 10-year bonds. In turn, this may lead to an inverted yield curve.

As you can see, several assumptions underlie this flow of logic. As with the negative YTMs, the inverted yield curve is a fact of financial markets that does not yet have a simple, clear, well-accepted explanation.

## HOW DO CENTRAL BANKS INFLUENCE MARKET INTEREST RATES?

The Fed and other central banks can influence market interest rates. How do they do it? Central banks have four ways of doing this: buying and selling loans; changing the interest rate on loans to banks; changing interest paid on banks' reserves with the Fed; and changing the deposit reserve ratio.

### Buying and selling loans

**When a central bank wants to reduce interest rates, it buys bonds in the bond market.** This increase in demand for bonds pushes their prices up, and reduces their YTM. Further, this puts more money with the bond sellers, which increases the money supply. On the other hand, **when a central bank**

**wants to increase interest rates, it sells bonds in the bond market.** This buying and selling of loans by a central bank is often called an open market operation.

**In March 2020, in response to the coronavirus, the Fed said it would buy bonds worth hundreds of billions of dollars.** Traditionally, central banks used to buy only government bonds, but that had changed in 2008, in response to the economic meltdown at that time. The Fed had shifted to purchasing a variety of bonds. In particular, the Fed would buy mortgage-backed securities, which we will discuss later in this chapter.

Further, the Fed would buy commercial paper. This term is financial jargon for no-collateral short-term loans of up to a few months taken out large firms. By buying these loans, the Fed took over the risk associated with these loans, which made it much easier for large companies to get these loans. The purchase also pumped up the money supply.

### Interest rate on loans to banks

The Fed lends money to banks that wish to add to their reserves. The rate at which the Fed lends money to banks is called the discount rate. We saw in Chapter 2 that this term has another interpretation. They are different concepts, so keep this difference in mind.

In March 2020, the Fed reduced the rate from 1.75% to 0.25%. As recently as April 2019, this rate was 3%. By lowering the discount rate, the Fed stood ready to increase the money supply, depending upon how much money banks borrowed from the Fed.

### Interest paid on banks' reserves with the Fed

In March 2020, the Fed cut the interest rate from 1.6% to 0.1%. The idea was to encourage the banks to lend more money in the market place, instead of keeping their funds as deposits with the Fed.

### Deposit reserve ratio requirements

We noted in Chapter 4 that the Fed reduced the deposit reserve ratio from 10% to 0%. This enabled banks to lend more, thus potentially increasing the money supply and cutting interest rates.

### Response to the coronavirus economic shock 2020

In response to the March 2020 coronavirus economic crisis, central banks have taken many other steps to make loans available to businesses and governments. For example, the Fed has said that it will enable loans worth $

2.3 trillion to those who need the money to tide them over. Further, the US government has announced that it will provide an economic stimulus package of $ 2.0 trillion, or even more.

Remember that the US government normally runs a budget deficit. Hence, **the US government will finance the stimulus package by borrowing money by issuing bonds of various maturities**. As usual, these bonds will be bought not only by US citizens and agencies but also by groups all around the world, who have faith in the US government.

**Once the US government has issued bonds, the Fed will buy some of them.** Some of the money for this purchase will come from the $ 2.3 trillion package announced by the Fed. Now, where does the Fed get this money from? Does the Fed have this much money sitting somewhere? No. **The Fed will pay for these bonds simply by depositing funds in the accounts of the sellers. All electronic – no need to print more money because electronic money is the same as paper money.**

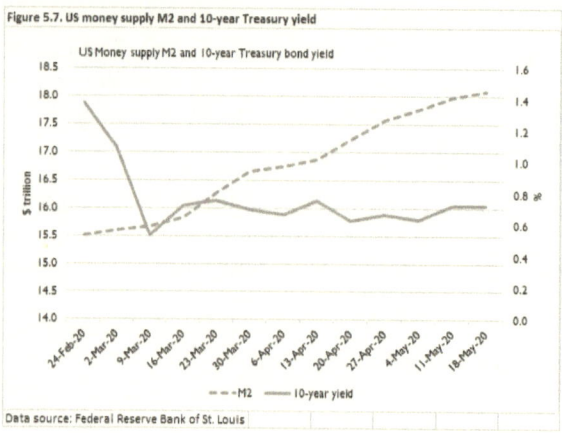

Figure 5.7. US money supply M2 and 10-year Treasury yield

The net effect is that the money supply will increase, and the yields on Treasury bonds will decline, as you can see in Figure 5.7 In turn, this change reduces the US government's cost of borrowing money to fund the stimulus.

**Isn't this all fake money? Isn't there some trick in it somewhere?** The answer lies in the discussion about money in Chapter 4. There we learned that money is money because people accept it as money. Or, a seller of bonds to the Fed accepts a payment from the Fed as legitimate money because this seller is confident that this deposit from the Fed can be used to buy something else – physical or financial – from someone else. **In the end, it works because people worldwide trust the US government and the dollar when it comes to money.**

## SECURITIZATION AND MORTGAGES

**Until the economic meltdown of 2008, securitization was an obscure term.** Financial-savvy people knew it, but other people knew about it vaguely, if at all.

Securitization became a public term when it turned out that one type of securitization was a key element of the financial transactions that had led to financial failures and, ultimately financial bailouts by the US government. This securitization was related to a large number of home mortgages issued to people with a significant risk that they would not be able to pay back the loans. These mortgages are called sub-prime loans, i.e., loans made to people who may not be able to pay back the loans, with full knowledge of this risk.

At that time, the news media had a hard time explaining these financial transactions to the general public. So, in some places and for some people, securitization became something to be avoided. They wished that the world would return to the old days, when financial transactions were simpler to undertake and understand.

But this is not the right way to look at securitization. Securitization is a useful financial tool that has been around for a long time. Like any other tool, it can be misused in particular cases. So, let's first look at securitization as a financial tool, and then see how it applies to mortgages in the US.

## Securitization concept

Securitization has two versions: pass-through securitization and collateralized debt obligations.

### *Pass-through securitization*

This is how pass-thru securitization works.

First, **create a pool of money flows from a variety of sources**. The sources can be of the same type, or of different types. For example, the money flows could come from the sale of different products that a company makes. Or, the money flows could come from interest and loan repayments made by large, well-established companies. The key point is that the money flows are pooled.

Now, you have a pool of money in which the source of the money is no longer significant. For example, a company such as Microsoft pools the profit flows from the various products and services it sells. Or, a money market mutual fund pools the money flows from the loans the fund has made to several companies.

Second, **sell shares in this pool of money. The key point is that your share is in the pool, not in any of the underlying sources**. For example, when you have a share in a mutual market mutual fund, you don't own a share in the companies that have borrowed money from this fund. Similarly, if you own a share in Microsoft, you don't have a share in the profits from any particular source such as Windows, or Microsoft Office, or their cloud services. What you have is a share in the pooled money.

**Your share is a security.** The money flows have been securitized.

Similarly, when you invest your funds in a mutual fund that buys shares in companies, you are not linked to any particular company. Your share in the stock mutual fund is a security that is linked to the pool of money.

## Collateralized debt obligation

The practical implementation of this concept comes in the form of asset-based securities (ABS) and mortgage-based securities (MBS). (Remember, in financial jargon, a loan is a lender's asset.)

These securities are shares in the pool of money arising from various sources. ABS are based on a pool of money resulting from repayments of several types of debt, such as loans other than mortgages or any other regular due payments, such as leases. MBS arise from mortgage payments.

Conceptually, ABS and MBS are similar, and we discuss only MBS here. Let's look at how mortgage finance work in the US.

### Step 1. Mortgage originator gives a mortgage loan with credit appraisal

**Many decades ago, banks were the principal agencies that issued mortgages.** The bank would lend you money to buy a house. This money came from the deposits that people had made in the bank. As we discussed in Chapter 4, these deposits are how the bank borrows money from savers.

For many decades, in the US, there are many non-bank commercial firms that make mortgage loans. Look around on the internet, and you will find them. These lenders do not take deposits to get the money they lend. Instead, they have a combination of their own money and funds borrowed on the financial markets.

Banks and non-bank lenders can be called mortgage originators, i.e., the agencies that give loans to homeowners.

Before giving a mortgage loan, the mortgage originators check the creditworthiness of the borrower. **Three agencies connected with the US government in different ways set the requirements for this credit check.** These agencies are generally known by their nicknames, Ginnie Mae, Fannie Mae, and Freddie Mac. These agencies work in different ways to make it easier for mortgage lenders to get the funds they need to make mortgage loans.

These guidelines have four elements. A mortgage loan that meets these guidelines is called a conforming loan, while a mortgage loan that does not meet these guidelines is called a non-conforming loan.

i.  **There must be a minimum down payment.** The borrower cannot borrow 100% of the value of the house, and must make a down payment. In some cases, the down payment can be as low as 3%, but is higher (around 20%) in most cases. The down payment is the borrower's initial equity.

The proportion of the principal amount borrowed relative to the equity the borrower makes as a down payment is known as the initial loan-to-value (LTV) ratio. The LTV usually goes down as the borrower pays down the loan over time and/or the value of the property increases, i.e., the borrower's equity generally increases over time.

ii.  **The loan amount must be below the loan limit.** The loan must be below the limit, which is changed periodically to take account of changes in house prices. In 2020, the general limit is $ 510,400. In designated high-cost areas such as New York and San Francisco, the limit is 50% higher at $ 765,600. Loans above this limit are called **jumbo loans,** which do not qualify as conforming loans.

iii.  **The borrower must have a good credit score.** The value of the minimum required credit score depends upon several factors. For many borrowers, the required scores would be above 680.

iv.  **The borrower must not have too much debt.** The lenders calculate the borrower's debt-to-income ratio, which is the ratio of all the borrower's monthly debt payments to your monthly income. The debt payments include monthly mortgage payments. In general, this ratio should be less than 36%, but higher limits up to 50% are also allowed in some circumstances.

One major reason for the US housing loan crisis in 2008 was that many loan originators made non-conforming loans in return for higher yields. In particular, there was not enough consideration in the preceding years of the credit score or the amount of the borrower's debt-to-income ratio. In short, the lender did not insist the borrower be creditworthy, and the borrowers paid a higher interest rate. These loans were called sub-prime loans, indicating that they had been given to borrowers with low creditworthiness.

### Step 2. Mortgage originator sells the loan to a loan buyer

Suppose that the mortgage originator keeps the loan, meaning that the originator does not sell the loan. This would limit the number of loans that the originator could make. For example, if a bank is making mortgage loans, the value of the loans would be limited by the deposits that the bank had.

Suppose that mortgage originators sell their loans. Then, originators that sell their loans get their money back. And, they can make more loans with this returned money. The homeowner is not affected by this sale, as the terms of the mortgage do not change. The only change is that the actual lender is now the loan buyer.

This sale and purchase of mortgages take place in what is called a secondary market in loans, where the primary market refers to the loan origination market.

In the US, it's normal for mortgage originators to sell their conforming loans. Fannie Mae and Freddie Mac are the common buyers of these conforming loans. These agencies do not buy non-conforming loans. However, there are private firms that will buy non-conforming loans. For example, Lehman Brothers, which became bankrupt in 2008, was a major buyer of non-conforming loans, including sub-prime loans.

### Step 3. Loan buyer creates a pool of money and sells mortgage-backed securities

A loan buyer buys many mortgages. They form a pool of money that comes from homeowners every month. In turn, the loan buyer looks to find some group that will buy the loans. This sale frees up the funds for new mortgage loans.

**Instead of selling the loans as loans, the loan buyer sells shares in the pool of money created by the mortgage payment inflows**. These shares are called securities. The buyers of the securities will receive their money from the mortgage principal and interest payments. **These shares are called mortgage-based securities.**

To recap. The homeowners make their monthly installment payments of the principal and interest on their loans. These payments do not go to the mortgage originators. Instead, this money flows into the pool created by the loan buyers. Then, the money flows out of this pool to the buyers of the mortgage-backed securities. **In effect, the MBS buyers are now the lenders to the homeowners.**

Who are the MBS buyers? In the US market, the buyers are not just in the United States – they are worldwide. The buyers could be retirement plans, insurance companies, or any other group looking for returns higher than those offered by government bonds.

In the case of conforming loans, the MBS buyers do not hold the risk of default by homeowners. The reason is that the payments due from homeowners are guaranteed by Fannie Mae and Freddie Mac. These entities take the risk of non-payment on conforming loans. However, in the case of non-conforming loans, the issuer of the MBS, possibly a bank or other financial entity, holds this risk.

## Tranched securities

The part about securitization that gave MBS a bad name in 2008 was the issuance of tranched securities. The idea underlying these tranched securities is to split up a large pool of loans into different layers known as tranches, based on different risks.

For example, suppose we have created a pool of money from 1,000 loans. Assume that about 1% of the borrowers may default, i.e., not make their payments. Based on this data, the pool of money is divided into tranches. To keep it simple, we have only Tranche 1 and Tranche 2.

People who put themselves in Tranche 1 have a higher priority in receiving the money flows from the pool as homeowners make their payments each month. People in Tranche 2 have a lower priority. In the case of default, Tranche 2 takes the first losses. Losses begin to hit Tranche 1 only after a pre-specified cutoff.

Why would anyone want to be in Tranche 2? Since the risk in Tranche 2 is higher, the return is also higher. Tranche 1 is the low-risk, low-return option.

That brings up the question: How are the different risk-return configurations set up? Typically, the differences would be based on the expected default rate, which is 1% in our example.

If the actual default rates turn out to be less than the expected 1%, then Tranche 2 will be happy. They will get a high return because few people defaulted, and Tranche 2 continued to get its share of the pooled money.

On the other hand, if the default rate turns out to be much higher, say 15%, then Tranche 2 will be hit with major losses. They may lose all that they have invested. And, even Tranche 1 may take some losses.

During the subprime crisis of 2008, subprime loans defaulted at rates that were much higher than expected. This was completely unexpected by most investors. These high default rates hurt financial institutions all around the world who had invested in the higher priority tranches, believing them to be low risk.

## KEY TAKEAWAYS

### Basics of bond market

1. A bond is just a loan. However, there are some important differences between the loans you and I take to buy homes and cars, and the loans underlying bonds. First, bonds represent loans taken by agencies, not individuals or households. Second, these entities borrow much more money at a time than individuals and households. Third, for most bonds, there is no collateral for the loan. Fourth, the repayment schedule for bonds is quite different from the repayment schedule for personal loans. For example, on a 10-year bond, the US government will pay interest twice a year, i.e., every six months. There's no repayment of the loan amount until the end of the loan period.

2. Each bond represents a loan amount, for which the jargon term is face value. Each bond has a coupon rate, which is the interest paid by the bond. Each bond has a maturity and a tenor. Maturity is the length of the loan. Tenor is the remaining period of a bond to maturity.

### Bond price and yield to maturity

3. Bonds are bought and sold in the bond market, where a bond's price is determined by supply and demand. A bond's price is closely linked to the bond's yield to maturity (YTM). The YTM is a measure of the expected return on the bond if it is held to maturity. A fundamental rule of the bond market is that when a bond's price goes up or down, the bond's yield to maturity goes in the other direction. For example, if the bond price goes up, the bond's yield to maturity comes down.

### Bond market experience in Greece and Germany

4. In 2010, the YTM of Greek government bonds increased significantly. In effect, the bond market had collectively voted against the Greek government's management of the economy. Greece was forced to seek a financial bailout.

5. The YTM of Germany's 10-year bonds has been negative since April 2019. The German government has been getting an unbelievably good deal when it borrows money.

## Details of the working of bond markets

6. Governments and companies set are the length of the loan, the coupon rate, and the total amount they want to borrow when they issue bonds by auction. They let the lenders determine the price, which is equivalent to determining the YTM.

7. There are three private firms that assess and rate borrowers. Their ratings affect the interest rate that the borrowers have to pay. Borrowers rated as riskier have to pay higher interest rates.

8. If you plot the yields on a particular day for loans of different durations, you get the daily yield curve. Normally, the yield curve is upward rising, reflecting the general rule that interest rates are higher for longer duration loans. A yield curve is said to be inverted when some parts of it are downward sloping. Some analysts believe that an inverted yield curve is an indication of a future economic slowdown.

## How do central banks influence market interest rates?

9. When a central bank wants to reduce interest rates, it buys bonds in the bond market. On the other hand, when a central bank wants to increase interest rates, it sells bonds in the bond market.

## Securitization and mortgages

10. Securitization is a useful financial tool that has been around for a long time. Like any other tool, it can be misused in particular cases.

11. Mortgage-based securities (MBS) are created from a pool of funds created by monthly mortgage payments from a large number of homeowners. The buyers of MBS are the ultimate lenders to the homeowners.

12. The part about securitization that gave MBS a bad name in the 2008 economic crisis was the issuance of tranched securities. The idea underlying these tranched securities is to split up a large pool of loans into different layers known as tranches, based on different risks. Unfortunately, the actual risks of US subprime loans were not properly disclosed, which ultimately led to substantial financial losses in many countries.

This concludes our discussion of financial markets. In the next chapter, we will turn to a discussion of unemployment

.

# SECTION III.   UNDERSTANDING AND MEASURING MAJOR ECONOMIC VARIABLES

In Chapter 1, we had introduced seven principal endogenous macroeconomic variables. We will discuss some of them in detail in this section. Our approach will be to focus on what they mean in the real world, and how they are measured. You will see that these variables are defined and measured in several different ways. You will also see that sometimes there is considerable discussion about which versions of the variables should be used in formulating policies.

We start by discussing **unemployment** (Chapter 6). This beginning is appropriate because getting and keeping a full-time job is one of the most important goals for most people. Then, we move to **inflation** (Chapter 7). As we saw in Chapter 4, many central banks have adopted an inflation target.

Professor Arthur Okun, a prominent economist with extensive real-world experience, defined a country's Economic Discomfort Index as a measure of how comfortable people are in economic terms. His index is the sum of the inflation and unemployment rates, given by the formula **Economic Discomfort Index = unemployment rate + inflation rate**. Based on this index, the aim of economic policies should be to keep both inflation and unemployment low, as this will reduce the people's discomfort.

During the 1976 US Presidential election campaign, Jimmy Carter pointed out that Economic Discomfort had gone up under President Ford. Then, in 1980, **Ronald Reagan renamed this index as the Misery Index.** He pointed out that under President Carter, the Misery Index had become even higher than under President Ford.

The use of the Misery Index in public discussions is a clear indication that the unemployment and inflation rates matter a lot to the average person. However, they are not the only variables that matter. One critical weakness of the Misery Index is that it does not take account of the **GDP growth rate**.

A high GDP growth rate was the aim of many countries even before the coronavirus hit their economies beginning in early 2020. As a result of the coronavirus, most countries have seen reductions in their GDP growth rates. Some countries are worried that their GDP will fall. At the same time, we note that some people say that we should not give much importance to GDP because it is a flawed measure. **We discuss the GDP and its flaws in Chapter 8.**

But, is a high GDP growth rate enough? What about the distribution of the economic benefits of economic growth to various groups? How equally are they distributed? **We look at poverty and economic inequality in Chapter 9.**

## CHAPTER 6.   JOB CREATION AND UNEMPLOYMENT

**For many people, one critical economic issue is: Do I have a job, or will I have a job in the future?** Most working-age people want a job. It's not because they love to work, though some do, but they see it as the best option to make a decent living. There is a revealing, somewhat flippant saying about jobs and job loss: "It's a recession when your neighbor loses their job. It's a depression when you lose your job."

For this reason, **creating enough jobs is a primary social goal of an economy**. Not just any jobs but jobs that pay reasonably well. What's a reasonable wage? That's a subjective value, which will vary from place to place, and over time.

A substantial amount of public discussion about job creation focuses on the current unemployment rate. However, it is equally **useful to understand how many jobs are needed in the future to get to or maintain future full employment.**

With this forecast of future job needs, we would have a clearer idea of the policies or actions that have to be taken now to meet future job needs.

### Chapter flow

This chapter has two main parts. In the first part, we discuss how many jobs have to be created in the future in various countries. We do not provide any numerical estimates. Instead, we lay out the broad steps that have to be taken to estimate this number in any country.

In the second part, we discuss how unemployment is measured in the US. While the discussion is US-specific, it brings out the practical complexity in defining and measuring unemployment. Since these issues are present in all countries, the lessons from the US system are broadly applicable.

### HOW MANY JOBS SHOULD AN ECONOMY CREATE EVERY YEAR?

It turns that it is quite complicated to estimate how many paid jobs an economy should create every year in the future. This number depends upon two broad variables.

**The first variable is the net new job seekers who will enter the labor force.** In turn, this depends upon how many people come of working-age and how many people move out of working-age. We discuss this below as estimating the future working-age population.

However, only some of the people who come of working age will be looking for paid work. Some of them will go for higher education, so they will look for paid work later. Others may follow tradition and become unpaid homemakers, and perhaps never look for a paid job. **The share of working-age people looking for work is called the labor force participation rate.**

The second variable is the number of existing working-age people who need new jobs in the future. If working-age people do not have jobs or are under-employed, then jobs will have to be created for them in the future. We can call this the backlog of people who will need a job in the future.

## First variable - net new job seekers

**The number of net new job seekers depends upon the future working-age population, and the future labor force participation rate.** The working-age population is the total number of people who would, in principle, be looking for a job. How many of them will be actually looking for a job will depend upon the labor force participation rate. Let's look at these two factors.

### *Estimate the future working-age population*

In the US, the working-age population is defined as people 16 years or older. In other countries, the working-age population consists of people 15-64 years old. **Let's use the 15-64 age group as a guideline as this will facilitate international comparison.**

### *Let's look at the working-age population in the next ten years*

**To do this, we create two age-based groups**. The first group is people 5-14 years old. In ten years, all of them will be part of the working-age population. Let's call them the entry group. On the other hand, the age group of 55-64 years old will no longer be part of the working-age population. Let's call them the exit group.

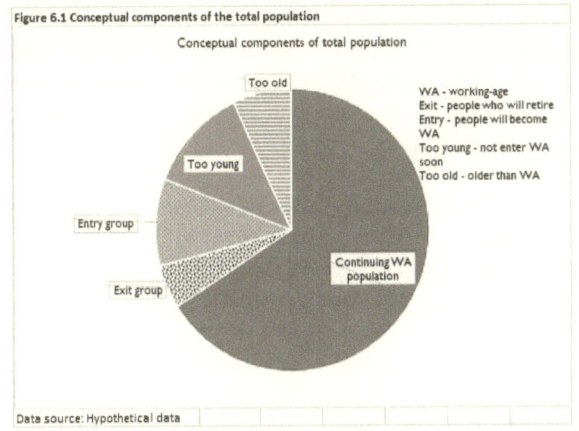

Figure 6.1 Conceptual components of the total population

The difference between the entry and exit groups' values indicates how much the working age population will increase in the next ten years. In turn, this is an indication of the number of jobs that the economy has to create.

In Figure 6.1, you can see the conceptual components of a country's total population. Within the working-age population, there is an exit group. Similarly, within the non-working-age population, there is an entry group.

In Figure 6.2, you can see the shares in the 2020 population of the entry and exit groups for several countries. We can also see each country's median age. By definition, half of the population is younger than the median age, and the other half is above the median age. **The median age is a key feature of a country's demographic profile**. From the demographic perspective, **countries with a low median age are considered young, while countries with a high median age are considered old.**

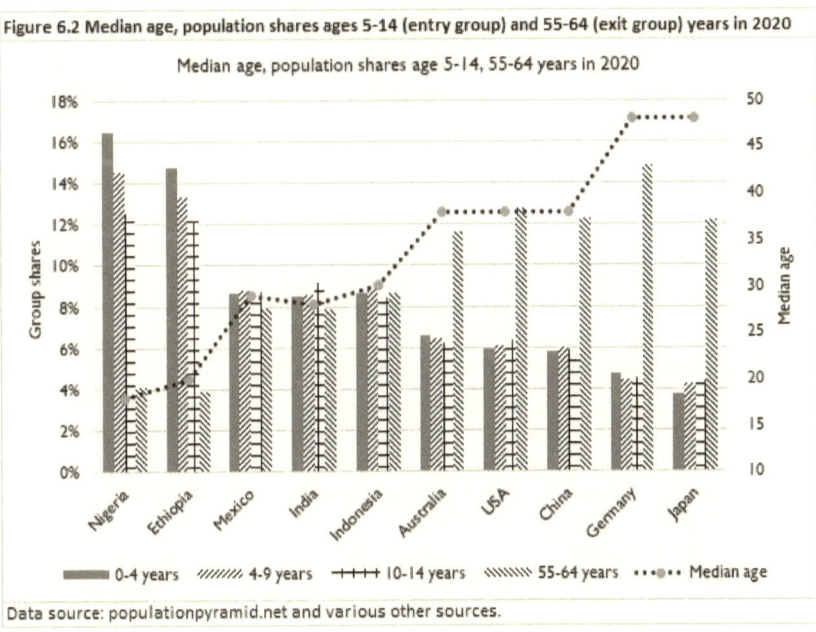

Figure 6.2 Median age, population shares ages 5-14 (entry group) and 55-64 (exit group) years in 2020

Data source: populationpyramid.net and various other sources.

In Figure 6.2, there are four categories of countries based on their median age, and the sizes of their entry and exit groups. While our analysis is related to just a few countries in each category, the results will broadly hold for other countries with similar demographic profiles.

**The first category consists of Nigeria and Ethiopia**. They are the two countries with the highest population in Africa. The median age here is below 20 years. They are very young countries. Their entry group is very large, while the exit group is rather small. **In these very young countries, there will be a need to create a huge number of jobs in the next ten years as the working-age populations will increase rapidly.**

**The second category consists of Mexico, India, and Indonesia.** Since their median age is close to 30 years, they are young countries. Here the entry group is large, though smaller than for Nigeria and Ethiopia. Further, the exit group is small, though larger than for Nigeria and Ethiopia**. These countries will need to create a large number of future jobs because their working-age populations will increase significantly in the next ten years.**

**The third category consists of Australia, the US, and China**. Their median age is close to 40 years, which makes them middle-age countries. China's presence in this category doesn't seem to fit. Based on per capita income, Australia and the US are high-income countries, while China is not – it is a middle-income country.

The reason China is a middle-age country is China's one-child policy. When two people have one child, the younger generation is smaller in numbers than the older generation. Some people in China broke the one-child policy and had more than one child. China gave up the policy in 2013. However, you can still see the policy's ongoing effects in the relatively low share of the entry group, and the high median age.

In this category, the values of the entry and exit groups are about equal. In these countries, there will be no disproportionate pressure to create jobs because there will not be any major change in the working-age population.

**The fourth category consists of Germany and Japan.** Their median age is close to 50 years, and they are aging countries. Here the share of the entry group is smaller than the exit group. The implication is that their working-age populations will shrink in the future. As a result, there will be no pressure at all to create jobs. Instead, they will be looking for some combination of automation, persuading people to keep working, and allowing migrants to come in. For example, Japan has changed its laws to encourage more immigration. Germany has also changed its laws to allow more immigration of skilled people.

**Hence, the burden of job creation in the next ten years is very different for countries with different demographic profiles.** Younger (by median age) countries will have to create many more jobs than older (by median age) countries. Further, each country will have to check whether its economic model is adapting suitably to the changing working-age population.

*Use labor force participation rate to determine the future labor force*

We started this chapter by saying that most people want jobs. The proportion of people looking to work is called the labor force participation rate, which is measured as a percentage. **The people looking for work, whether or not they have jobs, form the labor force.** People who are not looking for a job are said to be not participating in the labor force, and are outside the labor force.

Note that the above discussion is somewhat informal because we have not defined what it means to look for work. Nor have we defined what exactly a job is. As you will see below, it is customary to assign precise definitions to these terms. However, **at this stage, we don't want to get bogged in these technical details. What we want to do is to get a broad sense of the proportion of people who will be looking for paid work in the next few years.**

**There are always some working-age people who are not looking for paid work**, whether as holding a job or being self-employed. There are several reasons why some people don't look for paid work.

First, historically, fewer women than men have looked for paid work primarily because women have been looking after their families full-time. However, the share of women looking for paid work has increased over time. If this trend continues, the number of people looking for paid work will increase.

Second, farmers and their families working on the farm are not in the market for paid outside work. However, over time, some of them will move out of agriculture and look for paid work. This move out has been the historical worldwide trend. It is expected to continue, which will increase the number of people looking for paid work.

In this chapter, we will look at just these two factors that determine the future labor force: changes in the proportion of working-age people who are looking for paid work, and the outflow from agriculture into other sectors. Since these are the major factors, our big picture analysis will still be valid.

But let's note that at least two other factors affect the number of people looking for work. One factor is that some working-age people are students who are currently not looking for paid work. Another factor is that some people retire early. In contrast, others want to continue to work even after they are older than 64 years, which is the upper end of the working age population.

***Let's look at the first factor – the labor force participation rate.***

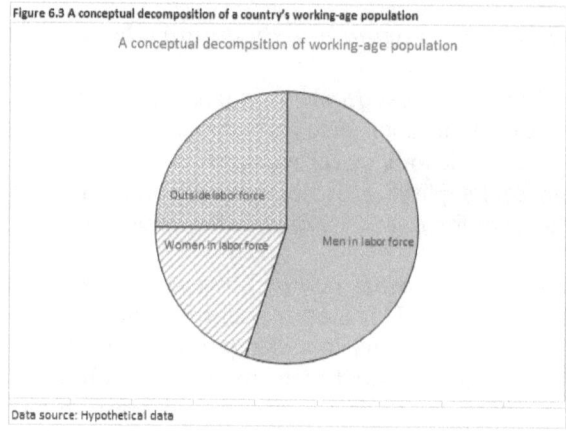

Figure 6.3 A conceptual decomposition of a country's working-age population

A conceptual decompsition of working-age population

Data source: Hypothetical data

In Figure 6.3, you can see a conceptual decomposition of a country's working-age population. Some people, men and women, are outside the labor force. The figure also shows the shares of men and women in the labor force.

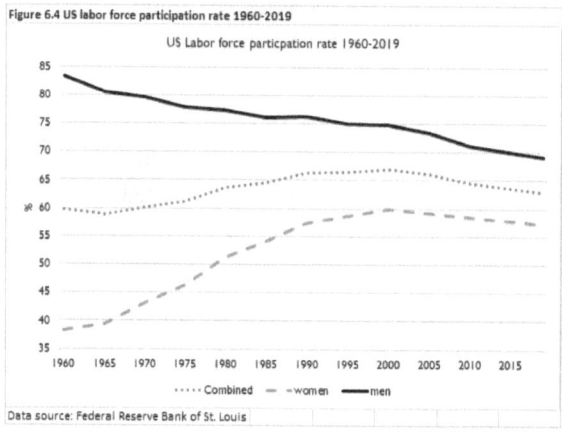

Figure 6.4 US labor force participation rate 1960-2019

US Labor force particpation rate 1960-2019

Data source: Federal Reserve Bank of St. Louis

In the US, the share of women participating in the labor force rose steadily from about 38% in 1960 to about 60% in 2000, and then has fallen a little bit. See Figure 6.4

In contrast, the share of men participating in the labor force has been falling steadily from about 83% in 1960 to about 69% in 2019. Thus, the combined share of men and women in the labor force has been declining in the US since 2000. If this declining trend continues, that will tend to reduce the number of jobs that would have to be created in the US.

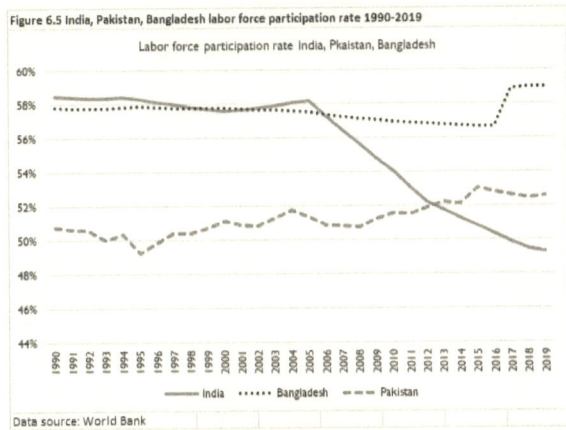

Figure 6.5 India, Pakistan, Bangladesh labor force participation rate 1990-2019

Labor force participation rate India, Pkaistan, Bangladesh

Data source: World Bank

Unfortunately, the available data on labor force participation rates for developing countries are not entirely credible. In Figure 6.5, you can see the data for India and its neighbors, Pakistan and Bangladesh. India's reported labor force participation rate is fairly steady at close to 58% over 1990-2005. After 2005, the rate declines every year to under 50% in 2019, which is much lower than the US labor force participation rate.

The people outside the labor force are not even looking for a job. As you see in Figure 6.2, in 2019, the US labor force participation rate was about 63%. Why would India's participation rate be only about 50%? Note the labor force includes unemployed people. So, the data says about half of the working-age people in India are not even looking for a job. This does not appear to be credible.

Let's compare India's data with its neighbors Pakistan and Bangladesh to check whether that helps to understand India's data. In Figure 6.5, you can also see the data for Pakistan and Bangladesh. The rate for Bangladesh dropped slowly from 1990 onwards, and then had a large increase in 2016. Pakistan's rate has a slight upwards trend. None of this helps to clarify India's data.

It's not clear whether the data reasonably reflect the ground reality. But, let's not get mired in a debate about the accuracy of this data. **What is important is that every country will have to project its own labor force participation rate accurately to figure out how many jobs have to be created in the future.**

*Let's look at the second factor – moving out of agriculture.*

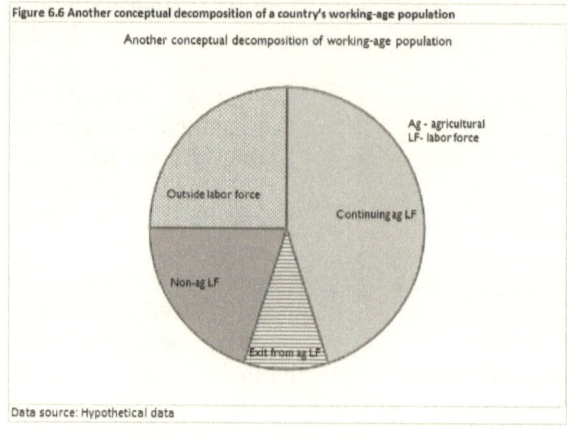

Figure 6.6 Another conceptual decomposition of a country's working-age population

Another conceptual decomposition of working-age population

Data source: Hypothetical data

In Figure 6.6, you can see another conceptual decomposition of a country's working-age population. As before, some people are outside the labor force. The figure also shows the shares of agriculture and non-agriculture in the labor force. Most importantly, the figure shows that some of the agricultural labor force will move out of agriculture. So, the question is: **how much of the agricultural labor force will leave agriculture?**

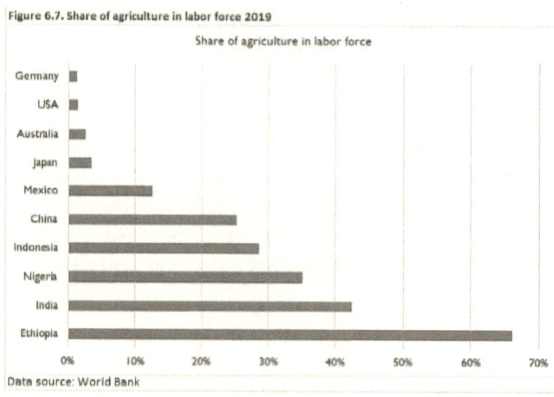

Figure 6.7. Share of agriculture in labor force 2019

Share of agriculture in labor force

Data source: World Bank

The share of agriculture in the labor force in several countries in 2019 is shown in Figure 6.7. As you can see, the share of the agricultural labor force in Germany, the US, Australia, and Japan is below 3%. At the other end, the share of agriculture is still large in Ethiopia and India, with the other countries lying in between.

We expect that countries with a large share of agriculture in the labor force will experience an outflow of workers from agriculture. This outflow will increase the number of jobs to be created. In part, the extent of the outflow depends on the job prospects in the cities. So, a country that is successful in creating many urban jobs will tend to attract more people to move to the cities. This will create a need for even more jobs to be created in cities. This response makes it hard to estimate how many jobs need to be created outside agriculture.

In Figure 6.8, you can see the historical outflow of workers from agriculture in recent years. In Mexico, agriculture has a low share, and this share has

138

declined just a little bit in the last 20 years. Thus, in Mexico, we would not expect a major outflow from agriculture in the next few years. On the other hand, China has seen a quick decline. This is likely to continue if China's industrial production continues to expand, and industries need additional workers.

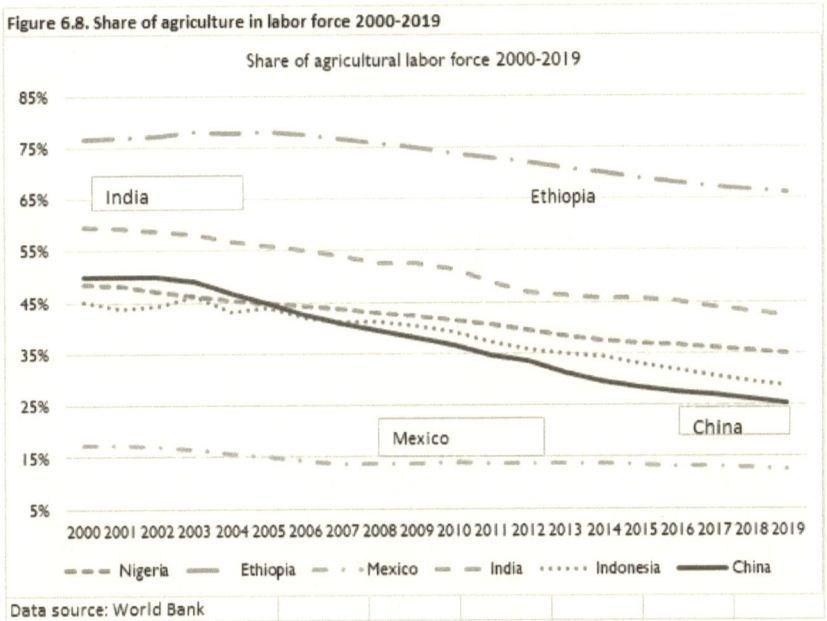

**Figure 6.8. Share of agriculture in labor force 2000-2019**

Apart from Mexico, the other countries are likely to experience moderate levels of outflow of workers from agriculture. Hence, **most developing countries must be prepared to create suitable jobs for the outflow of workers from agriculture.**

### *Which type of people will move out of agriculture?*

**What is likely to be the nature of the people who move out of agriculture?** While this will vary from country to country, there will likely be two common characteristics. First, most of the migrants are likely to be young and relatively poor, who have not yet found a way to make a living in their villages.

Second, they are likely to have low levels of skills. We have seen in Chapter 3 that schools in many developing countries don't provide high-quality education, and the situation in the rural areas is usually worse than in the cities. And, even those who finish high school are unlikely to go to college because there is likely to be a pressing need to earn an income.

Thus, we can expect that cities in many developing countries will get a significant influx of poorly-educated young people looking for a job. Hence, the economy in these countries must be able to create jobs suitable for them.

And, many of the young migrants will probably have just a high school degree or less. Thus, in the coming years, many African and Asian economies will need to be able to absorb low or mid-skill people in their cities' labor force. These labor force entrants are quite different from the labor force entrants in industrialized countries, where most people have already moved out of agriculture.

## Estimate the backlog of unemployed people

In order to calculate the backlog of unemployed people, you have to define who is unemployed. We saw in Chapter 1 that the US uses two different variables, U-3 and U-6, to measure the unemployment rate. We will look in detail at the differences between U-3 and U-6 later in this chapter. Here we just note that in the US, the backlog of unemployed is higher with U-6 than with U-3.

**In most countries, the labor market has two parts: the formal sector and the informal sector**. The formal sector consists of jobs in companies that are usually registered with the government in some fashion, pay taxes, offer jobs that pay wages in accordance with wage regulations, and have working conditions that meet regulations. For example, jobs in a car company, in a software company, or a financial institution.

The informal sector consists of jobs where these conditions are absent, and often deal on a cash basis. The informal sector is usually small in high-income countries but is quite large in developing countries.

In recent years, the gig economy has emerged as a new form of employment. Workers in the gig economy are treated as self-employed contractors even when they are closely associated on a regular basis with a large, well-established firm. For example, Uber and Lyft insist that their drivers are not their employees but are self-employed contractors who happen to use the companies' apps.

The gig economy is a controversial legal and economic issue but not important for our discussion of the backlog of unemployed people. The reason is that a gig worker is not unemployed for the purpose of determining the backlog of unemployed people.

**In developing countries, there is a real issue about whether some of the informal sector workers are actually employed.** It is common to say that some of the informal sector workers are underemployed. For example, how do you classify the people who sell cold water bottles at traffic lights in many developing countries? They work hard in the hot sun and polluted air the whole day for small amounts of money. But, are they fully employed?

This is often the condition of workers who have limited skills and work without much equipment. As a result, their productivity is low, no matter how hard they work. Hence, their earnings are low. No doubt, they would like to make more than they are earning now. But, without some training so that they have more skills, they are unlikely to get a better paying job, and even then, such a job may not be available.

So, should such people be included in the backlog of those unemployed? In practical terms, it is rare to see governments launching any programs to assist such people. **In effect, the real-world answer seems to be to treat informal sector workers as employed.**

## MEASURING UNEMPLOYMENT IN THE US

In Chapter 1, we introduced the U-3 and U-6 measures of unemployment in the US. So, what about the other U values? The US has six different unemployment rates, with U-1 as the narrowest definition of unemployment, and U-6 as the broadest definition of unemployment. Hence, U-1 is the lowest calculated unemployment rate, U-6 is the highest calculated unemployment rate, and U-3 is in the middle.

The government treats U-3 as the official estimate of the unemployment rate. However, in recent years, there has been considerable discussion of U-6, which some people call the true unemployment rate.

### Why does the US have so many unemployment rates?

Why does the US have so many measures of the unemployment rate? The basic idea seems so simple. Look at the total number of people who want a job. Split them into people who have a job and those who don't have a job. Then, divide the number of those without a job by the total number who want a job. That's your unemployment rate. What's the complication? There is no complication in principle.

**The difficulties arise from applying these concepts objectively to a large number of people.** For example, what exactly does it mean to want a job? Do you just ask this as a question, and record a Yes or No response? Or, do you have some objective definition of what "want a job" means in this context? That would make your measure more objective.

And, further, what exactly does it mean to say that you are employed? Are you employed when you work 1 hour per week? When you work part-time, does it matter whether you truly want to work part-time, or you are forced to work part-time because you cannot get full-time work?

To avoid subjectivity, the government has defined precise, objective questions that are used to collect the data that underlie the unemployment rates.

You will see similar issues arising in the measurement of other variables, such as inflation. As a result, it takes a considerable effort to even understand all the details associated with the measurement of economic variables. Here, I have restricted the discussion to the key features. However, I know that even this can be quite complicated and daunting at times. If that happens to you, just go over the material a second time, and you will get it.

## Data for calculating unemployment rates

The US calculates the unemployment rate every month. Where does the data come from? It would be prohibitively expensive and time-consuming to contact everyone in the US. Instead, **the unemployment rates are calculated from a representative sample.**

Every month, the US government conducts the Current Population Survey (CPS). The sample consists of 60,000 households chosen to be representative of the whole country. The selected households do change slowly over time. About 75% of the households remain the same from month to month, with 50% staying the same from year to year.

Every month, the government contacts the sample households, and asks them pre-set questions. The questions relate to the status of all household members during the survey reference week. The questions are about the labor force activities or non-labor force status of the household members.

All unemployment calculations are based on this sample data. **There's always a margin of error when we use a sample instead of the full population.** However, this is a large sample, which means that the margin of error is relatively small. If the estimated unemployment rate is 6%, then the actual unemployment rate could be in the range of 5.8% to 6.2%. Thus, small changes in the estimated unemployment rate may not represent any change in the actual unemployment rate.

## U-3 and U-6 measures of the US unemployment rate

You can see a conceptual decomposition of the US working age-population in Figure 6.9. The figure brings out the differences between U-3 and U-6.

Figure 6.9 Conceptual decomposition of the US working-age population

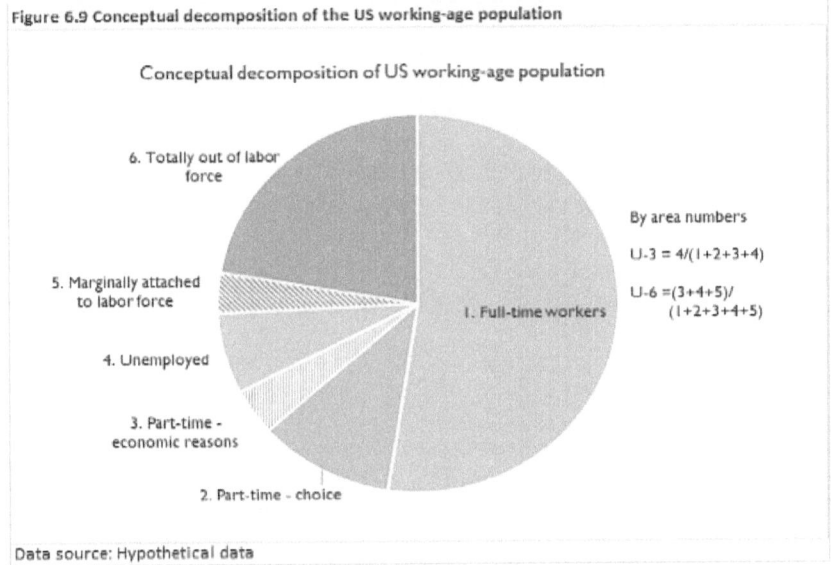

Conceptual decomposition of US working-age population

6. Totally out of labor force

5. Marginally attached to labor force

4. Unemployed

3. Part-time - economic reasons

2. Part-time - choice

1. Full-time workers

By area numbers

U-3 = 4/(1+2+3+4)

U-6 =(3+4+5)/ (1+2+3+4+5)

Data source: Hypothetical data

## U-3 measure of unemployment

**U-3 is defined as all the unemployed people as a percent of the civilian labor force.** To make this calculation, you need to define who is included in the civilian labor force. The civilian labor force includes all the people interested in paid employment. Within the civilian labor force, we define who is counted as unemployed.

In Figure 6.9, all the unemployed are shown as area 4. The civilian labor force is the sum of those employed full-time (area 1), those employed part-time by choice (area 2), those employed part-time because they cannot get a full-time job (area 3), and those who are unemployed (area 4). In other words, the civilian labor force is given by areas 1+2+3+4.

*U-3 = area 4/ (areas 1+2+3+4) in Figure 6-9, calculated as a percentage.*

Note that the civilian labor force is not the same as the working-age population. In the US, the working-age population consists of people who are 16 years old or older. In Figure 6.9, the working-age population is shown by the sum of all the areas 1-6. If you are of working-age but not looking for work, you are not part of the civilian labor force.

## U-6 measure of unemployment

U-6 is defined as (all unemployed workers + all marginally attached workers + all employed part-time for economic reasons) as a percent of (the civilian labor force + all marginally attached workers.)

In Figure 6-9, all unemployed workers = area 3, all marginally attached workers = area 5, and all employed part-time for economic reasons = area 4. Hence, the numerator of U-6 is given by areas 3 + 4 + 5.

Next, in Figure 6.9, the civilian labor force = areas 1 + 2 + 3 + 4, and all marginally attached workers = area 5. Hence, the denominator of U-6 is given by areas 1 + 2+ 3 + 4 + 5.

*U-6 = (areas 3+ 4 + 5)/ (areas 1+2+3+4+5) in Figure 6-9, calculated as a percentage.*

There are two differences between U-3 and U-6.

The first difference is how they classify people who work part-time because they cannot get a full-time job, shown as area 3 in Figure 6.9. Under U-3, these people are treated as employed. However, under U-6, this group is treated as unemployed.

The second difference between U-3 and U-6 is the group of marginally attached workers, shown in area 5 in Figure 6.9. A marginally attached worker is a person who is currently neither working nor looking for work, but indicates that they want and are available for a job and have looked for work sometime in the recent past. For example, suppose that you had a steady job, but were laid off some months ago. After searching for a new job for a couple of months, you have given up looking because you have failed to get a job. However, you would take a job if you were offered one. That makes you a marginally attached worker.

Under U-3, marginally attached workers are treated as outside the labor force. However, under U-6, marginally attached workers are treated as unemployed.

Both the differences mean that U-6 classifies more people as unemployed than U-3. Hence, U-6 is a broader measure of unemployment than U-3.

### U-3 and U-6 trends

Let's see the practical difference between U-3 and U-6, as shown in Figure 6.10. Note U-6 is not available for 1993 and earlier. As expected, U-6 is always above U-3. In recent years, the ratio of U-6 to U-3 is just below 2, which means that U-6 is nearly twice as high as U-3. Hence, **it makes a significant difference whether you use U-6 or U-3 to measure the unemployment rate.**

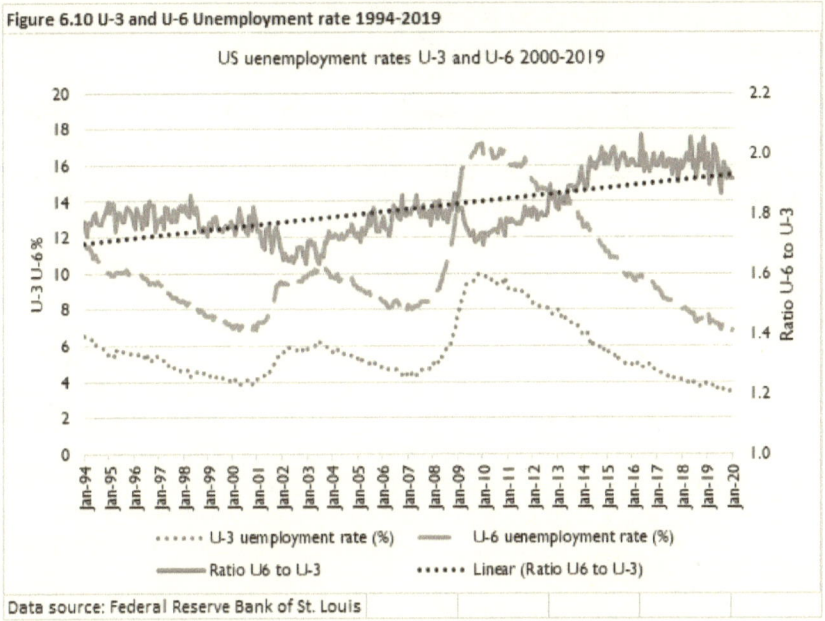

Figure 6.10 U-3 and U-6 Unemployment rate 1994-2019

In Figure 6.10, the trend line shows **an upward trend over time in the ratio of U-6 to U-3**. This trend means that the difference between U-6 and U-3 has increased over time. Why has this happened? There are reports that this increase in the ratio is due to increasing part-time employment even though the workers want full-time work. If this is indeed the case, it's a disturbing trend that U-3 cannot capture because U-3 classifies part-time workers as employed.

It is clear that you are not getting the complete picture if you rely only on U-3 to measure the unemployment rate. In particular, **if you are thinking about how many jobs need to be created in the future, then it is useful to consider both U-3 and U-6, not just U-3.**

## Seasonal adjustment of the unemployment rate

**Many economic variables, including the employment rate, fluctuate with the season.** For example, in the US, in the period between Thanksgiving and Christmas, physical stores and online sellers hire additional people to cope with the high volume of sales at that time. This tends to reduce the unemployment rate. Young people graduate from high school and college in May and begin to look for jobs. This tends to increase the unemployment rate at that time.

These kinds of changes happen in every country, though possibly at different times. For example, in India, the volume of sales increases around Diwali.

China's mega-shopping event is Singles Day in November. Again, they tend to reduce the unemployment rate at that time.

The official statistics that are usually reported take account of these predictable seasonal changes by a statistical method called seasonal adjustment. The mathematical techniques underlying seasonal adjustment are best left to specialists. Instead, here it's enough to see what the effect of seasonal adjustment is.

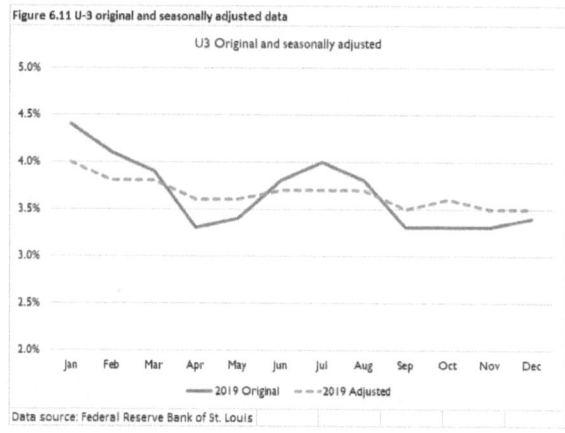

Figure 6.11 U-3 original and seasonally adjusted data

Data source: Federal Reserve Bank of St. Louis

In Figure 6.11, you can see the original and adjusted unemployment rates by month for 2019. You can see that there is a definite seasonal pattern in the unemployment rate.

The original data that is not seasonally adjusted in rarely reported by the news media, and does not figure is policy discussions. Still, it's worth knowing that what you are seeing in data has been adjusted by a statistical technique.

## KEY TAKEAWAYS

### Jobs to be created in the future

1. The number of jobs that have to be created in the future years depends upon two broad factors. The first factor is the number of net new job seekers in the future. The second factor is the size of the backlog of people who are currently unemployed.

2. There are clear indications that developing countries in Africa and Asia with a low median age (under 30 years) will face much pressure to create new jobs in the future. In contrast, higher-income countries such as Germany and Japan with a high median age (around 50 years) will not face such pressure. Countries with a median age of about 40 years) will be in between.

## US unemployment measurement system

3. The US has six different unemployment rates U-1 to U-6, with U-1 being the lowest rate and U-6 being the highest. While the official unemployment rate is U-3, there is significant public discussion about U-6, which is about twice as large as U-3, with some people calling U-6 as the real unemployment rate.

4. The complexities and issues present in the US specification and measurement of the unemployment rate are not specific to the US, and are relevant for calculating the unemployment rate in any country.

In the next chapter, we look at inflation, which is the other component of the Misery Index.

# CHAPTER 7.   INFLATION

In simple language, the inflation rate is the average of the percent changes in the prices in various goods and services in a given year or month over the previous period. **Across the world, the most commonly used measure of inflation is the Consumer Price Index (CPI).** People are familiar with it since the news media report the inflation rate based on the CPI.

**Governments began calculating the CPI as a tool that people could use to negotiate wage increases to compensate for price increases.** The idea is simple: "Because prices went up by 5% last year, my wages should go up by at least 5% to compensate me for the higher cost of living."

And, it's not just wages that have to be adjusted. Many governments also adjust their pensions. For example, Australia has created a variant of the CPI called the Pensioner and Beneficiary Living Cost Index to compensate retirees and other government beneficiaries for price increases. India uses the CPI to calculate the dearness allowance to compensate government employees and retirees for price increases. Here, the word dearness is used in the British sense, with dearer meaning more expensive.

**Let's call this the compensatory objective for measuring inflation.**

In the CPI, the average of the price increases is calculated by a formula called the Laspeyres index, named after the economist who devised this approach many decades ago.

**Economists have long complained that the Laspeyres index overstates the inflation rate. The reason for the overstatement is called the substitution bias**. The complaint is not about the Laspeyres method. Instead, the charge is that it is not the right way to measure inflation.

**Nevertheless, governments continue to use the Laspeyres index to calculate the CPI.** The main reason for this continuing practice is political resistance. Governments find it hard to defend a change that will lead to a lower estimate of inflation because that will lead to lower annual wage and pension increases.

**There is another objective for measuring inflation. In Chapter 4, we saw that many central banks have adopted inflation targets. Let's call this the policy objective for measuring inflation.**

**Economists have developed several alternatives to the CPI for measuring inflation for this purpose.** When your objective is to keep inflation in check, it makes no sense to use a method that you believe overestimates inflation. Further, central banks cannot wait one year, as is usual in the compensatory objective, to control inflation. Instead, central banks respond to last month's inflation rate. The method of calculating inflation has to take account of this monthly focus.

**Most central banks use inflation measures other than the CPI for the policy objective, though they don't ignore the CPI.**

### Chapter flow

This chapter has seven major parts. We begin our discussion by looking at the CPI and the Laspeyres index. Then, we look at a fundamental flaw in the use of the Laspeyres index to calculate the inflation rate. In the third part, we look at the alternative indexes used to measure inflation. In the fourth part, we consider various inflation measures attuned to the policy objective. Then, we discuss the practical problems in measuring the costs of owner-occupied housing. In the sixth part, we look at real interest rates, which are calculated on the basis of the inflation rate. Finally, we look at the inflation rates in various countries. This chapter has an optional annex, which is a primer on index numbers.

## LET'S LOOK AT THE CPI

We have stated above that the CPI is based on the Laspeyres formula or the Laspeyres price index. The Laspeyres index has two distinguishing features. First, it uses a weighted arithmetic mean formula to calculate the inflation rate. Second, the weights are derived from the expenditure share of each commodity in total expenditure in some past period, called the reference period. The quantities of the goods and services bought in the reference period constitute the past market basket used in the Laspeyres index.

In practice, when the inflation rate is calculated for many years, the weights don't change every year because they are derived from the past market basket. **Hence, they are called fixed weights, and the Laspeyres method is called a fixed-weight index.**

The fixed-weight feature of the Laspeyres index is the source of the substitution bias. The other methods used to calculate inflation use variable weights, not fixed weights.

Let's look at a simplified example of the Laspeyres index to understand these features.

## A hypothetical example of the Laspeyres price index

In Table 7.1, you can see the consumption data for a consumer named Cee.

| Table 7.1. Inflation rate calculated by Laspeyres index | Year 1 | Year 2 | Inflation |
|---|---|---|---|
| **Good A** | | | |
| Price | $7.00 | $7.84 | 12.00% |
| Quantity bought | 6.90 | 5.90 | |
| Actual Expenditure | $48.30 | $46.26 | |
| *Hypothetical expenditure (based on year 2 price, year 1 quantity)* | N/A | $54.10 | |
| Expenditure share | 83.4% | | |
| Weight | 0.834 | | |
| **Good B** | | | |
| Price | $3.00 | $3.12 | 4.00% |
| Quantity bought | 3.20 | 3.00 | |
| Actual Expenditure | $9.60 | $9.36 | |
| *Hypothetical expenditure (based on year 2 price, year 1 quantity)* | N/A | $9.98 | |
| Expenditure share | 16.6% | | |
| Weight | 0.166 | | |
| **Good A and Good B** | | | |
| Total Actual Expenditure | $57.90 | $55.62 | |
| Total Hypothetical Expenditure | | $64.08 | |
| **Laspeyres inflation rate (Hypothetical expenditure Year 2 over Actual Expenditure Year 1)** | | | 10.67% |

Data source: Hypothetical

In Year 1, Cee bought 6.9 units of Good A and 3.2 units of Good B. We call this combination as Cee's market basket for Year 1. **We will calculate the weights from the Year 1 market basket.**

In Year 2, Good A's price went up by 12%, and Good B's price went up by 4%. Cee changed the quantities Cee bought in response to the price changes, as shown in Table 7.1.

### Deriving the fixed weights

We derive the weights from the expenditure shares. From Table 7.1:

- In Year 1, the expenditure share of Good A is 83.4%. So, the weight of Good A is 0.834.

- In Year 1, the expenditure share of Good B is 16.6%. So, the weight of Good B is 0.166.

## Calculating the weighted average

To get the inflation rate, we calculate the weighted average of 12% and 8%. The calculation is:

$$0.834*12\% + 0.166*4* = 10.67\%$$

The answer in Table is 10.67%, not the value of 8% that we would get with the standard average formula.

Why is the weighted average higher? Is it always this way? No, it's not always higher. It's higher in this example because Good A's inflation rate of 12% has a high weight. This high weight pulls the weighted average closer to 12% than the standard average formula.

## Economic rationale for the weighted-average method

A weighted average is a mathematical tool. What is the economic rationale for this method?
.

The economic question that the Laspeyres index asks and answers is: How much more money does Cee need to spend this year to buy last year's market basket quantities at this year's prices?

The idea behind this question is that Cee's cost of living has gone up this year as prices have gone up. In the Laspeyres index, we focus on the market basket of Year 1. The total cost of the Year 1 market basket is $ 57.90.

Next, we calculate the cost of buying the Year 1 market basket in Year 2 at Year 2 prices.

This is a hypothetical calculation of expenditure in Year 2 because Year 1 prices are not prevalent in Year 2, and the actual expenditure in Year 2 would be at Year 2 prices. But we are not looking at the actual expenditure in Year 2; we are calculating a hypothetical expenditure in Year 2. In Table 7.1, the total hypothetical expenditure in Year 2 is $ 64.08.

Next, we compare the hypothetical expenditure in Year 2 with the actual expenditure in Year 1, which is $ 57.90. We find the percentage difference between $ 64.08 and $ 57.90. I am sure that you will not be surprised that the difference is 10.67%.

**So, the weighted average inflation rate is the same as the percentage increase in the cost of buying the previous year's market basket at this year's price. This is the economic rationale for using the Laspeyres index.**

## General Laspeyres formula

We can define the general formula in this way.

First, find the cost of the fixed market basket of goods at the past prices, i.e., the prices of the year in which the fixed weights were set. Its value will not change over time. This will appear in the denominator of the Laspeyres Price Index. In Table 7.1, this is $ 57.90 for Year 1.

Second, for each successive year, find the cost of the fixed market basket at current prices. This is a hypothetical value, which will change every year. This will appear in the numerator of the Laspeyres Price Index. In Table 7.1, this is $ 64.08 for Year 2.

Then, we can write the Laspeyres Price Index for the current year as

*100\*(Hypothetical expenditure, current prices, old quantities)/ (Actual expenditure, old prices, old quantities)*

The multiplication by 100 is to convert a proportion into a percentage. For example, in Table 7.1, the (Hypothetical expenditure, current prices, old quantities) = $ 64.08, and the (Actual expenditure, old prices, old quantities) = $ 57.90.

Thus, in our example.

*Laspeyres price index for Year 1 = 100\*(57.90/57.90) = 100.00*

*Laspeyres price index for Year 2 = 100\*(64.08/57.90) = 110.67*

Note that the numerator will change every year while the denominator will stay fixed. So, in any future year, we don't need any data about the quantities that the consumers buy.

## Economic justification – or lack of it - for the Laspeyres index

The economic justification for the Laspeyres formula is that the inflation rate it calculates can be interpreted as measuring the increase in the cost of living.

**This is a controversial statement, though it's common to use this justification in the real world.** For example, the US government uses the term cost-of-living adjustment (COLA) to describe the changes made in Social Security retirement payments when the CPI changes.

However, **the Laspeyres formula is not consistent with the definition of the cost of living in economic theory.** Since the debate about the relationship between the Laspeyres index and the cost of living is highly technical in terms of economic theory, I will not go into it here. Instead, let me just quote what the US Bureau of Labor Statistics (BLS), which is responsible for publishing the CPI, says.

The BLS website says:

> "The CPI frequently is called a cost-of-living index, but it differs in important ways from a complete cost-of-living measure. We use a cost-of-living framework in making practical decisions about questions that arise in constructing the CPI. ... Since the CPI does not attempt to quantify all the factors that affect the cost-of-living, it is sometimes termed a conditional cost-of-living index."

In other words, the BLS says that the CPI measures something that seems to be somewhat like the change in the cost of living. Or, the BLS does not claim that the CPI measures the change in the cost of living. Since this is where the state-of-the-art is, let's leave it that way.

## Three versions of CPI in the US

To collect the price and quantity data for the fixed market basket, a government surveys a representative sample of households, and collects their detailed expenditure data. The government derives the weights from this data. Then, the government uses these weights to calculate the weighted average for several years into the future. After that, the government conducts a new survey, and changes the weights. In the US, the government conducts a new survey every two years, but some countries take longer.

The US has three versions of the Consumer Price Index: CPI-W, CPI-U, and CPI-E. The weights in each version represent the fixed market basket of the different sets of households covered by the index. In Figure 7.1, you can see the values of the three variants in the last few years. As you can see, the differences between the three versions are relatively small, quite unlike the difference between U-3 and U-6 for unemployment in Chapter 6.

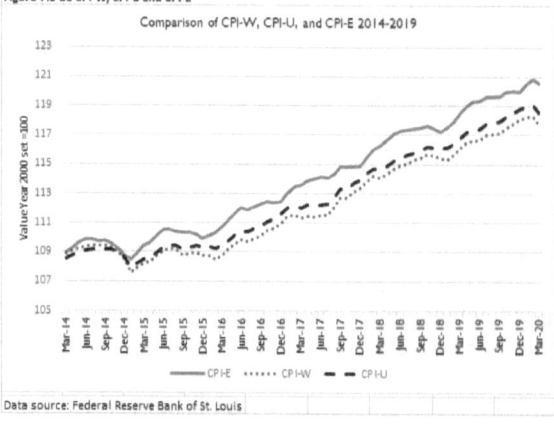

Figure 7.1 US CPI-W, CPI-U and CPI-E

Comparison of CPI-W, CPI-U, and CPI-E 2014-2019

Data source: Federal Reserve Bank of St. Louis

## The US Consumer Price Index for Urban Wage Earners and Clerical Workers CPI-W

The CPI-W is formally called the Consumer Price Index for Urban Wage Earners and Clerical Workers. **In CPI-W, the wights are based on the expenditure patterns of** a group of urban people who are wage earners and clerical workers. For a household to be included in the qualified pool, more than one-half of the household's income must come from clerical or wage occupations, and at least one of the household's earners must have been employed for at least 37 weeks during the previous 12 months.

The CPI-W was first published in 1919. Today, the CPI-W group covers about 29 percent of the US population. **In Figure 7.2, you can see the weights in the US CPI-W**. The highest weight is around 40% for housing, which includes utilities, furnishings, and other things – not just the cost of the home. The lowest weight is about 3% for apparel.

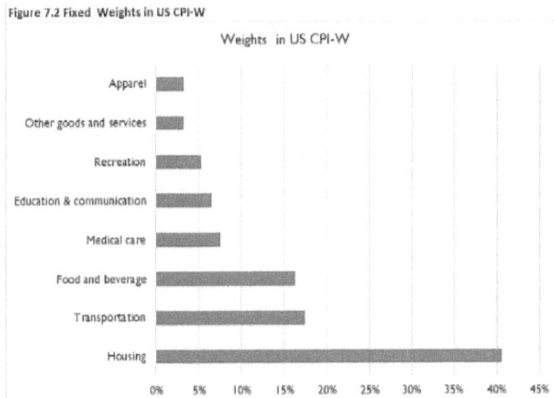

Figure 7.2 Fixed Weights in US CPI-W

Weights in US CPI-W

Data source: US Bureau of Labor Statistics

The US government uses CPI-W to adjust retirement payments. Since the CPI-W is not based on the market basket of senior citizens, there have been repeated proposals to change this. We will discuss the US government's response under CPI-E.

## The US Consumer Price Index for All Urban Consumers CPI-U

The CPI-U covers about 93% of the people in the US. The news media usually report the inflation rate based on the CPI-U. So, this is the number that is widely used for calculating annual wage increases in the US.

As you can expect, the weights in CPI-W and CPI-U are different, but, as we see in Figure 7.1, these two variants of the CPI give similar results.

## The US Consumer Price Index Experimental CPI-E

**The CPI-E calculates the weights in the market basket based on the expenditure patterns of people older than 62 years**. However, note that E does not stand for Elderly – it stands for Experimental. Thus, the US government considers the CPI-E as experimental, even though it has been available for several decades.

As you can see in Figure 7.1, the CPI-E yields a higher inflation rate than the CPI-W, which is what the US government uses for adjusting Social Security retirement payments. In contrast, as we noted at the beginning of the chapter, Australia has defined a separate variant of the CPI specifically for retirees.

## A FUNDAMENTAL ISSUE WITH THE USE OF THE LASPEYRES INDEX TO MEASURE INFLATION

There are no issues with the Laspeyres method as a mathematical formula. However, there is a fundamental economic issue with this index when it is used to measure inflation. **The issue is that the Laspeyres method leads to what economists call as substitution bias. While we will discuss the technical detail below, in simple language, the Laspeyres method puts undue importance on the past market basket.**

We have seen above that the Laspeyres index for each year is calculated with reference to the quantities of the goods and services that were bought several years ago. What's so important about what consumers bought years ago? What they bought in the past depended on the prices at that time, the things available at that time, and incomes at that time. These days, the economic world changes quickly and frequently. Why don't we take account of these changes in measuring inflation?

### Substitution bias in the Laspeyres index

**The substitution bias in the Laspeyres index comes from ignoring the response of consumers to changes in prices over time.** In effect, the Laspeyres index presumes that consumers would like to buy the same fixed market basket year after year. Perhaps this is what they would like to do. But **economic theory teaches us that consumers change their buying behavior in response to price changes**.

**In particular, if a commodity's price goes up, some consumers will shift to some extent to a substitute.** For example, if the price of apples goes up, some consumers will shift to bananas, which are a substitute for apples. Or if the price of pizzas goes up, some people will switch some of their purchases to hamburgers.

In short, consumers switch to some extent to cheaper substitutes. As a result of these switches, their actual expenditures will not increase as much as the hypothetical expenditure of buying the fixed market basket at this year's prices. **Hence, the hypothetical cost of the same market basket at this year's** prices is too high because it ignores the substitution that is a normal part of consumer behavior in response to price changes. This is the substitution bias in the Laspeyres index.

## Extent of substitution bias in the US

In 1996, a commission led by Professor Boskin issued a report *Toward a More Accurate Measure of the Cost of Living* related to the substitution bias. The commission's primary finding was that, in the US, the CPI overestimated the inflation rate by about 1.1% percentage points every year. In other words, if the actual inflation rate were 3%, the CPI would measure it as 4.1%. In response, the US government has made several changes in its methodology to reduce the substitution bias

## ALTERNATIVES TO THE LASPEYRES INDEX FOR MEASURING INFLATION

There are many alternatives available to the Laspeyres index. The most relevant formulas are the Paasche, Fisher, and Törnqvist indexes. Since the Fisher and Törnqvist belong to a category of index numbers called superlative indexes, we will discuss them under this grouping.

From an economist's viewpoint, a key common characteristic of these indexes is that, unlike the Laspeyres formula, the weights change in every period. In general, these indexes give a lower inflation rate than the Laspeyres index.

Let's now take a brief look at the technical details of these alternative formulas.

### Paasche index

The Paasche index is not directly used in any inflation measure. However, this index is a component of the Fisher index, which we discuss below. Further, the Paasche formula is the conceptual base for an inflation measure called the Implicit GDP Deflator, which we discuss later.

The economic question addressed by the Paasche index is different from the question asked by the Laspeyres index.

The specific question is: How does my actual expenditure in the current year compare with my hypothetical expenditure if I had bought my current market basket with the past prices?

The Paasche index derives the weights from the current year's market basket, not the past market basket. Hence, the Paasche index uses variable weights, not fixed weights. Since the variable weights are based on the current purchases, the Paasche index does not have the substitution bias.

Like the Laspeyres index, the Paasche index compares an actual expenditure with a hypothetical expenditure. You can see the differences between the two indexes in Table 7.2.

Table 7.2 Comparison of Laspeyres and Paasche formulas

|  | Current Period | Past period | Index = Current/Past |
|---|---|---|---|
| Laspeyres | Hypothetical expenditure | Actual expenditure | Hypothetical expenditure *divided by* Actual expenditure |
| Paasche | Actual expenditure | Hypothetical expenditure | Actual expenditure *divided by* Hypothetical expenditure |

### General Paasche formula

We can define the general formula in this way.

First, find the cost of this year's market basket of goods at this year's prices. This is an actual expenditure, which will change every year. This expenditure will appear in the numerator of the Paasche index.

Second, for the reference year in the past, find the cost of this year's market basket at the past prices. This is a hypothetical value. It will appear in the denominator of the Paasche index.

Then, we can write the Paasche price index for the current year as:

100*(Actual expenditure, current prices, current quantities)/ (Hypothetical expenditure, old prices, current quantities)

In the Paasche index, both the numerator and denominator change every year.

It is generally the case that Paasche price index is lower than the Laspeyres price index.

## Superlative indexes

The term superlative index is used to categorize several formulas that have desirable statistical properties. There are several superlative indexes available in the literature. Here we discuss only the two superlative indexes that are most relevant for measuring inflation: the Fisher index and the Törnqvist index.

### *Fisher index*

**The Fisher index is the geometric mean of the Laspeyres and Paasche index value for a particular period.** Since we are calculating the geometric mean of only two variables, the calculation is straightforward. Multiply the two numbers and find the square root. For example, arbitrarily, if the Laspeyres index is 160.2, and the Paasche index is 158.7. Multiply them, and the answer is 25,423.74. Now take the square root, which is 159.45. That's the Fisher index value. Note that, as in this example, the Fisher index will be between the Laspeyres and Paasche index values.

Since the Fisher index uses the Paasche formula as part of its formula, the Fisher index has variable weights.

### *Törnqvist index*

**The Törnqvist index is a weighted geometric mean.** The weighted geometric mean of what? When we are creating the index number values, and not calculating the inflation rate directly, we are taking the average of the price ratios of the different commodities. For example, in Table 7.1, the price ratio for Good A is 7.84/7.00 = 1.12. Similarly, in Table 7.2, the price ratio for Good B is 3.12/3.00 = 1.04. Thus, the Törnqvist index is a weighted geometric mean of the price ratios of the various goods and services.

**The weights in the Törnqvist formula are based on the actual expenditure share of a particular commodity in both periods.** There are no hypothetical calculations. The weights are based on the average values of the expenditure share in the two periods. In Table 7.1, the share of Good A in Year 1 is 83.3. Then, find the actual share of Good A in Year 2, and calculate their arithmetic mean. That's the weight of Good A. Similarly, for Good B.

Let's not get bogged down in these formulas. Let's see how they are used in the real world. These alternative formulas are generally used in inflation measures attuned to the policy objective.

## INFLATION MEASURES ATTUNED TO THE POLICY OBJECTIVE

In this part, we look at chained indexes, the Implicit GDP Deflator, and core inflation.

### Chained indexes

The most important practical implementation of the **Törnqvist formula is in chained inflation indexes.** One of the chained indexes in common use is the US Chained CPI-U, abbreviated as C-CPI-U.

The key characteristic of a chained inflation measure is that it has variable weights, based on the data for the current period and the past period. For example, March's inflation rate is based on weights calculated from the data for February and March. Then, the rate for April is based on the data for March and April. In this way, the weights form an interlinked chain, which is why this is called chained inflation.

*Chained CPI-U*

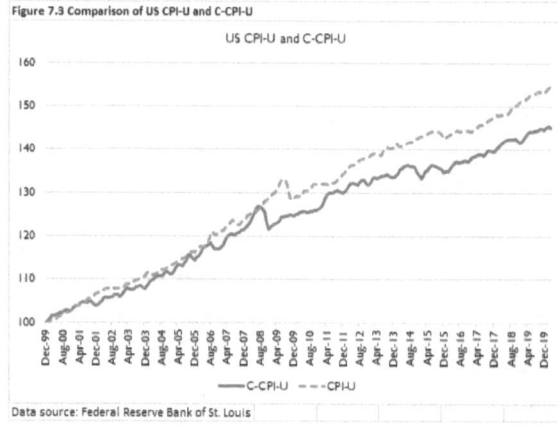

Figure 7.3 Comparison of US CPI-U and C-CPI-U

Data source: Federal Reserve Bank of St. Louis

**In the US, C-CPI-U is the chained version of the CPI-U.** In general, C-CPI-U is expected to give a lower inflation rate than CPI-U. That has been the case, as you can see in Figure 7.3, where the chart begins in December 1999 because that's the earliest available date for C-CPI-U.

*Uses of C-CPI-U*

The Fed sees C-CPI-U as a better of inflation than CPI-U because C-CPI-U does not have the substitution bias caused by fixed weights. Further, C-CPI-U is in sync with changes in what consumers buy because the flexible weights are based on data that is always current, not frozen in the past. Hence, **the Fed uses C-CPI-U in keeping track of its inflation target.**

In 2017, the US government began to use C-CPI-U to make automatic changes in the income tax brackets, which are called income tax slabs in some countries. In this context, automatic means that the changes take place every year according to a pre-approved formula, and the government does not have to get legislative approval for each year's tax brackets. This change in the limits of the tax brackets is done to avoid what is called bracket creep, which tends to increase the tax that people have to pay when their incomes go up because of inflation.

Let's look at a real-world example of automatic adjustment.

For incomes earned in 2019, in the US, a single taxpayer had to pay a tax of 10% on income in the bracket $ 0-9,700, and 12% on income in the bracket $ 9,701-39,475. Consider a single taxpayer with an income of $ 9,690 in 2019. Since this is within the 10% tax bracket, this person will pay only 10% of their income as tax. And this taxpayer does not come into the next 12% tax bracket at all.

Suppose that the inflation rate is 1.8%, and the taxpayer's earnings are linked to the inflation rate. Hence, the taxpayer's income rises by 1.8% from $ 9,690 to $ 9,875. This puts the taxpayer's income above the 10% limit of $ 9,700. That means the taxpayer will have to pay some tax at the rate of 12%. This is called bracket creep. The way to avoid bracket creep is to increase the upper limits of the tax brackets.

For example, in the US, for 2020, the upper limit on the 10% tax bracket has been increased from $ 9,700 to $9,875. This is an increase of 1.8%, again based on the inflation rate. With this increased upper limit, our single taxpayer will stay within the 10% tax bracket, and will not be pushed into the 12% tax bracket.

*Controversy about C-CPI-U*

**There is considerable controversy about the use of C-CPI-U**. The supporters say that it is a better measure of inflation than CPI-U. So, let's use C-CPI-U. However, some people think that C-CPI-U is nothing but mathematical jugglery designed to reduce the measured inflation rate, and give people a lower wage/pension increase.

In 2013, the US government floated a proposal to link Social Security payments to C-CPI-U instead of CPI-W. However, seven years have passed without this proposal being approved. The reason is the fear that this will slow down the annual increase in Social Security payments.

## Implicit GDP Deflator

**The Paasche formula forms the conceptual base for the Implicit GDP Deflator (IGD).** As its name implies, the IGD is based on the goods and

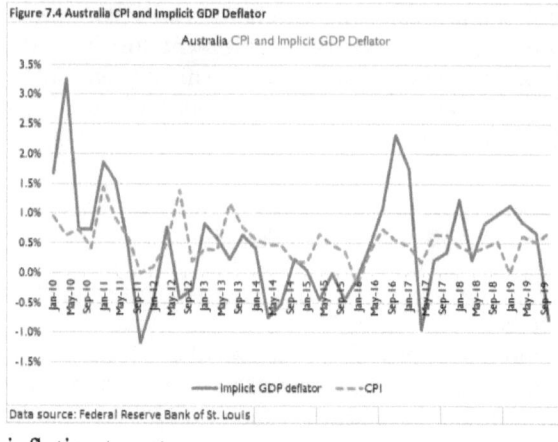

Figure 7.4 Australia CPI and Implicit GDP Deflator

Data source: Federal Reserve Bank of St. Louis

services included in the GDP, i.e., all the goods and services produced in the country in a particular year. Hence, the IGD excludes the prices of imported goods, which are included in the CPI.

Many central banks look at the IGD in checking whether they are meeting their inflation target.

As in the Paasche formula, we first calculate the actual value of the GDP each year. This is the market value of all the goods and services at the market prices that year. For example, the GDP of 2019 will be the value of the quantities produced in 2019 calculated at the 2019 prices. **This is called the nominal GDP for 2019.**

Then, we calculate the real GDP, also called inflation-adjusted GDP, each year. What's the real GDP? It's the value of the goods and services produced this year, calculated at the past prices in the reference year. For example, if the reference year is 2015, then we calculate the market value of what we produce in 2019 at the prices that prevailed in 2015. **This is the real GDP for 2019.** Then,

IGD price index for 2019 = 100*Nominal GDP for 2019/Real GDP for 2019.

This formula holds good for every year.

In this formula, I have taken the past prices of a particular year to calculate the real GDP. However, it is possible to use some average of the prices of several years as the past prices.

For our purposes, what's important is that the results from the CPI will not be the same as the results from the IGD. It's also important to note that many central banks look at the IGD in assessing whether they are meeting their inflation targets.

As you can expect, the CPI and IGD give different results. In Figure 7.4 (below), you can see the quarterly CPI and IGD inflation rates for the last ten years in Australia. The IGD inflation rate was negative in some months, but the CPI inflation rate was always positive. Keep in mind that this pattern is

162

specific to Australia over 2010-2019, and may or may not apply to other countries or other periods.

## Core inflation

One of the most significant differences from the viewpoint of the policy objective is the difference between standard and core inflation. Many central banks use core inflation, not standard inflation, for checking their inflation targets.

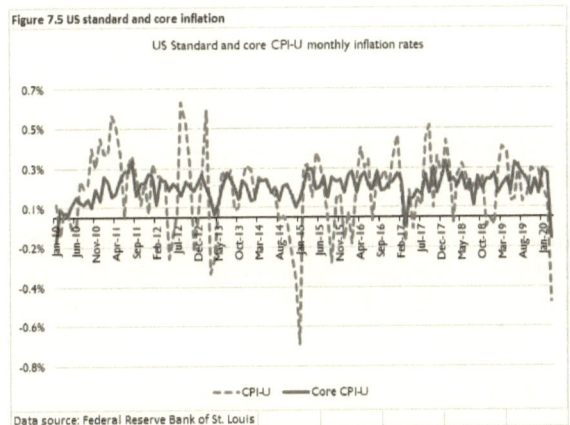

Figure 7.5 US standard and core inflation

Before we go into the details of core inflation, it's helpful to compare the inflation rate as measured by standard and core inflation. You can see in Figure 7.5 the monthly inflation rate in the US as measured by CPI-U and its core version, Core CPI-U.

You will see that the standard inflation rate goes up and down quite a bit, while the core inflation is relatively steady. And, that's the point of calculating core inflation – to focus on the steady changes in prices.

The technical difference between standard and core inflation is that core inflation excludes some goods and services in calculating the inflation rate.

Why would you exclude some of the goods and services that people pay for and consume? Will this exclusion not bias the calculation of the inflation rate? And, won't that, in turn, affect the increase in salaries that people should get to compensate for inflation?

These questions are certainly valid. The answer is straightforward. **Core inflation is not used for indexing any economic variable, including wages and salaries.** As core inflation measures are used only for the policy objective, not for adjusting economic variables, these measures will not affect the calculation of inflation for the compensatory objective.

Still, the question is: why leave out some commodities in the calculation of inflation? The reason is that the extreme swings in the prices of some commodities create large swings in the inflation rate that have nothing to do with monetary policy.

## Averages are affected by outliers

The usual formula used to calculate an average, i.e., the arithmetic mean, is affected by all the values. It does not differentiate between extreme values that may be called outliers, and what may be called normal values. This is why economists often use the median instead of the arithmetic mean, as in median wages and median housing prices.

But the median ignores most of the values whose average is to be calculated. What we need is an average formula that is based on most of the values but excludes the outliers. But what's an outlier?

## Two modified ways to calculate the average

We will look at two ways to modify the average calculation: the trimmed means method and the pre-identified commodities method.

First, we look at an averaging system that many people are familiar with. **This is the scoring system used in Olympic events such as diving or skating**. Here we have multiple judges, say, seven judges. Each judge scores a performer on a 1-10 scale, with higher scores being better.

How do they calculate the average score?

They throw out the lowest and highest score because these scores may reflect some bias. Then they calculate the average of the other five scores. **The calculation system that throws out the extreme scores and calculates the average from the remaining scores is considered better than taking the average of all the judges.**

This is called the **trimmed mean method**. It reflects the idea that the dataset is trimmed by excluding extreme values. Under this method, any particular Olympic judge is not identified as an outlier. Instead, what is excluded is the outlier value coming from any judge. **Under the trimmed mean method, the commodities to be excluded for core inflation are not pre-specified. Instead, they are whichever commodities happen to have extreme price swings at that time.**

**Under the second method, some particular sources are identified as leading to outlier values**. It would be like saying that some judges are biased, and we will not include their scores in calculating the average score. That would make no sense in the scoring an Olympics event. Why would you let a biased judge continue? You would not.

However, this method can work in the calculation of inflation. **You would identify particular commodities that tend to have outlier values again and**

**again.** Then, you would calculate the inflation rate based on the arithmetic mean of the remaining commodities.

We can call this **the pre-identified commodities method.** We focus on this method, as this is what is followed by most countries.

### Pre-identified commodities method

This method excludes commodities whose prices are known to swing up and down frequently. Food and energy are the two commodities that have had major swings in prices in the past. They are excluded in the calculation of core inflation, as in Figure 7.5.

For example, when the coronavirus-induced economic slump hit the oil market, the price of oil dropped dramatically, becoming negative at one point. In turn, the price of gasoline fell. For example, in the US, the gasoline price in early March 2020 was around $ 2.50/gallon. In early May 2020, the price had dropped to about $ 1.88/gallon, a fall of 33%.

The policy question is; Should a central bank count this fall in gasoline prices as the outcome of a successful monetary policy?

The obvious answer is No. Monetary policy had nothing to do with bringing down the gasoline price.

Similarly, suppose that the price of some commodity goes up suddenly because of a crop failure or some other factor. Say that locusts suddenly sweep an African country, and destroy quite a bit of the local crops. As a result, the prices of crops quickly rise much higher.

Is this rise in the prices of crops due to a failure of monetary policy? The answer is No. Monetary policy had nothing to do with it.

In other words, when you see sudden, extreme swings in the prices of some commodities, these changes often have nothing to do with monetary policy. So, it makes sense to exclude these extreme swings when asking how successful the central bank's monetary policy is in meeting its inflation target.

We can now define the difference between the standard and core inflation more precisely. Standard inflation is calculated from all commodities, while core inflation is calculated after excluding commodities with extreme swings in prices.

*Skepticism about core inflation*

Some people react with skepticism when they find out that the US Fed uses the pre-identified commodities method of core inflation to check whether inflation is in control. They ask: Don't those people in Washington, DC buy food and gasoline? If they do, why do they ignore the prices of these commodities? The answer again is that this calculation is only for assessing the success of monetary policy in keeping inflation in check. Core inflation is not used for inflation calculations related to the compensatory objective.

## PROBLEMS IN MEASURING COSTS OF OWNER-OCCUPIED HOUSING

As housing is usually a big part of everyone's budget, we must make sure that the housing prices are correctly tracked over the years. Some people rent their homes. Their costs are easy to measure. But when it comes to owner-occupied housing, it's not clear how to measure the price.

We all know that the prices of houses change every year, and they usually go up. While the current price of an existing house is unknown, it is not difficult to estimate its price. How do we account for this changing price for a person living in their own home? People don't buy a home every month. They buy it once in a few years or even decades. **How do we calculate the price of an owner-occupied home every month, and use it in the monthly CPI?**

Suppose you have bought a house with a mortgage loan. To keep the discussion simple, assume that your monthly mortgage payment is fixed. And, once you have paid off the loan, you have no monthly costs. Then, you may think of your housing costs in this way.

I make a fixed mortgage payment every month to repay my loan. So, that is my monthly cost of housing. It doesn't change every month. So, there's no inflation in my housing costs. I know that house prices are going up, but that does not alter my costs. I understand that the rent people pay is going up every month. But, since I have bought my home, changes in what others are paying has no impact on my costs. So, there's still no inflation in my housing costs. And once I have paid off the loan, I will be living free. So, there will be no inflation in my housing costs – they will be zero.

That's not how the CPI of any country takes account of housing prices. **However, there's no universally accepted method to include the price of owner-occupied housing in measuring inflation.** We discuss four methods below, though calling the last way a method is a bit of a stretch.

## Four methods to take account of owner-occupied housing prices

One method is the **rental-equivalent method**. This is used in the US and several other countries. The specific term in the US is "owner's equivalent rent," which is sometimes called imputed rent.

In simple language, this is the rent you would get if you rented out your home. Now, you have no intention of renting out your home – you want to live there. It doesn't matter. What this means is that your housing price goes up if the rents in your area go up. This is the case even if your actual payments, such as your mortgage payment, remain the same.

What sense does this make? What's the relevance of this hypothetical rent?

Let's go back to our discussion of opportunity costs in Chapter 3. In simple terms, by staying in your house, you are giving up the opportunity to earn rent every month. Of course, this is different from your financial outlay – but that's the whole point of opportunity cost. Still, this method continues to be debated, with various proposals to modify it.

A second way to handle housing prices is through the **acquisitions method**. This applies only to newly constructed houses – not to sales of existing houses. Here, the housing price is measured by the prices of new houses. Nothing complicated about it. Australia and New Zealand use this method. However, this method ignores the prices of existing homes, which is a significant omission.

A third way to include housing prices is the **user cost method**. This is a complicated implementation of the idea of opportunity costs. The user cost has two parts: some observed financial outlays and some unobserved economic costs. The observed expenditures are normal maintenance expenditures and property taxes. The unobserved costs are depreciation expenses, interest not earned because of funds used to buy the house such as the down payment, and any profit or loss due to a change in the value of the home.

Though this method has support from economic theory, **it is so complicated in practical terms that no country uses it.** Canada uses a simplified version that adds mortgage interest costs but excludes the foregone interest and the profit/loss.

A fourth way is to **leave out the costs of owner-occupied housing**. The EU countries calculate inflation according to the guidelines in the Harmonized Index of Consumer Prices (HICP). The HICP guidelines aim to ensure that all EU countries measure inflation in the same way. Surprisingly, the cost of owner-occupied housing is totally missing from the HICP. However, there is an ongoing debate about how to include these costs.

## NOMINAL AND REAL INTEREST RATES

**We call the interest rates we observe in the market place nominal interest rates.** These interest rates have an element of inflation built into them. Suppose you have made a loan of 10,000 pesos at an interest rate of 5% for five years, set up like a bond. So, you will get an annual payment of 500 pesos every year, and then a repayment of 10,000 pesos at the end of the five years.

Suppose that dinner at your neighborhood restaurant costs 250 pesos per person. So, the amount of money you have loaned out is worth 40 meals.

You plan to use your interest earnings of 500 pesos to eat there with someone you love. At the end of the first year, you take your 500 pesos, and go to the restaurant. Surprise! Dinner now costs 260 pesos per person, an increase of 4%. You will have to dip into your funds to pay the dinner bill. Further, your loan amount will no longer buy 40 dinners. It will buy only about 38.5 meals.

And, then you realize that if the dinner price increases at the end of the second year to about 270 pesos per person, you will have to dig deeper into your pockets for the two meals. And, now the repayment of 10,000 pesos will buy you only 37 meals.

What's happening is that the purchasing power of your money is coming down because of inflation. How can you take account of inflation in calculating what you are earning? **Instead of looking at the nominal interest rate, you can look at your inflation-adjusted interest rate, which is called the real interest rate.**

(This is the amazing thing about the jargon that we economists use. The interest rate you see in the real world is not the real interest rate – it's just the nominal interest rate. The real interest rate is the rate you calculate according to a formula.)

Ok, what's the formula for the real interest rate?

Real (inflation-adjusted) interest rate = nominal interest rate – inflation rate

In the above example, the real interest rate = 5% (nominal interest rate) - 4% (inflation rate) = 1%. So, while you see that you are earning 55 interest, you are really earning 1% interest.

In general, the higher the inflation rate in a country, the higher the interest rate will be. In the US, in 1979, the market interest rate on 30-year mortgages was about 13%. Wow! How could people afford to take a loan when interest rates were so high? However, the inflation rate at that time was around 12%, (and annual wage increases were correspondingly high.) Hence, the real interest rate was only 1%.

## INTERNATIONAL COMPARISON OF INFLATION

In a real-world presentation of the CPI, there is a base year for which the CPI value is set equal to 100. In the US, this period is currently set as 1982-84. This makes it easier to compare the price level over time. For example, the US CPI value for September 1974 is 50.6, which indicates that prices in September 1974 were about half as high as in 1982-84. Or, prices doubled in about 10 years. And, the US CPI was about 199.7 in March 2006. So, it took about 22 years for prices to double again in the US.

However, it's easy to change the base year. For example, we can reset the base period for the US CPI, and make it September 1974, just to illustrate the point. With the CPI for 1974 set at 100, what would be the CPI value for March 2006? It would be 100*199.7/50.6 = 394.7. As expected, this shows that prices in March 2006 were about four times higher than in September 1974.

This change of the base period is useful in international comparisons. For example, I have set the CPI values for January 2000 equal to 100 for several countries. You can see the resulting CPI values in Figure 7.6.

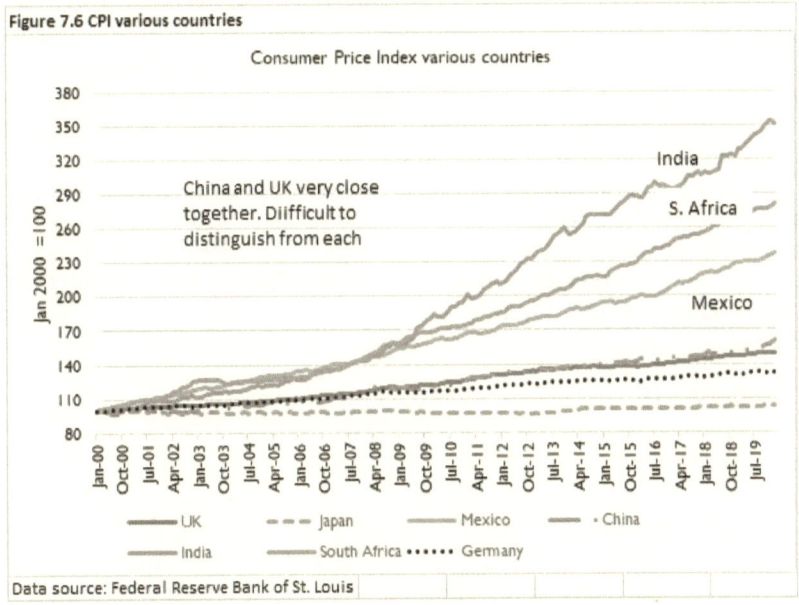

Figure 7.6 CPI various countries

169

In Figure 7.6, you can see that Japan had nearly zero inflation in these twenty years. In some years, the inflation rate has been negative! However, this low inflation rate is not a sign that Japan's economy is doing well. For the last twenty years, Japan's economy has been growing slowly, with a decline in real GDP on several occasions.

In recent years, Japan has been trying to stimulate economic growth. Japan is also looking to increase its inflation rate. Japan's government has borrowed heavily to stimulate the economy. At the end of 2019, Japan's debt/GDP ratio was the highest in the world at around 230%, up from around 100% in 2000. In comparison, the US debt/GDP ratio in 2019 was approximately 105%, up from about 55% in 2000.

Japan's inability to achieve higher GDP and inflation rates in the face of significant government borrowing to finance a stimulus is a puzzle for which there is no solution available so far. And, it is worth noting that in 2009-10, when Greece reached a debt/GDP ratio of around 125, the bond market raised the yields of Greek bonds to unaffordable levels. However, in 2019, the yields on the Japanese government bonds were close to zero or negative. Thus, the debt/GDP ratio alone is not a reliable indicator of inflation or bond yields.

On the other hand, you can see from Figure 7.6 that India had the highest inflation rate, with a CPI value of about 350 for February 2020. This means that in India, on average, what cost 100 rupees in January 2000 had a price of 350 rupees in February 2020. Again, this is not a sign that the Indian economy is doing badly. While there are some questions about the accuracy of Indian GDP data, the World Bank data show that India's real GDP growth has been in the 4-8% range over 2000-2019.

Germany, the UK, and China have had low inflation rates. The rates in China and the UK were close enough that it is hard to distinguish between them in Figure 7.6. While the inflation rates are similar, China had a significant GDP boom in this period, with a growth rate higher than 10% in some years. Mexico and South Africa had lower inflation rates than India but higher than the other countries in the graph.

## KEY TAKEAWAYS

### Let's look at the CPI

1.  The CPI is based on the Laspeyres price index, which has two distinguishing features. First, it uses a weighted arithmetic mean formula to calculate the inflation rate. Second, the weights are derived from the expenditure share of each commodity in total expenditure at some time

in the past. Since these weights don't change every year, the Laspeyres method is called a fixed-weight index.

## A fundamental issue with the use of the Laspeyres index to measure inflation

2. The fixed-weight feature of the Laspeyres index is the source of a flaw called the substitution bias, which implies that the CPI overestimates the inflation rate.

## Alternatives to the Laspeyres index for measuring inflation

3. There are many alternatives to the Laspeyres formula index available to calculate price indexes. The most relevant formulas are the Paasche, Fisher, and Törnqvist (sometimes called Törnqvist-Theil) indexes.

4. From an economist's viewpoint, a key common characteristic of these indexes is that, unlike the Laspeyres formula, the weights change in every period. In general, these indexes give a lower inflation rate than the Laspeyres index.

## Inflation measures attuned to the policy objective

5. The chained indexes, the Implicit GDP Deflator, and core inflation measures are used by central banks for checking whether they are meeting their inflation targets.

## Problems in measuring costs of owner-occupied housing

6. How do we calculate the price of an owner-occupied home every month, and use it in the monthly CPI? Different countries use different methods, and there's no universally accepted method.

## Nominal and real interest rates

7. Economists call the interest rates observed in the market as nominal interest rates. What economists call as real interest rates are nominal interest rates adjusted for inflation.

## International comparisons

8. Developing countries such as India, Mexico, and South Africa have had higher inflation rates than higher-income countries. While a controlled inflation rate is an indication of sound economic management, it is not meaningful to assess a country's economic condition by looking at just the inflation rate.

In Section III, we have so far looked at unemployment and inflation. Suppose we have low unemployment and low inflation. That's good. But, what's the annual income? Without that, the economic picture is not complete. We turn to this issue in the next chapter.

## OPTIONAL - A PRIMER ON INDEX NUMBERS

Let's see how index numbers are used in measuring inflation. There are a lot of numbers and calculations ahead of us. So, let me give you the conclusion upfront so that you know where this is leading to.

A price index is a convenient way to set a comparison period, usually a year, to which prices in other years are compared. Then, the current inflation rate is the percent change in the value of the price index for the current period over the previous period.

**The idea of an index number series comes not from Economics but from Statistics**. Economists just use the available concepts and methods. To make this clear, in the example below, I am applying the idea of an index not to prices but to another economic variable. This is the value of dollar bills in circulation, which we saw in Chapter 4.

In Table 7.2, you can see the value of dollar bills in circulation and the annual growth rate in the value. This table also has two index numbers series. Let's look at the index series labeled 2012 =100. Impossible, right? How can 2012 = 100? It's a short way to say that we have the set the year 2012 as the comparison year – to which the values of other years will be compared. In the jargon, the comparison year is usually called the reference base year, or just the base year.

Table 7.2. Value of dollar bills in circulation $ billion

|  | 2011 | 2012 | 2013 | 2014 | 2015 | 2016 | 2017 | 2018 |
|---|---|---|---|---|---|---|---|---|
| Value $ bills in circulation | $1,034.5 | $1,127.1 | $1,198.3 | $1,299.1 | $1,380.0 | $1,463.4 | $1,571.1 | $1,671.9 |
| Growth rate | N/A | 9.0% | 6.3% | 8.4% | 6.2% | 6.0% | 7.4% | 6.4% |
| Index 2012 =100 | 91.8 | 100.0 | 106.3 | 115.3 | 122.4 | 129.8 | 139.4 | 148.3 |
| Index 2014-15 =100 | 77.2 | 84.1 | 89.5 | 97.0 | 103.0 | 109.2 | 117.3 | 124.8 |

Data source: Federal Reserve Bank of St. Louis

In Table 7.2, you can also see an index series labeled 2104-2015 = 100. Why are we looking at an index that uses two years as the comparison period? The answer is simple. In the US, all the CPIs use the period 1982-1984 as the comparison period. So, I want to show you how to use several years as the comparison period.

**To make 2012 as the comparison year, we set the value of the original data (dollar bills) in that year equal to 100.** This is simple. Divide the reported value of 1,127.1 by 1,1271.1, and the answer is 1. Then, multiply by 100, and you get 100. Easy.

Then, let's find the index value for 2013. Now divide the original value for 2013 by the original value for the comparison year, which means 1,198.3/1,271.1. The answer is 1.063. Multiply by 100 to get 106.3. This is the value you see for 2013.

The value of 106.3 for 2013 is interpreted as saying that the value of dollar bills in 2013 was 6.3% higher than in 2012. In other words, the growth rate was 6.3%. Similarly, the index value of 139.4 for 2017 shows that the value of dollar bills in 2017 was 39.4% than in 2012. To calculate the growth rate for 2017, we compare the index value of 139.4 for 2017, with the index value of 129.8 for 2016. This gives a growth rate of 7.4%, the same as with the original data.

To make 2014-2015 as the comparison period, we use the average value for 2014-2015 as the number we divide by, instead of the value of 2012. The average of 2014-15 is $1,339.6. So, we divide all the original values by 1,339.6, and multiply by 100. For example, for 2011, we divide 1.034.5 by 1,339.6, and the answer is 0.772. Then, multiply by 100, and you get 77.2 as the value of the index for 2011.

## CHAPTER 8.    GROSS DOMESTIC PRODUCT

**We know our individual incomes. That's not enough. We also want to understand how our country, or a region within our country, is doing**. One reason may be that we think that our financial prospects will be brighter if the country is doing well. For example, we saw in Chapter 5 that some professionals left Greece after the 2010 economic problems because they felt that the Greek economy would not do well in the next few years, and that would restrict their job prospects.

**There are two related but different objectives in measuring how the economy is doing**. One aim is to understand and measure what is happening, i.e., **to measure the level of economic activity in the economy. The GDP is a well-known measure of the level of economic activity in an economy.** The economic activity leads to incomes or self-production and consumption, which is the usual reason for economic activity.

Another objective is to measure the economy's income level, i.e., **to measure the country's total income.** While a substantial amount of the country's income comes from domestic economic activity, some of it comes from external activities. For example, one of the reasons why countries and civilizations built political empires was to gain income from activities outside the country.

While we don't have political empires anymore, large companies do make profits abroad and send them back home. And migrant workers do send money back to their families. **The World Bank uses the Gross National Income (GNI) as a measure of national income. In brief, the GNI adds the net international financial income inflows to GDP, which looks at only in-country production and income**.

The difference between GDP and GNI is meaningful for some countries, and should be kept in mind for these countries. Nevertheless, the jobs created within the country are directly linked to GDP, not GNI.

**There is considerable public policy discussion about the use of GDP as a measure of how well the economy and people are doing**. One issue is whether the GDP is a measure of well-being or happiness. The short answer is that the GDP is not such a measure.

175

Another issue is whether developing countries should focus heavily on GDP or look at some alternative measures such as the Human Development Index in planning their development. The short answer is that there is no reason to look at just the GDP, but we should look at the strengths and weaknesses of all the measures we look at.

A third issue is whether the GDP alone presents the full picture, or whether we should look at other measures also. The short answer is that we should look at other measures. we have already looked at unemployment and inflation, and we will look at poverty and income inequality in the next chapter.

We will look at only GDP in this chapter.

## Two clarifications

**First, in calculating GDP, we need not stick to a country. We can reduce or expand the region covered**. Instead of a country, we can look at a part of a country, such as a State, or a group of countries. Sometimes we add the letter S, and make it GSDP to indicate we are looking at a State. For example, California's GSDP is so large that its GDP would be the fifth highest in the world if it were a country on its own.

Or we can look at several countries together. They could be the Eurozone, OECD, South Asia, Francophone Africa, Gulf Cooperation Council, or Central America – whichever group we are interested in. Then, we need to find some way to convert the GDP of each country, which is calculated in the local currency, to a common currency.

**Second,** the **GDP reporting period is usually a quarter or a year**. While unemployment and inflation data are commonly published monthly, no country officially publishes monthly GDP data. It takes time to compile and process all the data at the end of the quarter. Hence, it is common to release preliminary estimates, often called flash estimates, soon after the quarter ends, and then issue revised data later.

But people are keen to know how the economy is doing right now. To meet this need, in the US, the Fed publishes an unofficial estimate called GDPNow. This uses a statistical model to produce a running estimate of real GDP growth based on available data for the current measured quarter. It is common to look at variables whose data are available monthly or weekly, such as electricity production or automobile sales.

**The Fed publishes another unofficial measure called the Weekly Economic Index (WEI).** The WEI is based on three groups of data. One group is consumer behavior, which is measured by same-store retail sales and is an indicator of consumer confidence. High values indicate that the economy is doing well. A second group measures employment and unemployment alternatives to the unemployment rate. They are the initial and continuing unemployment insurance claims, an index of temporary and contract employment, and federal tax withholding data. The third group includes production and sales data for four key industries: steel, electricity, fuel sales, and railroad traffic.

## Chapter flow

This chapter has five main parts. We begin by looking at how to define and measure GDP. Here we say that there are three different methods to do this. They are the output method, the expenditure method, and the income method. In the second, third, and fourth parts, we look at each method, and bring out the insights we get from the three methods. The fifth part has a comparison of the GDPs of different countries.

## THREE WAYS TO DEFINE AND MEASURE GDP

There are three fundamental questions in measuring and using GDP as a measure of national income. Think of the economy as a group of people who work together to make their living.

The first question is: **What do you do to earn your joint income?** The answer would be that we produce various things. We sell most of them in the market, but keep some for our own use. What is the value of goods that this group produces? **At the national level, this leads to what we call the output definition and measurement of GDP.**

The second question is: **What do you do with your output?** Again, we do various things with what we produce. First, we save some of it, which will be our investment so that we can increase our production in the future. Then, we set aside some of it for collective spending, which is like paying taxes to finance government spending. Then, we export some of what we produce. Finally, we come to our total consumption, which includes our imports. **At the national level, this leads to what we call the expenditure definition and measurement of GDP.**

The third question is: **Who gets what share of your output?** To answer this, we have to create some sub-groups within our group. Then, we can tell you what their shares are. **At the national level, this leads to what we call the income definition and measurement of GDP.**

So far, we have seen various top-down division of the group's production. We are dividing the same thing into its components in three different ways.

At the national level, we don't look at top-down divisions. Instead, we make bottom-up additions. For this, we get data about the components and add them up.

If a country does its accounts properly, the bottom-up addition by the output, expenditure, and income definitions will give the same answer. In practice, there may be ignorable differences between the three different answers.

This means that we can define and measure GDP in three ways, and they all mean the same thing. However, **it is common to define GDP in terms of the output method.**

If the three different methods give the same answer, isn't it enough to look at just one method? Why do we have to look at all three? Because we get different insights by looking at GDP in these three ways.

Let's look at the three methods.

## GDP – OUTPUT METHOD

It is conventional to define GDP by the output method. It makes sense because the P in GDP stands for product, which is what output is. We will follow the convention here. So, here's the definition.

**GDP is the current market value of all the final goods and services produced in a country in a particular period.** The term final is used to indicate that we don't count both the final product and its inputs. When we look at the value of cars produced, we don't count the value of the seats, tires, and other parts. Similarly, when we look at bread, we don't add the value of the flour used in the bread. Their values are all built into the final product value.

**Let's now look at the implications of each of the key phrases in the GDP definition.** The key three terms are current market value, all the final goods and services, and produced.

### Implications of *current market value*

The term itself is clear. We are calculating the value of the output at the current market price. However, the words current and market value both raise some important issues.

## *Implications of* current *– need to use real GDP*

When we use current market prices, we know that they change every period due to inflation. Hence, the GDP's value will change with price changes, even if we produce precisely the same quantities. So, **we call the GDP estimate at current market prices as the nominal GDP.** Then, we also calculate **the real GDP, which is the value of the final goods and services produced at prices from some past period.**

**Real GDP is much more important than nominal GDP in assessing how an economy is doing.** This is particularly important in countries with high inflation rates, as their nominal GDP will rise, not because they are producing more, but because their prices have increased. For this reason, it is useful to check whether the news media are reporting the nominal or real GDP, though it is common to report the real GDP growth numbers, not nominal GDP growth numbers.

## *Implications of* market value

While the term itself is clear, **one issue is how does GDP handle goods and services that are not sold through the market?** There are two types of goods and services that are not transacted in the market place.

First, there are goods and services produced by household members for the family's use. For example, some farmers in developing countries may produce food mainly for their own use. It is usual to devise some way to estimate the value, called the imputed value, of the food that subsistence farmers produce for themselves. This is doable because some of the product is sold, and there is a market price for the product.

However, there is usually no way to calculate the value of the household services that women have traditionally provided and continue to provide. This is indeed a serious shortcoming, but there's no clear method to find the right money value for these services. This omission implies that the value of GDP increases as people shift, over time, from self-production to commercial production. For example, fifty years ago, families used to eat proportionately more home-made food than today.

Even if you make pizza at home, you may have bought a ready-to-bake pizza at the grocery store, and you are just baking it at home, not making the dough yourself. And, in international comparisons, the GDP of countries where self-production for household services is high will be under-estimated compared to countries where self-production is lower.

**Second, the government produces a variety of goods and services that do not go through the market place.** What's the value of the judicial system? Of the police? One solution is to evaluate the work based on the cost of production. That's easy to do because the government does pay its employees.

## Implications of *all* the final goods and services *produced*

### *Implications of* all

**In the attempt to include all the goods and services, we run into two problems.** There are some goods and services that the providers don't want to disclose to any person in authority. This would include things that may have been declared illegal, such as drugs, prostitution, gambling, and alcohol. **There is simply no way to get accurate data about these illegal goods and services, even though they are sold in the market place.**

Next, every economy has some economic activities that are legal, but people don't want to report them to the government. Some people just want to avoid paying taxes. You go to someone's home, repair something, get paid in cash, and buy some stuff on your way home. **The things you buy show up in the GDP, but not the repair work you did.**

This off-the-books work can be substantial in developing countries with a significant number of people in the informal sector.

### *Implications of* produced

This term says that we focus only on what is produced. **The implication is that we don't include what is lost.** For example, suppose I crash my car, and it becomes unusable. That's a loss. But this loss will not be recorded in the GDP. On the other hand, when I buy a new car to replace my crashed car, the new car's value will be in the GDP. In short, the GDP ignores losses.

**The biggest loss ignored by the GDP is the loss of the environment arising from the production of goods and services.** At the global level, the loss is due to the climate change brought about by the production processes that lead to greenhouse gas emissions. At the local level, we may see the loss in the form of worsening water and air quality. And, that's just a small part of the environmental loss.

In order to take account of this loss, we define Green GDP as GDP minus the environmental loss. And, then use Green GDP instead of GDP. The idea is clear and straightforward. However, so far, there is no consensus on how to calculate the environmental loss in a methodologically sound, objective way.

It's not for lack of trying. Economists and others have been trying to come up with ways to resolve this, but there is no solution yet. But efforts are ongoing. For example, the European Commission has launched a "Beyond GDP" initiative to develop indicators as well-defined as GDP, but more inclusive of environmental and social aspects of progress. In the next few years, we may get a measure that goes beyond the level of economic activity to reflect other parameters.

## Insights from GDP output method

**It is standard practice to measure the individual contributions of agriculture, industry, and services to a country's GDP.** Manufacturing is a sub-group within industry. The shares of the sectors in GDP are a measure of the importance of the three sectors in the economy.

### *Shares of various sectors in GDP*

In Figure 8.1, you can see that in all the countries, **services is the largest component, followed by industry, with agriculture at the bottom.** While we don't have GDP data for 1900, we do know the labor force in most countries in 1900 was in agriculture. **Overall, the world has managed to produce enough food to feed itself, though not equally across countries, and shift workers to industries and services. The current trend is a decline in industry's share, and a rise in the share of services.**

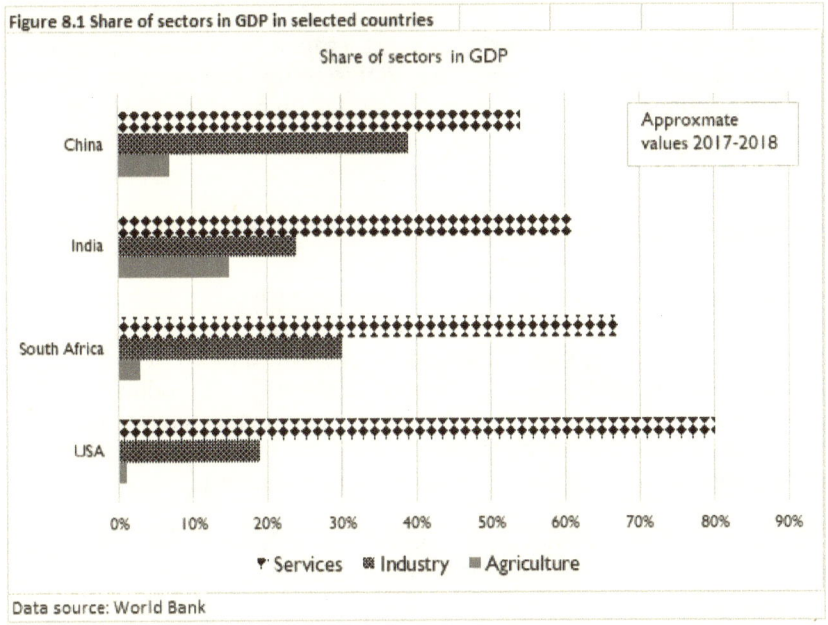

Figure 8.1 Share of sectors in GDP in selected countries

Data source: World Bank

The issue for this century is the extent to which the share of industry will decline over time on a worldwide basis, with an increase in the share of services. And, if the share of services rises, will they be similar services across the world, or will there be significant differences? And, if it materializes, will this trend create enough jobs, particularly in what we called in Chapter 6 as low median age countries? Right now, there are no clear answers that I am aware of, so there seems to be a clear need for further analysis here.

In this group, **agriculture's share in the highest in India**. We saw in Chapter 6 that India has around 40% of its labor force is in agriculture. Here we see that agriculture's share in India's GDP is around 15%. It follows that India's labor force is less productive in agriculture than in manufacturing or services. **So, it's no surprise that India is looking to promote is its industrial sector, specially manufacturing, though with limited success so far.**

In **China, the share of agriculture is higher than in long-industrialized countries like Germany and the US.** And, we saw in Chapter 6 that China still has more than 20% of its labor force in agriculture. This is an indication that China's transformation away from an agriculture-dependent economy is not yet complete. Nevertheless, in this group of countries, **industry's share is the highest in China, and much higher than of any other country.**

In this group of countries, the US has the lowest share of industry in GDP. Thus, the contrast between China and the US is clear. As expected, the share of services in the highest in the US.

Even in China, the share of services is higher than the share of industry. In fact, this is the case in all the countries in this group. This is a clear sign that **services are the most important sector in GDP on a worldwide basis**. And, this is the case even though we don't count the value of household services in GDP.

### Evolution of manufacturing over time

You can see from Figure 8.2 (below) that China has the highest share of manufacturing in GDP, and China's share is far higher than the share of any other country in this group. This is consistent with the common perception that China has become the world's factory. Made in China products made sell all over the world. However, in China, the share of manufacturing has begun to decline, with a rise in the share of services. Thus, China's economy is moving away slowly from heavy reliance on manufacturing.

Mexico is the only country whose share of manufacturing has gone up but only slightly. In Germany, the share of manufacturing has been fairly steady at around 20%.

South Africa and India have been looking to increase the importance of manufacturing in their economies. Manufacturing's share has not increased in India, and has declined in South Africa.

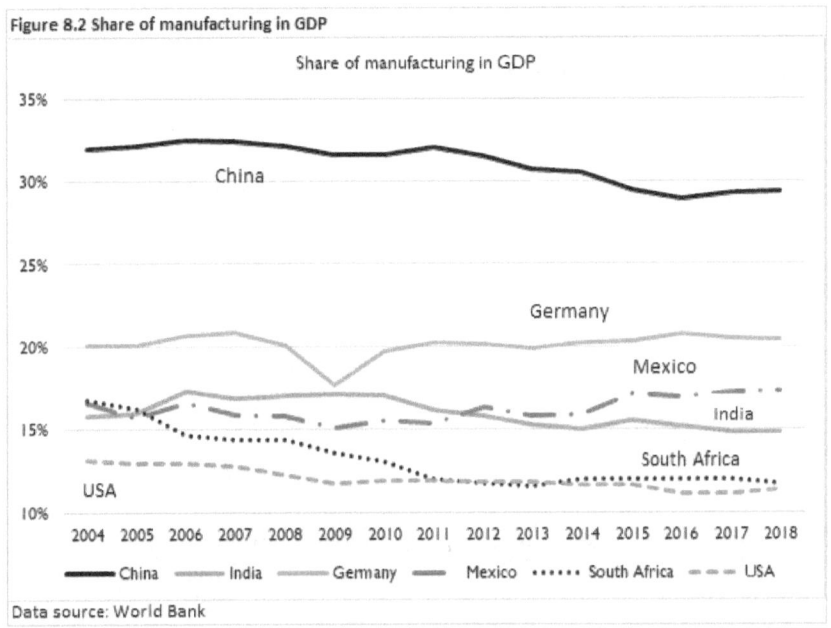

Figure 8.2 Share of manufacturing in GDP

## Manufacturing and finance in the US

We see in Figure 8.2 that the share of manufacturing in the US is lower than in other countries, and has declined slowly over time. There has been much discussion in the US that manufacturing has declined over time, while the role of financial services has increased. This difference between manufacturing and finance is confirmed by the data for the last two decades.

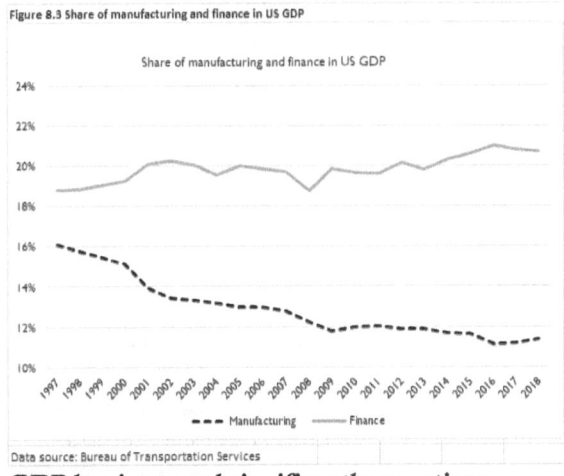

Figure 8.3 Share of manufacturing and finance in US GDP

In Figure 8.3, you can see that in the US while the share of manufacturing in GDP has declined slowly over time, the share of finance, which includes insurance, real estate, rental, and leasing, has increased slowly over time. **As a result, the difference between the shares of manufacturing and finance in the US GDP has increased significantly over time.**

## GDP – EXPENDITURE METHOD

Under this method, the GDP is based on the expenditures of four groups.

The first group is people, whose expenditure is conventionally denoted by the letter C.

The second group is firms, whose expenditure is conventionally denoted by the letter I, for investment. If you look for real-world data related to I, it is likely to be written as Gross Fixed Capital Formation.

The third group is the government, whose expenditure is denoted by the letter G. Note that some of government outlays, such as social security payments, are not expenditures, but simply financial transfers. They are not part of G.

The last group comprises of foreigners, who spend money on what we call out country's exports, whose expenditures are denoted by the letter X.

We have to take account of the fact that some of these expenditures will be on imported products, which are not part of GDP. It is conventional to denote these expenditures by the letter M.

Then, we write GDP by the expenditure method as

$$GDP = C + I + G + X - M$$

Why do we subtract imports when we are adding all the other expenditures? Because we want to focus on the expenditures on goods and services that are produced within the country. Remember the output definition of GDP? If we included expenditures on imports in the expenditure method, we would not get the same answer by output and expenditure methods.

Sometimes, the term X- M is written as $N = X - M$, where N stands for net exports. Note that N can be negative, meaning that the exports are less than the imports. With this, we can write GDP by the expenditure method as:

$$GDP = C + I + G + N$$

### Implications derived from expenditure method formula

**This version of the GDP definition makes it easier to understand why the GDP is going up or down.** For example, if consumer sentiment is low, and people are holding back on their consumption, then C will be down. And that will tend to reduce the GDP. Similarly, if firms are not sure about the economy, then I will be low.

### How to boost GDP in an economic slowdown

In case C and I are down, what are the options to boost the GDP?

First, **you can increase G directly, which is a well-known form of an economic stimulus to try to boost GDP**. However, it is not easy to increase government expenditure. As President Obama found out, it's hard to find "shovel-ready" projects on which the government can spend its money. Still, government procedures take time, and the projects that the government wants to fund need many approvals and clearances. It all takes time.

Second, **you can transfer some funds directly to people, and hope to boost C**. Some people will spend the money they get from the government quickly, while others may hold back. In general, poorer people will tend to spend more of the government transfers. Poorer people have tight budgets, and they may be eager to spend some more money. This transfer can be done fairly quickly, and the money will tend to be spent much faster than by increasing G.

Third, **you can try to give some incentives to firms, and hope to boost I.** These incentives can be in the form of lower interest rates via monetary policy, or profit boosts via lower tax rates. But, in the end, firms must be confident that they can sell more and make a profit on what they sell. In any case, it may take some time for firms to respond to the incentives.

Finally, **you try to boost exports or reduce imports.** Most countries cannot boost exports quickly because it takes time to find new markets or sell more of your materials. One option is to devalue your currency, which makes your exports cheaper for the buyers. Suppose you want to see a product in the US for 100 pesos. If the exchange rate is $ 1 = 20 pesos, then you need to sell it for $ 5. However, if the exchange rate becomes $ 1 = 25 pesos, then it's enough to sell your product for $ 4, as this will give you 100 pesos. On the other hand, with this change in the exchange rate, your imports will become more expensive. So, **devaluation can boost exports and reduce imports, i.e., increase net exports N.**

However, devaluation comes with many side effects that hurt your economy, which we will discuss in Volume II of this book. Here, we just note that devaluation has to be undertaken carefully, and is generally low on the priority list of options to boost the economy.

Another way to look at the structure of the economy is by the shares of the various groups in total expenditure. We turn to this next.

## International variations in Consumption share in GDP

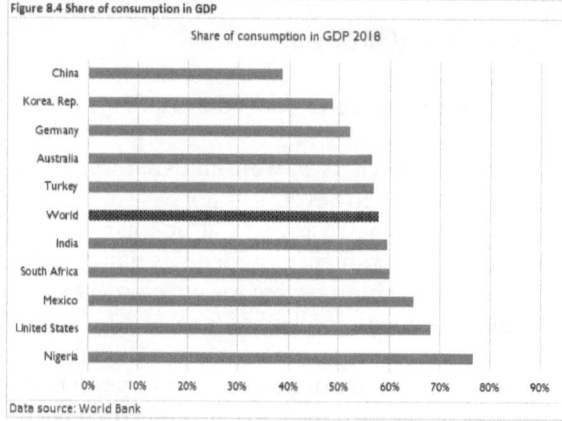

Figure 8.4 Share of consumption in GDP

Data source: World Bank

In Figure 8.4 you can see the share of consumption in selected countries. The contrast between the US and China is clear. The US has a high share of consumption, while China has a low share of consumption. The US has the highest GDP in the world (though international comparisons of GDP are not straightforward, as we discuss later in this chapter), and high consumption levels.

**This makes the US the largest market in the world.** Further, the US has been historically open to imports. That makes it a large, attractive market for all countries looking for export markets. As a result, a slowdown or recession in the US is felt around the world as US imports come down. Thus, **the US is currently one of the major drivers of the world economy**.

**China has the second-highest GDP in the world, and China still has a high economic growth rate.** While China's consumption share is low, the share will likely increase in the future. Further, China does import inputs for its industrial production, which makes China an attractive market for firms that make industrial inputs. **That makes China a growing, attractive market.**

For example, nearly 40% of Australia's exports go to China, composed mainly of iron ore, gas, and coal, with education and tourism increasing in recent years. About 7% of US exports go to China, composed primarily of aircraft, various types of machinery and instruments, and vehicles.

India has seen high economic growth rates in the last two decades, though not as high as in China. India has a relatively high share of consumption. This makes India another growing, attractive market for other countries.

In general, countries with a low share of consumption have a high share of investment, as we see in Figure 8.5.

## International variations in Investment share in GDP

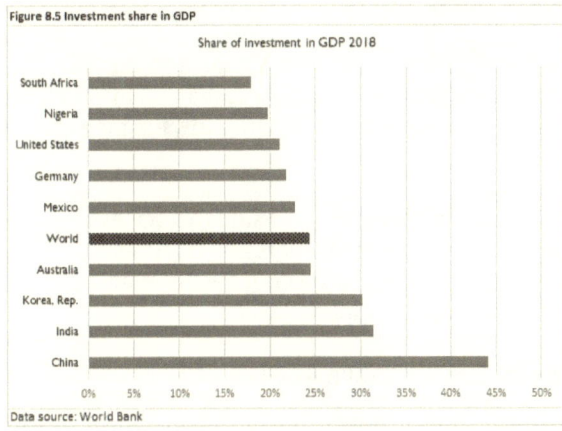

Figure 8.5 Investment share in GDP

Share of investment in GDP 2018

Data source: World Bank

In Figure 8.5, we can see that China and the US are again at the different ends of the spectrum of investment shares. **The US investment share is about only 20% of the GDP, while China's share is the highest in this group at nearly 45%.** India and South Korea also have high investment shares.

High investment levels are closely associated with high economic growth. It is no surprise that China and India have had high economic growth rates in recent years.

However, China's high investment levels are perhaps a bit too high. **Economists measure the effectiveness of investment by a term called the incremental capital-output ratio (ICOR).** A higher value of ICOR shows that you need more investment for an additional unit of output than with a lower value of ICOR. It follows that your investment is more effective if you have a low value for your ICOR.

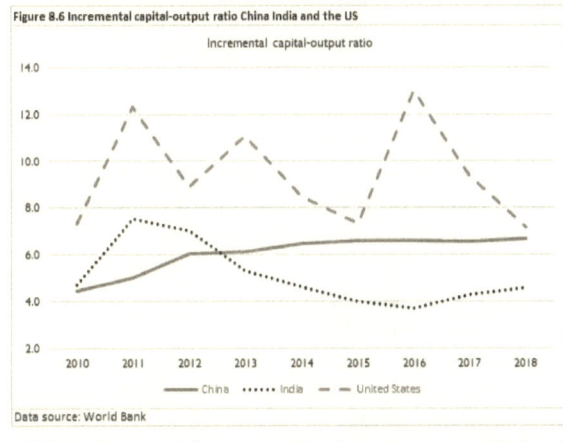

Figure 8.6 Incremental capital-output ratio China India and the US

Incremental capital-output ratio

China ······ India — — United States

Data source: World Bank

In Figure 8.6, you can see that the ICOR for China, India, and the US. Here, I have calculated the ICOR as the investment share of GDP divided by the GDP growth rate.

**You can see that China's ICOR has been rising over the years.** Is this increase taking place because China is not able to use its investments efficiently? Is there an increase in misplaced investments that don't yield good results? Or, is it that production in China is increasingly more capital-intensive, so that you need more capital

187

than earlier? Probably, it is some combination of these two factors. **In any case, the implication of the rising ICOR is that China will have to invest more to maintain high growth rates.**

On the other hand, **India's ICOR is lower than for China and the US.** This means that India can achieve higher growth rates than China and the US from the same level of investment. However, India's ICOR shows some signs of rising in recent years.

Overall, every country has to figure out how to make sure that its investments are efficient and productive. Higher investment shares in GDP that come at the expense of consumption shares may not be sustainable for many years, as people may begin to press for higher consumption levels.

## International variations in Export share in GDP

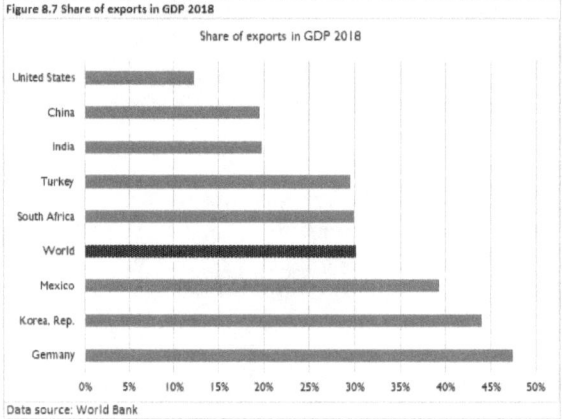

Figure 8.7 Share of exports in GDP 2018

Data source: World Bank

In Figure 8.7, you can see the export share in the GDP of various countries.

Given China's reputation as the world's factory, it would be natural to think China's economy depends heavily on exports. However, this is not the case. China's share of exports in GDP is quite low at around 20%. In this group, only the US has a lower share, at around 12%.

Then, how did China get a reputation as an economy that is heavily dependent upon exports? You can see the answer in Figure 8.8 (below). Here we see that **in China the share of exports in GDP increased steadily since 1990 but hit its peak in 2005-2007, and has declined since then.**

**In contrast, Germany has steadily increased its export share over the years.** But, how come we don't see German goods being sold all over the world, like we see goods from China? Because apart from cars, Germany exports mainly machinery of various kinds and some pharmaceutical products. Not what you and I look out for in our daily shopping forays.

**Mexico's share of exports has also increased steadily over the years**. You can see a big bump up in 1995, which is due to the North American Free Trade Agreement (NAFTA) coming into effect in 1994.

**India was quite closed to international trade until the policy changed in 1991.** In Figure 8.8, you can see that India's export share had more than tripled by 2013, after which there has been some decline in the export share.

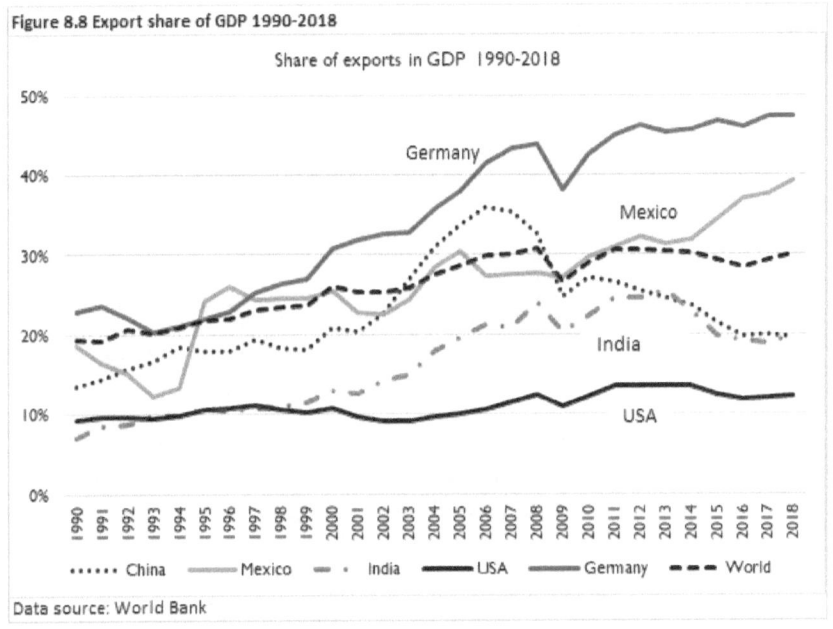

Figure 8.8 Export share of GDP 1990-2018

Data source: World Bank

Over these years, **the US export share has stayed low, without any significant changes**. The US economy is much more dependent upon its sizeable domestic market than on exports.

Finally, in Figure 8.8, you can see how **the world has become globalized over the last three decades**. In 1990, the share of exports in the global GDP was around 20%. This share increased fairly steadily to about 31% by 2008. Then, there was a significant dip due to the economic crisis at that time. Since then, the share has recovered but is still near, not above, the old peak.

## GDP – INCOME METHOD

**Under the income method, we look at the decomposition of the GDP into the earnings of various groups.** The US calculates the GDP as the total of (i) employee compensation; (ii) net taxes paid; (iii) net operating surplus, which is basically profits, and (iv) consumption of fixed capital, which is basically depreciation.

## Implications derived from income method formula

**Our focus is on the changes in labor's share of the GDP over time**. This is not an issue that has attracted much public discussion, where the focus has more been on income inequality, minimum wages, and poverty. However, the changes in the labor's share have been discussed frequently in the economic literature.

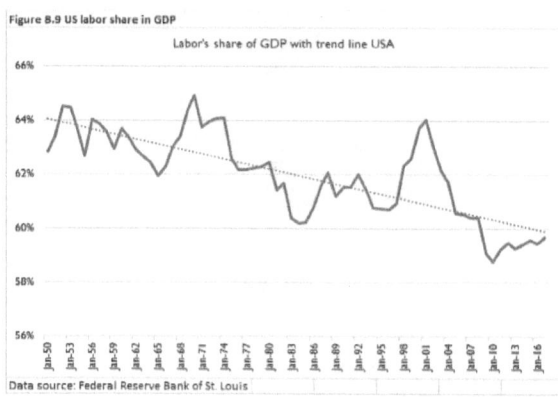

Figure 8.9 US labor share in GDP

Data source: Federal Reserve Bank of St. Louis

In Figure 8.9, you can see the changes in the labor share of GDP in the US. In the US, there has been a decline of the labor share in the GDP from 1950 onward. The fall is particularly noticeable in this century from a high of around 65% in 2001 to about 60% in 2017.

The US is not alone. Based on several studies, there is a worldwide trend that the share of labor in the GDP has declined over time. There are many possible explanations for this decline. One simple explanation is that countries have increasingly shifted from labor-intensive production to capital-intensive production. In capital-intensive production, labor's share is lower than in labor-intensive production. Other explanations are more complex. These include globalization, and the reduction in the bargaining power of labor. It may be the case that the explanation differs from country to country, or from one group of countries to another group of countries.

More importantly, there is no consensus that governments should adopt policies that aim to increase labor's share. Further, there are no well-established policies to try to increase labor's share.

## INTERNATIONAL COMPARISONS OF GDP

**It is common to ask which are the top countries in terms of GDP.** In particular, these days, there is considerable debate about whether the US is still ahead of China, or China has overtaken the US. There are no clear answers to these questions because **the international comparison of GDP is**

**full of pitfalls.** The most critical issue is **which exchange rate we should use in converting the GDPs of different countries into a common currency.**

## Purchasing power parity (PPP) exchange rates

**It is customary to use the market exchange rate to convert the GDP of one country into another currency.** Given the US dollar's dominance as a global currency, it is customary to convert the GDP of other countries, measured in their local currencies, into their values in US dollars. **Here, the use of the market exchange rate creates a serious problem.**

Consider a high-quality haircut in a comfortable, pleasant place. If it is similar across two countries, it should be worth the same amount in the GDP of both countries. According to a website that keeps track of prices in various countries, such a haircut costs about 92 yuan in Beijing. Using the current approximate market exchange rate of $ 1 = 7 yuans, this haircut's cost is about $ 13. But you would pay more, say $ 20, for such a haircut in the US, particularly in Washington, DC.

So, **the same haircut adds $ 13 to China's GDP and $ 20 to the US GDP.** That clearly inflates the US GDP compared to China's GDP. The problem is that the market exchange rate is not the right way to convert the haircut value. So, how should we convert it? Which exchange rate should we use?

In the above example, we should use an exchange rate that converts 92 yuan to $ 20 – the two prices for the same haircut in the two countries. Then, the exchange rate is 92/20, which gives us $ 1 = 4.5 yuans, different from the market exchange rate of $ 1 = 7 yuans.

But, that's only for haircuts. What about other commodities? You have to repeat this exercise for other commodities. And, then take the average of these calculated rates. That gives you **the purchasing power parity (PPP) exchange rate.**

Thus, in theory, **PPP exchange rates, not market exchange rates, are the right way to convert the GDP of another country into US dollars.** So, why don't we use the PPP exchange rate? First, it is tedious and time-consuming to derive the PPP exchange rate. The World Bank runs a large program to calculate PPP exchange rates. In May 2020, the World Bank's website shows a PPP exchange rate of $ 1 = 3.54 yuans – but this is for 2018, not today. Second, there are elements of subjectivity in these calculations.

Hence, the common practice is to continue to use the market exchange rate and recognize that the PPP exchange rate would give a different answer. **For example, the US GDP in 2019 was about $ 21 trillion, and China's GDP was about $ 14 trillion at the market exchange rate. However, at the PPP** exchange rate, the US was still at $ 21 trillion, but China was at about $ 27 trillion – far ahead of the US.

Economists would prefer to use the PPP exchange rate to compare living conditions in different countries. However, companies selling their products in another country will not be able to convert their profits back at the PPP exchange rate. They will have to convert their money at the market exchange rate.

Nevertheless, this is not just a theoretical debate. People in the US sometimes travel abroad for medical treatment because the market exchange rate makes the cost in the destination country much lower than in the US. Some retirees move abroad to places where the cost of living is lower, but the market exchange rate does not take into account this.

## International ranking of GDP

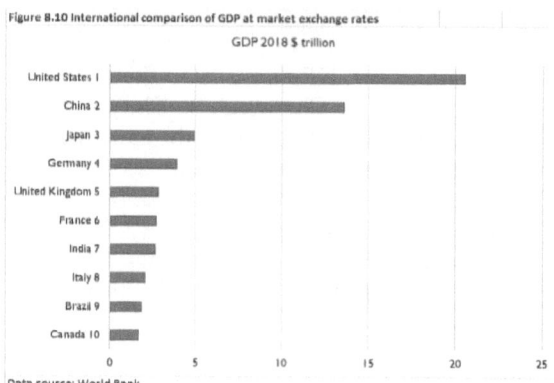

Figure 8.10 International comparison of GDP at market exchange rates

Data source: World Bank

In Figure 8.10, you can see the top ten countries ranked by the size of their GDP in 2018, calculated at market exchange rates. **The US is at the top, as it has been for many years.**

Two of the ten countries – the US and Canada – are from North America. Three countries – Germany, France, and Italy – are from Europe. Three countries – Japan, China, and India - are from Asia. The only country from South America is Brazil. The tenth country is the United Kingdom – I leave it to you to decide which continent it is located in.

### Change since 2000

There have been only limited changes in the GDP ranks since 2000. The most significant change is that India moved up from outside the top ten (rank was 13 in 2000) into the top ten at rank 7. India was close to France (rank 6) and the United Kingdom (rank 5) in 2018. **According to some reports**, in 2019, **India moved ahead of France and the UK into the fifth rank.**

**China has jumped from rank 6 to rank 2.** Given the significant difference between the US and China GDP at market exchange rates, this ranking may persist for the next few years.

Since India entered the top ten, some country had to move out. This was Mexico, which dropped from rank 9 in 2000 to rank 15 in 2018.

| Table 8.1 GDP ranks in 2000 and 2018 | | |
|---|---|---|
| | **GDP Rank 2018** | **GDP Rank 2000** |
| USA | 1 | 1 |
| China | 2 | 6 |
| Japan | 3 | 2 |
| Germany | 4 | 3 |
| United Kingdom | 5 | 4 |
| France | 6 | 5 |
| India | 7 | 13 |
| Italy | 8 | 7 |
| Brazil | 9 | 10 |
| Canada | 10 | 8 |
| Mexico | 15 | 9 |
| Data source: World Bank | | |

## KEY TAKEAWAYS

### Measuring GDP and insights

1. GDP is conventionally defined as the market value of all the final goods and services produced in a country in a particular period. This definition corresponds to the output method of defining and measuring GDP. The expenditure and income methods of measuring GDP give the same answer as the output method.

2. There are several problems in the measurement of GDP. One major problem is that the GDP ignores the services provided by homemakers, who have historically been women, to their families. Another major problem is that the GDP ignores the environmental loss arising from the production of goods and services.

3. The output measured by GDP comes from the agricultural, industrial, and service sectors. The shares of the three sectors differ across countries. China has the highest share for industry across countries, but this share has been declining with an increase in the share of the services. In the US, the industrial sector has a low share, while the share of the service sector is high.

4. From the expenditure method, we learn that the US has a high share of consumption in GDP. This makes the US the largest market in the world. China and India have high shares of investment in GDP, which facilitates their high GDP growth rates. Germany has a high share of exports in GDP, while the US has a much lower export share. China's export share in GDP peaked around 2007, and has been falling since then.

5. The income method shows that labor's share of GDP has been falling over time on a worldwide basis. However, there is no consensus on what to do about this, or how to reverse this fall.

## International comparisons of GDP

6. Conventional international comparisons of GDP are based on the GDP of different countries converted by the market exchange rates. This method underestimates the dollar value of the GDP of countries with lower costs of living. However, the theoretically superior purchasing power parity (PPP) exchange rate is difficult to calculate, even for major international agencies. And there are many subjective elements in the determination of the PPP exchange rate. Hence, the market exchange rate method continues to be used in international comparisons.

7. The top ten countries in 2018 in terms of GDP are the US, China, Japan, Germany, the UK, France, India, Italy, Brazil, and Canada. The only new entrant in the top ten since 2000 is India. China moved up from rank 6 in 2000 to rank 2 in 2018. Mexico dropped out of the top ten.

In this chapter, we saw that labor's share in the GDP has declined over time. This sets the stage for the next chapter, where we will discuss poverty and income inequality

.

## CHAPTER 9.   POVERTY AND ECONOMIC INEQUALITY

**In Chapter 1, we introduced the major economic variables in an economy. That list did not include the poverty rate. Why? That's because economic theory does not provide an explicit definition of poverty**. And, poverty does not figure significantly in the popular US economics textbooks related to Microeconomics and Macroeconomics.

Nonetheless, the poverty rate has great significance in developing countries, where poverty and hunger were widespread just a few decades ago. In China, millions of people died in a famine in 1959-1961. While India did not have such a large number of deaths after it became independent in 1947, food shortages persisted for many years. Getting rid of poverty was a major social goal in these and other developing countries.

Europe does not have the kind of poverty seen in developing countries. However, the European Union (EU) uses a broad definition of poverty, and has a policy goal of reducing the poverty rate.

**Income and wealth inequality are related to poverty, but the two are conceptually different**. It is entirely possible for a country to reduce its poverty rate significantly but still increase income and wealth inequality. Further, two countries with similar income inequalities could have very different poverty levels. Hence, it is best to look at inequality separately from poverty.

### Chapter flow

This chapter has two main parts. **In the first part, we look at poverty**.

Is this person poor or not poor? It seems to be an easy question to answer. We can just look to decide whether a person is poor. But the real world is more complicated than that even when you look at just one country at a time. When you compare poverty rates across countries, you run into even more complications than those in the comparison of their GDPs. **We look at the poverty measurement system in the US, developing countries, and Europe,**

**In the second part, we look at economic inequality.** Most of the focus is on how to measure inequality, and the recent worldwide trends in inequality. Our discussion about how to reduce inequality is brief. First, many high-income countries have relatively low levels of inequality, so high inequality is not a pervasive problem in these countries. For low-income countries, it remains a challenge to achieve high levels of economic growth with low levels of income equality.

## US POVERTY MEASURES

**The US uses an income measure to classify people as poor or not poor.** The US Federal government sets income limits every year for this purpose. If you are below the applicable income limit, then you are poor. Otherwise, you are not poor.

**While this seems a straightforward exercise, in practice, the US system is complex.** Specifically, the US Federal government uses one method to decide whether you are poor. And, then, it uses another approach to decide whether you qualify for Federal anti-poverty and subsidy programs. Wait. There's yet another way to determine whether you are eligible for low-income housing. Further, many States and cities use their own measures because they find that the Federal limits don't reflect their local economic realities.

### Measuring poverty in the US

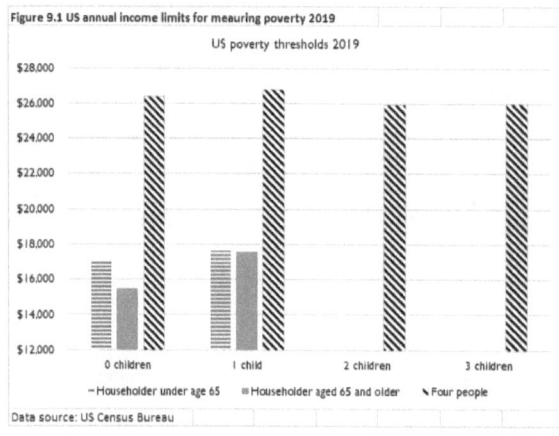

Figure 9.1 US annual income limits for meauring poverty 2019

The US Federal government measures the poverty rate by income limits that are called poverty thresholds. These dollar limits, which you can see in Figure 9.1, vary based on age and number of children. The income limits for households with a person older than 65 are lower than those of younger people.

For example, in households with no children, the limit is about $ 15,540 if a senior citizen is present. However, if there is no senior citizen present, then the limit is about $ 17,100. Above these income levels, this household is not poor.

**Children add less to the income limit than adults.** For example, a four-person household with no children has a limit of about $ 26,400. However, the limit is only about $ 25,900 for a four-person household with two children.

Two underlying issues reduce the validity of the US estimates of the poverty rate. One issue relates to the methodology used. The other issue is a failure to recognize the regional differences within the US.

## US poverty rate methodology is flawed

The poverty thresholds were first developed in 1963-1964 in an ad-hoc manner by an employee of the Social Security Administration. She started with the data from a 1955 household consumption survey. That was the most recent data available at that time.

The data showed that a family of three persons spent about one-third of its after-tax income on food in 1955. This led to the concept that you could determine the income limit as some multiple, close to 3, of a poor family's **hypothetical** expenditure on food. This hypothetical expenditure would then be multiplied by 3, or some number close to 3, to determine the income limit for poverty.

Why hypothetical? Why not actual? Because they wanted the base to come from an estimate of the minimum expenditure necessary to live acceptably well. Where would this estimate come from? At that time, the Department of Agriculture had something called the economy food plan. This plan was said to show what a budget-constrained family would buy and be able to eat reasonably well.

So, they calculated the cost of this plan for different family sizes. Then, they multiplied this dollar value by a number not far from 3 to find the income limit. For example, the poverty line for a two-person family was calculated by multiplying the hypothetical dollar cost of the economy food plan by 3.7.

**Soon, there were concerns about the methodology and the data used to calculate the poverty income limits**. One significant effort to change these limits came in 1976. At this time, an inter-agency task force submitted a comprehensive report to the US Congress. The only change was some minor amendments in the methodology. The core of the ad-hoc methodology continued.

In 1995, a panel of the National Research Council proposed a new approach for measuring poverty. But no change took place. The old 1963 methodology continues to be used in the official poverty estimates, and is still in use.

However, in 2011, the US government started issuing an unofficial estimate of the poverty rate. This unofficial estimate is called the Supplemental Poverty Measure (SPM). In Figure 9.2, you can see that the unofficial poverty rate is higher than the official poverty rate, though the difference is not large. However, even the unofficial poverty rate underestimates the true rate. The reason for underestimation is the second methodological issue, which we discuss below.

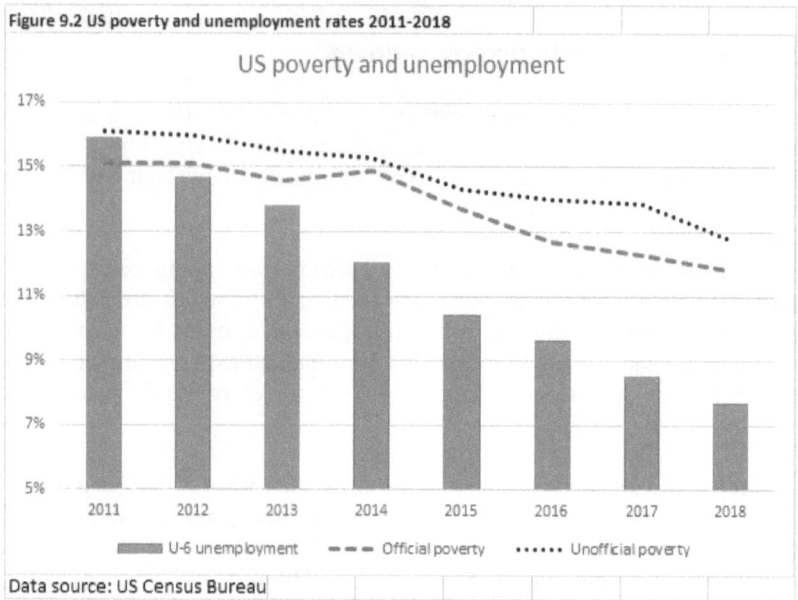

Figure 9.2 US poverty and unemployment rates 2011-2018

Data source: US Census Bureau

## Insights from estimated official and unofficial poverty rates

Even though the official and unofficial poverty rates are underestimates, **we can still derive some insights from their values.**

**First, both the official and unofficial poverty rates do respond to economic changes.** In Figure 9.2, we can see that the unemployment rate U-6 and the poverty rates have declined in recent years. However, the poverty rate is higher than U-6, the broadest measure of unemployment. Further, the poverty rate has declined at a slower rate than the decline in the unemployment rate. **The implication is that a reduction in unemployment will reduce poverty to some extent. Still, there will likely be some poverty in the US, even with a low unemployment rate.**

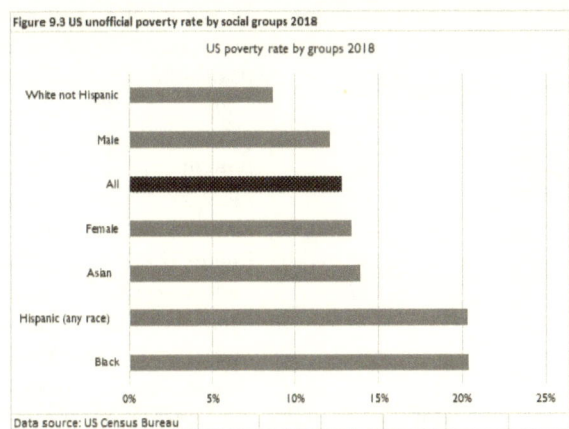

Figure 9.3 US unofficial poverty rate by social groups 2018

Second, **there is considerable variation in the poverty rate for different social groups.** In Figure 9.3, you can see that the unofficial poverty rate is the lowest for the group Whites not Hispanic, and the highest for the Black and Hispanic groups. Further, the poverty rate for males is lower than for females.

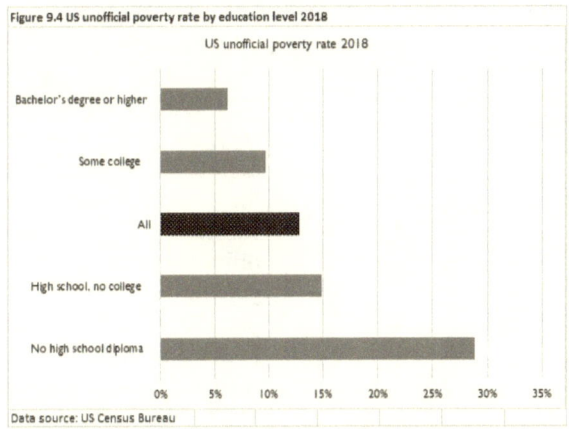

Figure 9.4 US unofficial poverty rate by education level 2018

In Figure 9.4, you can see the unofficial poverty rate by educational level. The poverty rate for people with college degrees was only around 6%. In sharp contrast, people without high school degrees had a poverty rate of about 29%. The implication is clear: **your chances of being poor come down as your education level goes up.**

## US poverty rate ignores regional differences

**The poverty thresholds used for measuring poverty are the same throughout the US.** However, the US is a vast country with considerable economic differences across various regions. For example, the amount of money that may be enough in a small town will not get you equally far in New York City. In recognition of this difference, many areas have developed their own poverty thresholds.

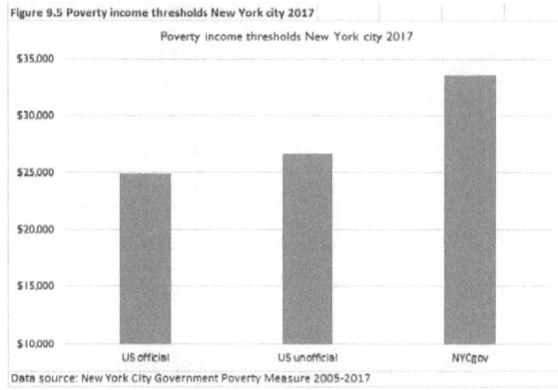

Figure 9.5 Poverty income thresholds New York city 2017

Data source: New York City Government Poverty Measure 2005-2017

In Figure 9.5, you can see the official US, unofficial US, and New York City's own poverty thresholds for a typical family. The New York City value is about $ 33,500, much higher than the official and unofficial limits. Thus, **both the official and unofficial thresholds under-**estimate the poverty rate in New York City and other expensive metropolitan areas.

## ELIGIBILITY LIMITS FOR POVERTY-RELATED SUBSIDIES IN THE US

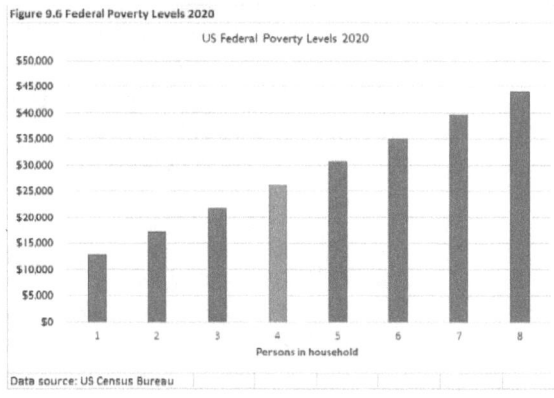

Figure 9.6 Federal Poverty Levels 2020

Data source: US Census Bureau

The US Federal government has a separate measure to define eligibility limits for poverty-related subsidies. These are officially called poverty guidelines, and popularly called the Federal Poverty Levels (FPL). These limits are much simpler than the poverty thresholds we just discussed. You can see the dollar limits in Figure 9.6. While they are different from the poverty thresholds, the difference is not large.

The dollar limits are the same across the US, except for Alaska and Hawaii, which have their own limits. This failure to capture regional differences ignores a crucial element of the economic ground reality.

### Cities and States set their own limits

Since the FPLs don't take account of the local cost, several States and cities use their own measures to set limits for their subsidy programs.

It's common to use available data with some modifications, instead of calculating these eligibility limits from scratch. Some places may use a multiple of the FPL. For example, the FPL for a family of four people is

$26,200. Some locations may increase it by 50% to raise the limit to $ 39,300. This is called 150% FPL.

In California, a family of four with income below $ 51,500 is eligible for subsidized electricity and natural gas. If your income is 0% – 138% of the FPL, then you qualify for Medi-Cal, California's name for the Federal Medicaid health insurance subsidy program.

### Low-income housing has its own measure

**The US Department of Housing and Urban (HUD) uses a different measure to judge eligibility for low-income housing.** Every year, HUD calculates the median income, called the Area Median Income (AMI), for each area. Then, HUD defines the income limits for that area for low-income housing. These limits vary according to household size. Further, HUD breaks down low-income people into three categories:

- Low income – household income less than 80% FPL

- Very low income – household income less than 50% FPL

- Extremely low income - household income less than 30% FPL

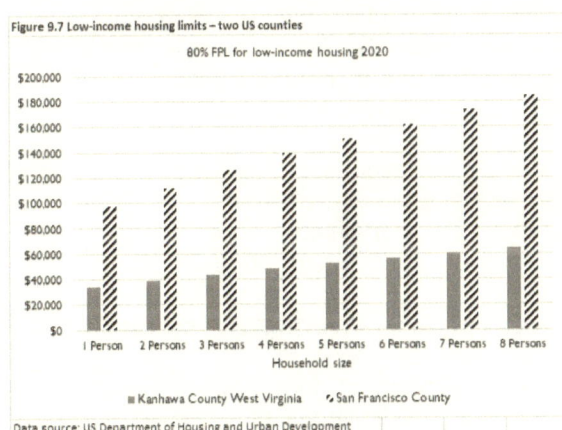

Figure 9.7 Low-income housing limits – two US counties

Data source: US Department of Housing and Urban Development

In Figure 9.7, you can see the 80% FPL limits for two distinctly different areas: San Francisco and Kanhawa, where the capital of West Virginia state is located. HUD's income limits for San Francisco are nearly three times the limits for Kanhawa, which shows the enormous difference in incomes across the US.

## INTERNATIONAL POVERTY MEASURES - WORLD BANK

The World Bank is an international agency affiliated to the United Nations (UN). However, the Bank is managed by its Board of Directors, which does not report to the UN. **The World Bank says that one element of its mission is to reduce the share of the global population that lives in extreme poverty** to 3% by 2030. This is the same as the United Nations' Sustainable Development Goals (SDG) 1.

## Measuring poverty worldwide -World Bank method

We have seen how complicated it is to measure poverty in the US. You would expect the issue to be even more complex when you consider so many countries worldwide, with their own currencies and different living costs. The only way out is for some agency to say this is how we are going to measure poverty, and for others to follow.

In 1990, the World Bank said that people who live on the equivalent of $ 1 per day per person are extremely poor. That definition has been widely accepted. Since then, the limit has been updated occasionally, and has been $ 1.90 per day since 2015. The limit is set in prices that prevailed in 2011, and the World Bank uses PPP exchange rates to convert the poverty line into the local currencies.

Many international groups follow the World Bank poverty line. For example, SDG 1 is set in terms of the World Bank poverty line. However, there is an alternative measure, which we discuss later in this chapter.

It's one thing for the World Bank to get many people and agencies to agree to use its international poverty line. It's another thing to get governments to provide the data for their countries regularly. **When you look at the World Bank's data-set on poverty, you find that it is full of holes.** Most countries have not reported their poverty rates on a systematic basis.

The World Bank poverty line looks at expenditures, not incomes. One reason for this is that in many countries the expenditure data is often more reliable than income data, particularly for households whose income comes intermittently from various sources.

## Current status of worldwide poverty -World Bank method

The United Nations publishes an annual report on the Sustainable Development Goals. This report for 2019 found that the world is not on track to meet its poverty reduction target, with a projected worldwide poverty rate of 6% instead of the target rate of 3% by 2030. You can see in Figure 9.8 that the poverty reduction rate has slowed down in recent years. The report found that, at present, poverty is mainly a rural phenomenon.

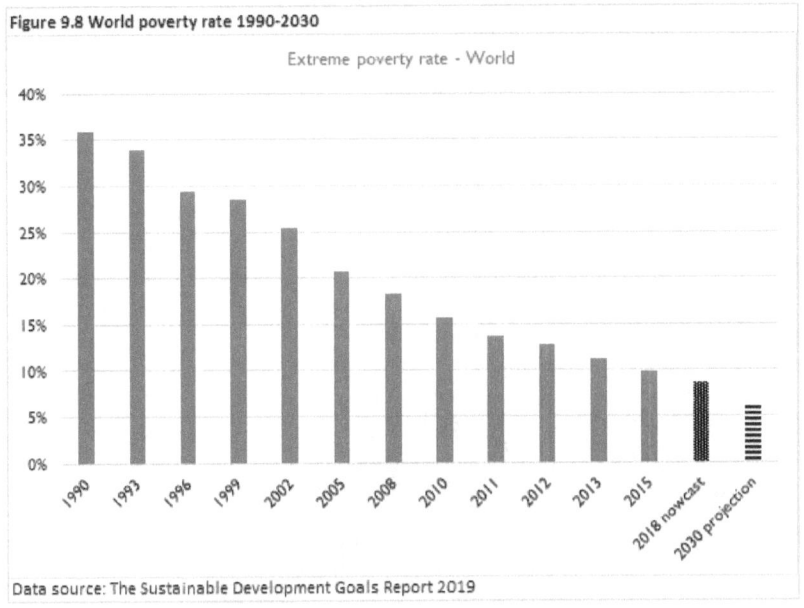

Figure 9.8 World poverty rate 1990-2030

Data source: The Sustainable Development Goals Report 2019

A World Bank report *Year in Review: 2019 in 14 Charts* published in December 2019 found that, in 2015, about 740 million people lived in extreme poverty.

### *Regional differences*

There are significant regional differences in poverty rates and progress in reducing poverty.

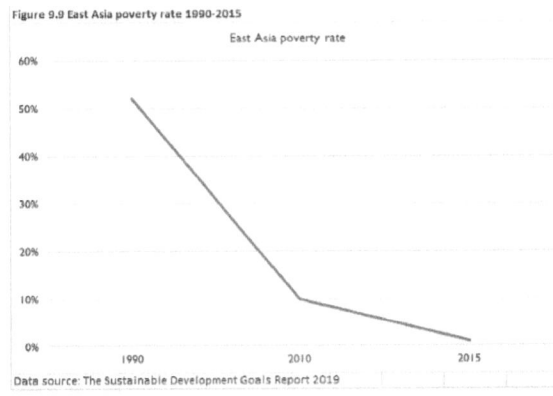

Figure 9.9 East Asia poverty rate 1990-2015

Data source: The Sustainable Development Goals Report 2019

**Eastern Asia has had a sharp decline in poverty rates**. As you can see in Figure 9.9, East Asia's poverty rate fell from 52% in 1990 to 10% in 2010, and then to less than 1% in 2015. **China**, as the most populous country in the world, is responsible for most of this decline. **Indonesia** cut its poverty rate from around 20% in 1999 to under 10% in 2019. **Vietnam** is another success, where the poverty rate fell from about 50% in the early 1990s to around 2% by 2018. **Thailand** has successfully reduced poverty over the past three decades, from over 65% in 1988 to under 10% in 2018.

Some East Asian countries do lag behind. For example, Cambodia's poverty rate was around 13% in 2018, and Laos had a poverty rate of about 23% in 2012.

**Extreme poverty is now concentrated in Sub-Saharan Africa and South Asia**. In 2015, Sub-Saharan Africa had about 55% of the world's poor people, followed by South Asia with about 30%, as you can see in Figure 9.10.

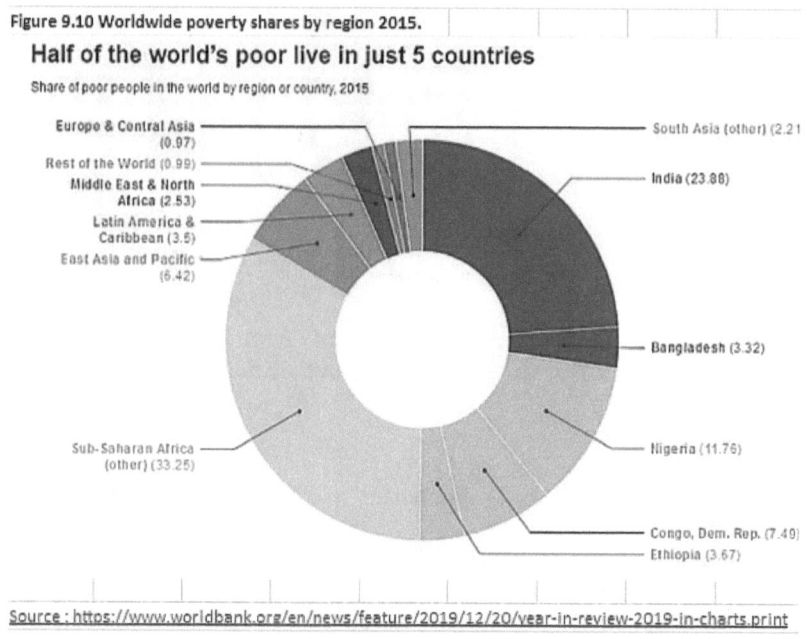

Figure 9.10 Worldwide poverty shares by region 2015.

**Half of the world's poor live in just 5 countries**

Share of poor people in the world by region or country, 2015

Europe & Central Asia (0.97)
Rest of the World (0.99)
Middle East & North Africa (2.53)
Latin America & Caribbean (3.5)
East Asia and Pacific (6.42)
Sub-Saharan Africa (other) (33.25)
South Asia (other) (2.21)
India (23.88)
Bangladesh (3.32)
Nigeria (11.76)
Congo, Dem. Rep. (7.49)
Ethiopia (3.67)

Source : https://www.worldbank.org/en/news/feature/2019/12/20/year-in-review-2019-in-charts.print

As you can see from Figure 9.10, in 2015, about half of the 740 million people in extreme poverty lived in five countries: India, Bangladesh, Nigeria, the Democratic Republic of Congo, and Ethiopia. Let's look at how these five countries have progressed over the years.

India, Bangladesh, and Ethiopia have had high GDP growth rates since 2014. In 2018, their GDP growth rates were near or above 7%. Congo had a GDP growth rate of around 6% in 2018. While high GDP growth rates are neither necessary nor sufficient for significant reductions in poverty rates, most countries that have had significant reductions in poverty rates have also had high GDP growth rates. Thus, it's likely that these three countries will be able to reduce their poverty rates in the future.

However, Nigeria has had low GDP growth rates in recent years, with a negative growth rate in 2016 and a 2018 growth rate of around 2%.

Thus, it is likely that the poverty rates in South Asia will fall faster than the poverty rates in Sub-Saharan Africa. As a result, poverty will increasingly be concentrated in Sub-Saharan Africa.

## Botswana – a success story in Sub-Saharan Africa

The World Bank classifies all its member countries into four groups, based on per capita incomes: low income, lower middle income, upper middle income, and high income. In this classification, China is an upper middle income country, and India is lower middle income country. **Botswana is one of the few countries in Sub-Saharan Africa that the World Bank classifies as an upper middle income country.**

Botswana was an impoverished country when it became independent in 1966. It had hardly any educated people – it is said that only 22 of its citizens had a college degree at that time. According to the World Bank, Botswana is a development success story. It has had good governance. There have been no major social flare-ups between the several ethnic groups in Botswana. In 2019, Transparency International ranked Botswana as the least corrupt country in Sub-Saharan Africa.

After independence, diamonds were found in Botswana, and they became the source of its wealth. **With sound economic management of its diamond wealth, Botswana's economy has grown tremendously.** However, in recent years, the growth rate has slowed down. The Gini coefficient is around 53%, indicating a high level of income inequality. The poverty rate is about 16% in 2016, which is still quite high.

Nevertheless, according to the World Bank, Botswana is aiming to become a high income country by 2036. One major constraint is that Botswana still does not have enough skilled workers, even though its education expenditure is high.

## INTERNATIONAL POVERTY MEASURES - UN AND OXFORD

The United Nations, in collaboration with Oxford University, calculates and publishes the Multidimensional Poverty Index (MPI). The MPI focuses on the extent to which a person is deprived of essential commodities. Let's first compare the MPI and the World Bank's main results before getting into the MPI details.

## Comparison of World Bank and MPI results

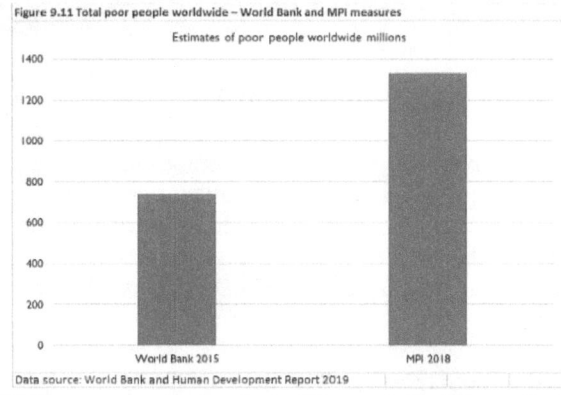

Figure 9.11 Total poor people worldwide – World Bank and MPI measures

Data source: World Bank and Human Development Report 2019

There is a significant difference between the number of people estimated as poor by the two measures. The World Bank found that there were around 740 million poor people in 2015, but the MPI concludes that there were about 1,300 million people in 2018, as you can see from Figure 9.11. Thus, **the MPI counts many more people as poor than does the World Bank.**

*Geographical concentration of poor people*

Like the World Bank measure, the **MPI also finds that the bulk of the poor lives in South Asia and Sub-Saharan Africa, as shown in Figure 9.12.** Further, the MPI also finds that the five countries listed by the World Bank – Bangladesh, Congo D.R., Ethiopia, India, and Nigeria – account for about 50% of the world's poor people.

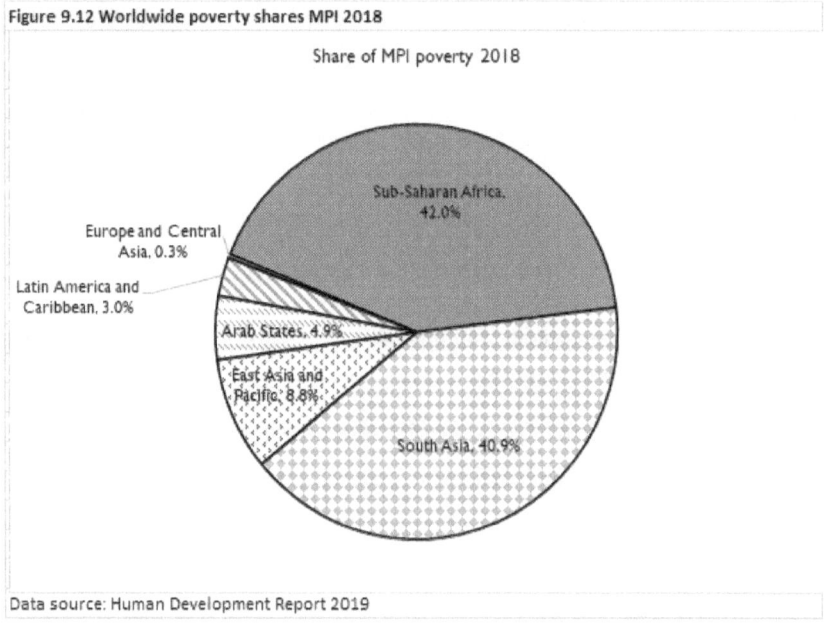

Figure 9.12 Worldwide poverty shares MPI 2018

Data source: Human Development Report 2019

206

However, the MPI finds that the shares of Sub-Saharan Africa and South Asia in the total number of people are similar. In contrast, the World Bank finds that Sub-Saharan Africa's share is much higher than that of South Asia.

## Comparison summary

The World Bank and MPI measures of poverty yield the same major conclusion that poverty on a worldwide basis now concentrated in Sub-Saharan Africa and South Asia. This similarity is reassuring because the MPI methodology is quite different from the World Bank methodology.

## MPI Methodology

The MPI methodology focuses on deprivation with a focus on health, education, and goods and services that reflect the standard of living. Each of these three factors has an equal weight in the index. Then, each of these factors is broken up into two or more components. The health and education factors have two components, while the standard of living group has six components, as shown in Table 9.1.

Table 9.1 Components of the Multidimensional Poverty Index

| Dimensions of Poverty | Indicator | Deprived if living in the household where. | Weight |
|---|---|---|---|
| Health Weight = 1/3 | Nutrition | An adult under 70 years of age or a child is undernourished. | 1/6 |
| | Child mortality | Any child has died in the family in the five-year period preceding the survey. | 1/6 |
| Education Weight =1/3 | Years of schooling | No household member aged 10 years or older has completed six years of schooling | 1/6 |
| | School attendance | Any school-aged child is not attending school up to the age at which he/she would complete class 8. | 1/6 |
| Standard of living Weight = 1/3 | Cooking Fuel | The household cooks with dung, wood, charcoal, or coal. | 1/18 |
| | Sanitation | The household's sanitation facility is not improved (according to SDG guidelines) or it is improved but shared with other households. | 1/18 |
| | Drinking Water | The household does not have access to improved drinking water (according to SDG guidelines) or safe drinking water is at least a 30-minute walk from home, round trip. | 1/18 |
| | Electricity | The household has no electricity. | 1/18 |
| | Housing | Housing materials for at least one of roof, walls and floor are inadequate: the floor is of natural materials and/or the roof and/or walls are of natural or rudimentary materials. | 1/18 |
| | Assets | The household does not own more than one of these assets: radio, TV, telephone, computer, animal cart, bicycle, motorbike, or refrigerator, and does not own a car or truck. | 1/18 |

Ssource: Human Development Report 2019

In Chapter 7, we saw that there is considerable debate on choosing the market basket and weights in calculating the inflation rate. So, it's natural to ask: where does the market basket in the MPI come from? Why is the amount of food consumed not included? **Why are telephones and computers in the same group as animal carts and bicycles?**

And, **where do the weights come from?** Why do the three broad groups have the same weight? And why do the components of each group have the same weight? Or compare the importance of schooling with the availability of electricity. If one child in the household drops out before the eighth grade, the deprivation has a weight of 1/6 = 16.67%. On the other hand, if the household does not have electricity in the home, the deprivation has a weight of 1/18 = 5.5%. Who decides that not going to school is so much more important than having electricity in your home?

The answers to these questions are the same as the answer to a similar question about the World Bank poverty measure. Why is precisely $ 1.90 PPP per day per person the right cut-off level for declaring a person poor? **The answer is that these numbers, in the end, represent the judgment of experts, who take account of the need for simplicity in formulating these measures**.

## EUROPEAN UNION POVERTY MEASURES

The EU has a comprehensive system of measuring poverty.

### EU poverty measurement system

The EU definition of poverty has two broad components: financial poverty and social exclusion. While the formal EU term is that you are at risk of poverty or social exclusion, I will call it Euro-poor for simplicity of discussion. These two components are measured by three indicators. Then, you are Euro-poor if you must meet any of these three indicators: low income, material deprivation, and part-time work.

**Thus, the Euro-poor concept is broader than any of the measures we have seen above**. Specifically, the Euro-poor concept pulls together the US income poverty criterion, the MPI deprivation criterion, and adds the part-time work criterion we saw in the U-6 measure of unemployment in the US.

**In Figure 9.13, you can see that about 21.7% of the EU's people were classified as poor in 2018.** About 85 million people were income poor, 33 million had part-time work, and about 28 million were materially deprived. However, some of the poor qualified on two or three criteria. On taking account of this overlap, the EU-28 countries had about 109 million poor people. The poverty rate was higher for women (22.3%) than for men (19.9%), though this is not shown in Figure 9.13.

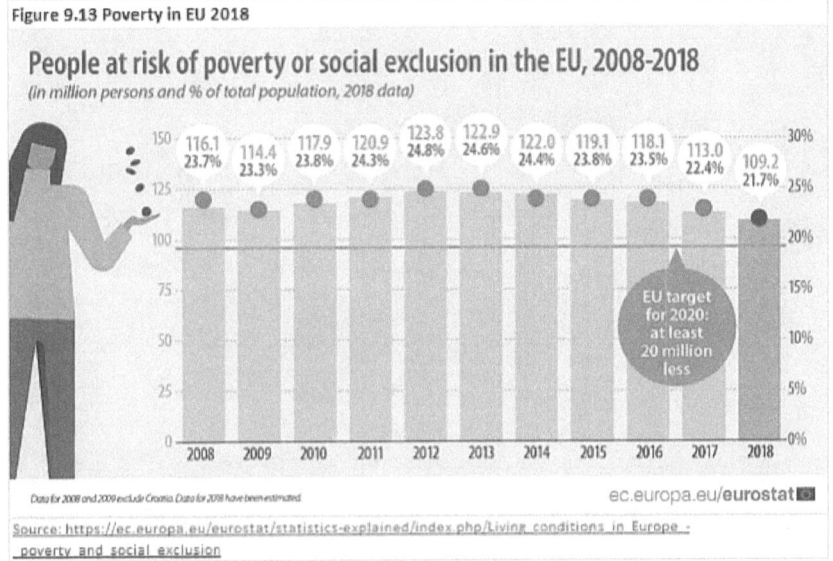

**Figure 9.13 Poverty in EU 2018**

**People at risk of poverty or social exclusion in the EU, 2008-2018**
*(in million persons and % of total population, 2018 data)*

Data for 2008 and 2009 exclude Croatia. Data for 2018 have been estimated.

ec.europa.eu/**eurostat**

Source: https://ec.europa.eu/eurostat/statistics-explained/index.php/Living_conditions_in_Europe_-_poverty_and_social_exclusion

In 2018, there were about 6.5 million people that met all three poverty criteria. Further, there were another 25.4 million people met two of the three poverty criteria. Together, 32 million people, about 6% of the total EU population, can be seen as a group of people who are entrenched in poverty.

The EU poverty rate has declined slowly over time, as you can see from Figure 9.14. Further, in 2018, the EU was not far from its poverty target for 2020. The target was not set in percentage terms. Instead, it was set to reduce the number of poor people in the EU by 20 million by 2020. (The economic crisis created in 2020 by the coronavirus will surely set back progress, and make it virtually impossible for the EU to attain its 2020 poverty target).

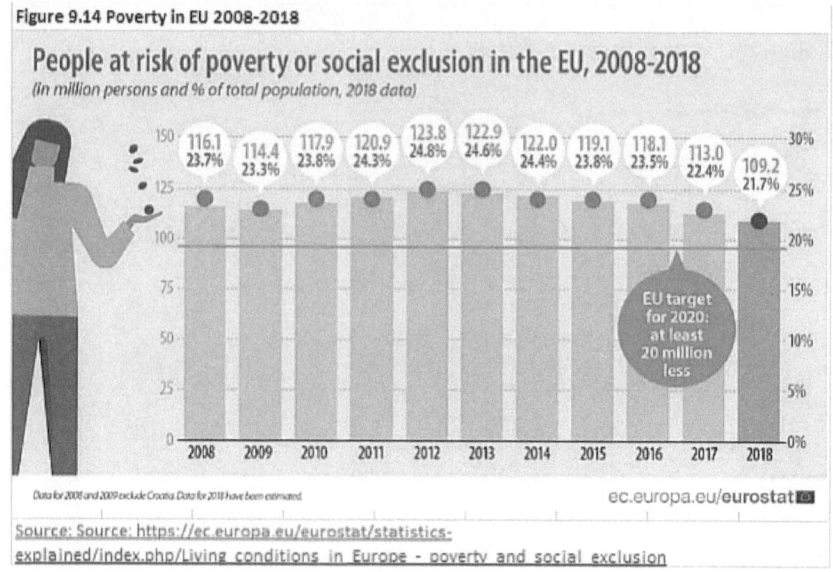

Figure 9.14 Poverty in EU 2008-2018

Source: Source: https://ec.europa.eu/eurostat/statistics-explained/index.php/Living conditions in Europe - poverty and social exclusion

**There is a considerable difference in the poverty rate among EU countries**, as shown in Figure 9.15. As you expect from what we have seen about Greece in earlier chapters, it has a high poverty rate. Spain also has a high poverty rate. On the other hand, Germany and Sweden have lower poverty rates.

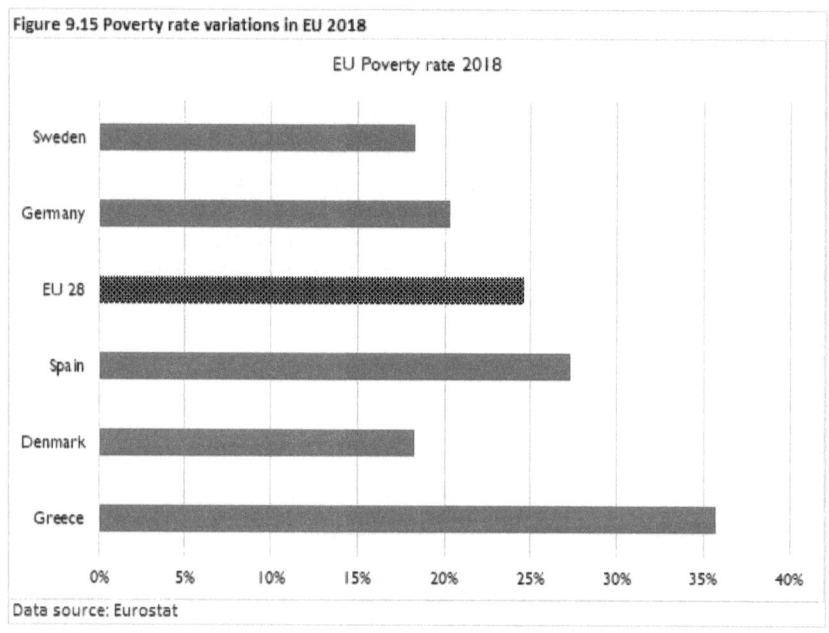

Figure 9.15 Poverty rate variations in EU 2018

Data source: Eurostat

Now that we have seen how the EU is faring on poverty, let's look at the details underlying the three criteria.

## EU Low-income criterion

We saw in Figure 9.13 that more people, nearly 85 million, in the EU met this criterion than the other two criteria. You meet the low-income standard if your adjusted disposable income is below a cut-off income level. The formal EU term is <u>equivalized</u>, but I find it simpler to call it <u>adjusted</u>.

What does the adjustment do? It adjusts the number of people in the household according to the modified OECD equivalence scale. This scale counts the household head as 1 person. Every additional adult is counted as a 0.5 person, and each child is counted as a 0.3 person. Thus, a family of two adults and three children would be counted as $1 + 0.5 + 3*0.3 = 2.5$ adults.

What is disposable income? It is the household's income after taxes and income transfers.

What is the specified income level? You need a two-part calculation to set this.

First, calculate the average household's disposable income in the country. Here we use the median, not the familiar arithmetic mean, to calculate the average income. For example, this value could be € 25,000.

Second, calculate 60% of this median value. In this example the answer would be $0.6*€ 25,000 = € 15,000$. You are poor if your household's adjusted disposable income is less than € 15,000.

**This concept of poverty judges you based on how well you are doing compared to other households in the country.** Hence, it does not always mean that a poor person has a low standard of living. It's just that your living standard is significantly below the average living standard.

**Thus, the Euro-poor approach is fundamentally different from the US Federal government's income method in both the official and unofficial poverty measures. The Euro-poor method is also fundamentally different from the expenditure approach used by the World Bank.**

Apart from classifying a household as poor or not poor in a given year, the EU also considers whether a particular household has continued to be in poverty for some time. This is called **persistent poverty. To be considered as persistently poor, you have to be poor this year and in at least two of the previous three years.**

## EU Part-time work criterion

We saw in Figure 9.13 that this criterion ranks second in the number of people who meet the three criteria. The EU's formal term for this criterion is low work intensity. You meet this criterion if you live in a household where adults worked no more than 20 % of their full work potential during the past year. In simple terms, you are classified as poor according to this criterion if your household members worked for only 20% or less of the available time.

## Material deprivation criterion

This is the third of the three criteria in the EU measure of poverty.

The EU has decided that nine material items are needed to lead an adequate quality of life. The first five items are the ability to:

i.    Cope with unexpected expenses;
ii.   Afford a week annual holiday away from home;
iii.  Avoid arrears (in mortgage or rent, utility bills or hire purchase installments);
iv.   Afford a meal with meat, chicken, fish, or vegetarian equivalent every second day;
v.    Keep the home adequately warm;

The next four items are about whether or not you:

vi.   Possess a washing machine;
vii.  Possess a color TV;
viii. Possess a telephone; and
ix.   Possess a personal car.

There are no weights attached to these nine items. The rule is straightforward. If your answer is No to four or more of these nine items, you are classified as severely materially deprived, i.e., poor.

Some of these nine items seem to be not comparable to the other items. For example, these days color TVs and phones are quite cheap. You can go to distant villages in Asia and Africa, and find plenty of people there have them. So, why would people in the EU not have a color TV or a telephone? However, most people in remote villages in Asia and Africa cannot even think of a week's annual holiday away from home or buying a car. So, why do the widespread, cheaper items have the same importance as the expensive items in the EU basket? While the answers to these questions are not obvious, perhaps, it's best to leave these decisions to local experts who have spent considerable time studying these issues.

When we compare the EU and MPI baskets, we see that health and education are missing from the EU basket, whereas they dominate the MPI basket. The absence of these items in the EU basket reflects the reality that reasonable health and education facilities are readily available to EU residents.

## MEASURING INEQUALITY

Economists generally focus on equality or inequality of the distribution of income or wealth. The same measures can be used for both variables. However, much more data is available for income inequality than for wealth inequality. Hence, we will focus mainly on income inequality in this chapter; we note that wealth inequality is generally expected to be higher than income inequality.

When we look at income inequality, it makes a difference whether we look at pre-tax income or post-tax income. In most countries, poor people receive some subsidies. This boosts their post-tax income, after adding the value of the subsidies to their income. Further, the better-off people do pay some taxes, though tax avoidance and evasion cannot be ignored.

In Chapter 1, we saw that a common measure of inequality is the Gini coefficient. Like the Gini coefficient, several other measures use statistical formulas to calculate inequality. While these measures are technically sound, they lack intuitive appeal. Hence, we find that many organizations use measures that are simpler to understand and relate to.

A major difficulty in looking at inequality is that most governments don't collect the data and report inequality measures regularly. For example, in the World Bank database, the most recent Gini coefficient for Jamaica is for 2004, and there are gaps in the data for China and Mexico.

In recent years, a group of researchers led by Professors Piketty and Saez have created a World Inequality Database, which collects and collates available information from various sources. I have used this database extensively for this chapter.

### Intuitive measures of inequality

The intuitive measures can be in the form of shares or ratios.

*Share measures*

The share measures are the simplest to understand. For example, **these days there is a lot of discussion about the income or wealth share of the top**

**0.1%, 1% or 10% of the people.** However, it is difficult to use these measures as most governments don't publish such data.

We can look at many shares at the same time. For example, we can look at the shares by quintiles, i.e., the share of the bottom 20% (lowest quintile), next 20% (second quintile), next 20% (third quintile), next 20% (fourth quintile), and top 20% (highest quintile). Or, we could even look at deciles, where we would start with the bottom 10% (lowest decile), and work our way up to the top 10%.

In Figure 9.16, you can see the share of the top 1% of the people in pre-tax national income in 1990, 2001, and 2015/16 (depending upon available data) for selected countries. **The share of the top 1% has increased for all the selected countries over time, particularly in India and South Africa.**

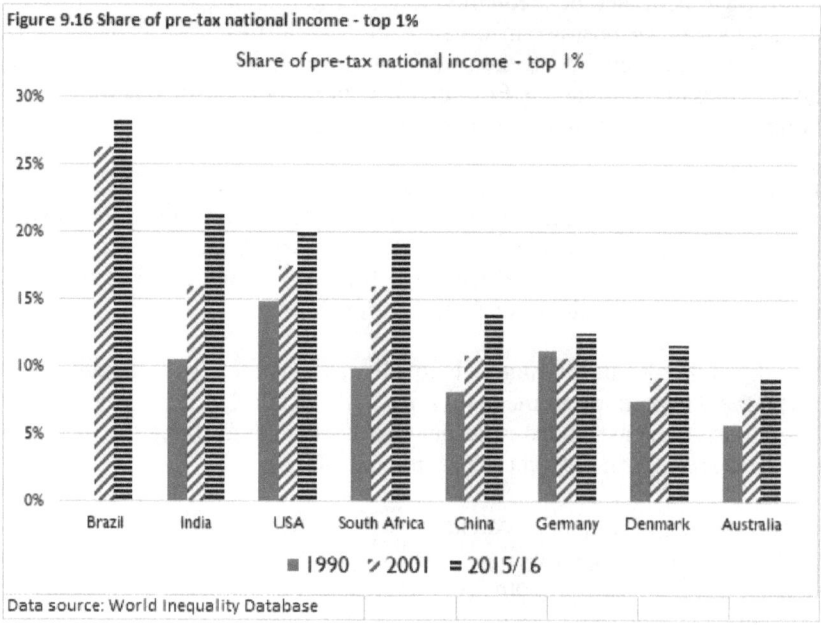

Figure 9.16 Share of pre-tax national income - top 1%

**There is considerable variation across countries.** In this group, Brazil had the highest share of the top 1%, reaching over 25% in 2015, while Germany, Denmark, and Australia had the lowest shares at under 12% in 2016.

**You can see the share of the top 10% in Figure 9.17 (below). The results are similar to the share of the top 1%.** The major difference is that South Africa has the highest share, reaching nearly 65% in 2015/16. Further, India's share in 2015/16 is similar to Brazil's share – both are close to 55%.

214

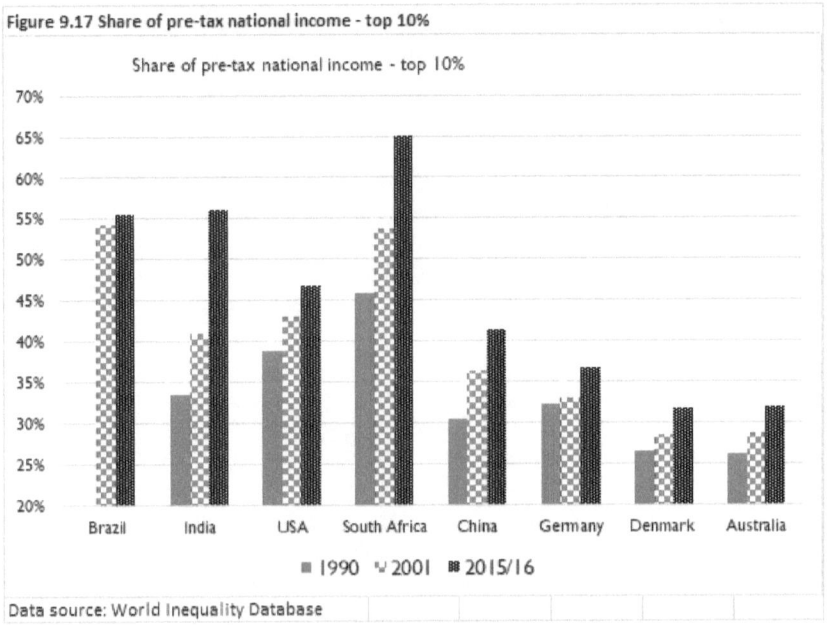

Figure 9.17 Share of pre-tax national income - top 10%

Another way to look at the income shares is by the regions of the world. You can see in Figure 9.18 that Europe has the lowest share of the top 10% in national income.

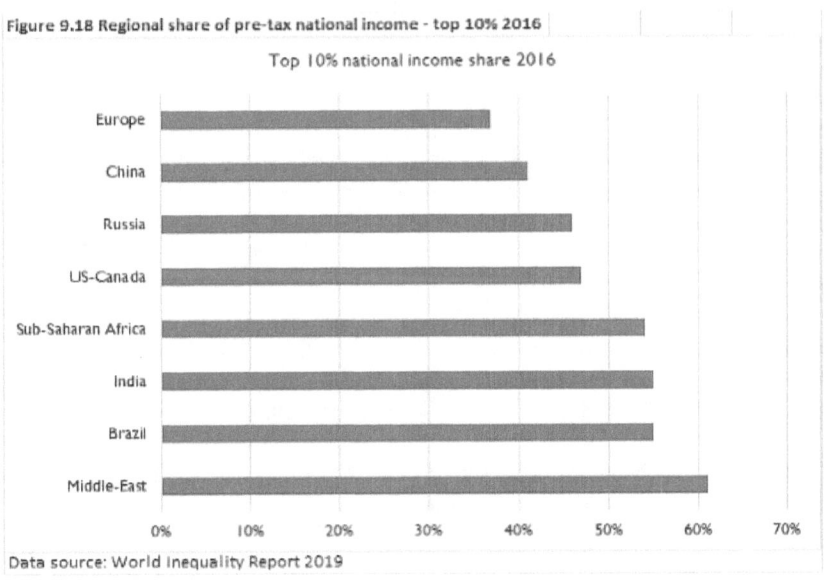

Figure 9.18 Regional share of pre-tax national income - top 10% 2016

215

The increasing and high shares of the top earners in India and South Africa are particularly noticeable because they still have a relatively large number of poor people.

In Figure 9.19, you can see the wealth share of the middle class and top earners across the world, with the world trend based on the experience of China, Europe, and the United States. This chart is notable for two reasons. First, it looks at the middle class, not just the people at the top and the bottom. Second, it looks at wealth, not income. **The message is straightforward: the wealth shares of the people at the top are rising at the expense of the middle class.**

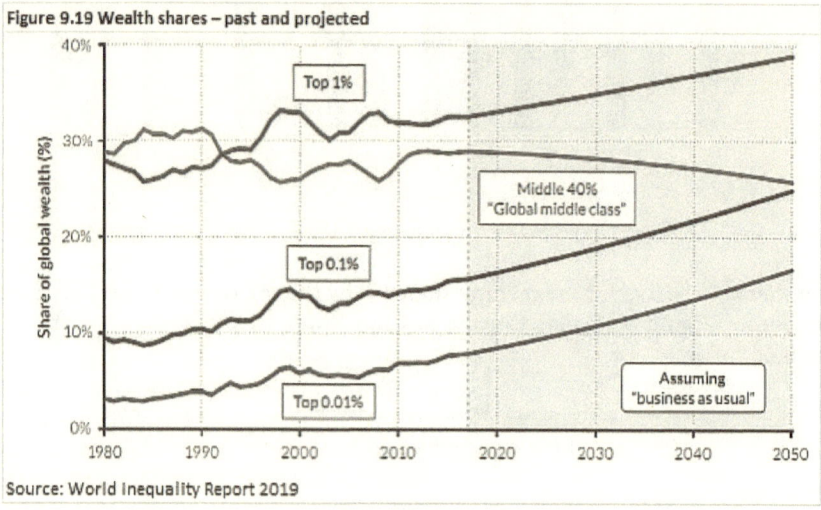

Figure 9.19 Wealth shares – past and projected

Source: World Inequality Report 2019

The World Inequality Report found that in the US, the income share of the top 1% has increased over time while the share of the bottom 50% has declined, as you can see in Figure 9.20 (below).

### Ratio measures

**You can create any ratio you like**. It could be the ratio of the top 1% to the bottom 50%, as we see implicitly in Figure 9.21. Or, it could be the top 10% to the bottom 10%. It depends upon what you want to highlight.

The EU reports the ratio of the top 20% to the bottom 20%. This is called the income quintile share ratio or the S80/S20 ratio.

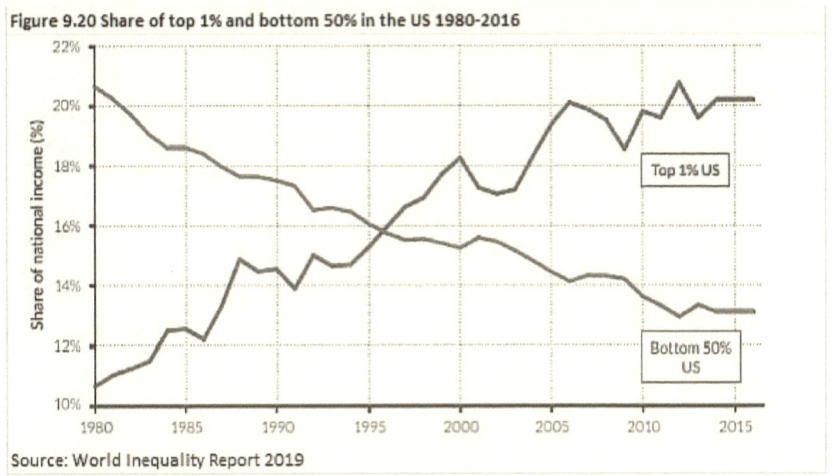

Figure 9.20 Share of top 1% and bottom 50% in the US 1980-2016

Source: World Inequality Report 2019

## Statistical measures of inequality

While the share and ratio measures consider only part of the available data, the statistical measures are based on all of the data. There are four main statistical measures.

### *Gini coefficient measure of inequality*

**This is the most well-established and commonly used measure of inequality**. However, there is no way to figure out whether changes in a country's Gini coefficient are coming from changes at the top, middle, or bottom, or some combination. We cannot figure out the reasons for changes in the Gini coefficient by looking deeper at the Gini coefficient itself. For example, the Gini coefficient tells us that income inequality has increased in South Africa. But, we cannot figure out which group lost and which group gained as the inequality increased.

### *Atkinson's measure of inequality*

**Professor Atkinson was a prominent economist. So, his measure of income inequality has a direct economic interpretation.** What is the percentage of total income that a country has to give up make the income distribution more equal? How much of the total income is "excessive" income – that's what we are trying to measure.

But how much equality do you want? That's a choice in Atkinson's measure. There's a choice variable labeled as e. A higher value of e indicates a desire for greater equality. The US government publishes Atkinson's measure with low (e = 0.25), medium (e = 0.50), and high values (e =0.75) of e.

217

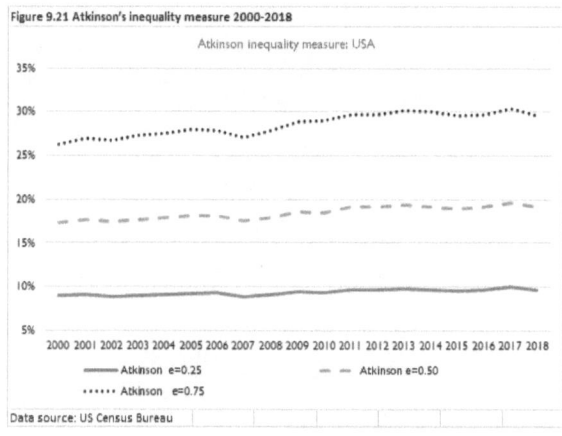

Figure 9.21 Atkinson's inequality measure 2000-2018

You can see in Figure 9.21 that, according to Atkinson's measure, income inequality has increased slowly in the US since 2000. However, as in the Gini coefficient, we cannot figure out the gainers and losers underlying the increase in inequality.

## Two other statistical measures of inequality

The other two statistical measures are Mean Logarithmic Deviation (MLD) and Theil's Index. Both of them are complicated ways of calculating the weighted average difference in income shares. I am not discussing them here because they are not commonly used.

Anyhow, in the US, they are highly correlated with other measures. In Table 9.2, you can see the correlation coefficients between all four statistical measures, including all three versions of Atkinson's measure. The Gini coefficient is highly correlated with the other measures. And, all the measures are highly correlated with each other. The exception is the combination of the Theil Index and MLD, where the correlation is 0.89, which is low only in relation to the other high values.

Table 9.2 Correlation coefficients between US inequality measures 2000-2018

|  | Gini | Mean log deviation | Theil | Atkinson e=0.25 | Atkinson e=0.50 | Atkinson e=0.75 |
|---|---|---|---|---|---|---|
| Gini | 1.000 |  |  |  |  |  |
| Mean log deviation | 0.969 | 1.000 |  |  |  |  |
| Theil | 0.970 | 0.891 | 1.000 |  |  |  |
| Atkinson e=0.25 | 0.992 | 0.937 | 0.993 | 1.000 |  |  |
| Atkinson e=0.50 | 0.999 | 0.970 | 0.973 | 0.993 | 1.000 |  |
| Atkinson e=0.75 | 0.993 | 0.991 | 0.941 | 0.974 | 0.993 | 1.000 |

Data source: US Census Bureau

The different statistical measures do give different results, and these differences are meaningful when you are looking to get a detailed understanding of inequality. However, **if you are looking for just the big**

218

picture, it is reasonable to use the well-established Gini coefficient for this purpose.

## WHAT SHOULD WE DO ABOUT INCOME AND WEALTH INEQUALITY?

### Kuznets hypothesis

The conventional answer in economic theory is that there is no need to worry much about these inequalities. Prof. Kuznets, a Nobel Prize winner we discussed in Chapter 2, wrote a seminal paper in the 1950s. Kuznets put forward a hypothesis, based on a pattern he found in the data, that inequality would initially increase with economic growth but would later decline with further growth. People interpreted this to mean that it would be enough to focus on maintaining full employment, and let inequalities be resolved on their own over time.

This hypothesis continues to discussed and debated in academic studies. And, Kuznets's hypothesis was later extended to environmental degradation. Meaning that the environment would degrade initially with economic growth but would improve later with further economic growth. This also continues to be debated and discussed in academic studies.

Perhaps the Kuznets hypothesis is correct. From a practical point of view, the Kuznets hypothesis's weakness is that it doesn't say when the inequalities will begin to reduce. Where's the tipping point? At what level of economic development would the inequality begin to decline? Would this tipping point vary across countries? If so, what would be the factors that determine the tipping point for different types of countries?

The answers to these questions could have emerged from the numerous related academic studies undertaken over the years. **However, my assessment is that consensus answers have not emerged so far**. That may come as no surprise to people who feel that economists are always saying, "Yes, but on the other hand ..." But my sense is that we are not even at the stage where we could summarize the debate in a simple two-handed manner.

For example, what do we make of the rising inequalities in the US? When will the tipping point towards declining inequalities come? Or, how come some countries have managed to have considerable economic growth without high levels of inequality? Are they on their own Kuznets curve? Further, how come some countries have extremely high levels of inequalities even though their level of economic development is low? How could this happen if inequalities are supposed to increase with income growth? Are these countries also on their own Kuznets curve?

## Recent work of Professors Piketty and Saez

The lack of clear-cut answers has left open a space in the thinking and understanding of economists. The recent analytical work of Professors Piketty and Saez has occupied this seemingly unoccupied space. They point out that there are major regional differences in inequality, but argue that the world will continue to see increasing inequalities in the coming decades.

**Suppose that their view is correct. So what?** Shouldn't the low-income countries, where most of the world lives, be more concerned about reducing their poverty rates than reducing inequalities? If their economic growth lifts nearly a billion people out of extreme poverty and some more out of near poverty, then wouldn't that be a remarkable achievement, even if inequalities increase?

Maybe. Maybe not. It depends upon your objectives. Do you want an economy that is judged to be fair and just? Then, your answer would probably be that this type of poverty reduction is not the right answer. Do you care more about poverty and hunger? Then, your answer would probably be that you will tolerate the inequalities.

Or, do you think that this is a false dichotomy, and you can have both economic growth and low inequality – a just and prosperous economy? Economists call this inclusive growth. However, it remains more of an idea than a reality in most countries.

Let's leave this issue here because the answers are not clear, and will continue to be debated and discussed. Instead, **let's turn to the recommendations in the World Inequality Report 2019**. It summarizes the views of the economists who are pushing hard against income and wealth inequalities.

## Recommendations of the World Inequality Report 2019

These recommendations have a global focus, which means that they go beyond what individual countries can and should do.

First, **put higher taxes on rich, high-income people**, which economists call progressive taxation. This should include significant inheritance taxes, particularly in low-income countries that have high levels of inequalities.

This is a well-established idea. However, in the real world, there are endless stories about how well-off people manage their affairs to avoid or evade taxes. So, if this idea is accepted, then those loopholes would have to be plugged, too. The economists promoting lower inequality know this, which leads to the second recommendation.

**Second, curb global tax evasion and money laundering practices.** To make this work, they recommend an international financial register recording the ownership of financial assets.

This is a new idea. Can it work? Possibly. However, we have not yet been able to get adequate global traction on fighting climate change. What are the odds that this recommendation will fare better?

**Third, focus some more on improving the prospects of the poor.** They recommend greater equality of access to education and well-paying jobs.

This is a well-established idea, which we can interpret as reducing the inequality of opportunity. This idea is consistent with reducing the poverty rate or improving the lives of poor and near-poor people. Hence, it may turn out to be widely accepted. So, the practical issue might be how to get it done, not whether to do it.

**Finally, governments should invest in the future.** They recommend public investments in education, health, and environmental protection. However, they recognize that many governments may not have the money they need to finance these investments.

Apart from money, there may be some operational issues also in getting this done. For example, we saw in Chapter 3 that many government-financed schools in developing countries fail to provide a good education. And rural health systems often lack, even in the US, the facilities to provide high quality health services in the local area.

## KEY TAKEAWAYS

### Poverty

1. While the US poverty measurement system is flawed, we can still conclude from it that a reduction in the unemployment rate tends to reduce the poverty rate. However, even low unemployment rates will likely leave the US with some poor people.

2. The world has about 0.75 billion to 1.3 billion extremely poor people, depending upon how you measure poverty. Global poverty is now concentrated in South Asia and Sub-Saharan Africa. While there will be some progress on reducing poverty in this decade, the world is not on track to meet the United Nations target of reducing extreme poverty to 3% of the people by 2030.

3. The EU has a comprehensive definition of poverty that goes beyond incomes and expenditures. Further, the income component of poverty compares your income to a modified form of the average income, not to a pre-set euro amount. In 2019, the EU was moving close to its target of reducing the number of people who qualified as poor by this comprehensive definition.

## Inequality

4. While there are several ways to measure income inequality, all of them show a pattern of wide variations in income inequality. It's low and mostly steady in Europe and a few other countries. It's rising in the US, India, and China, and is high in some countries in Sub-Saharan Africa.

5. There is no consensus on the extent to which the world should aim to reduce income inequalities, and how to do it. However, these inequalities have emerged as a major public policy issue in some countries.

This chapter brings us to the end of this book. The next set of economic issues will be in Volume II, which is currently under preparation. In Volume II, we will look at macroeconomic policies; sectoral issues such as health, education, and environment; international economics; and, a quick dip into Statistics and Econometrics. No doubt, some mathematics will be needed in the last section. Still, the discussion will focus on interpreting published results, not on formulas and equations.

# Subodh Mathur

I was born in Alwar, a small town in India. My parents moved around Rajasthan until we reached Jaipur in 1958, where I graduated from high school. After that, I got my BA and MA degrees in Economics from Delhi University. Then, I went back to Jaipur to teach at Rajasthan University. It was a fun time, with Professor Raj Krishna as the Head of the Economics Department.

After that, I got my Ph. D. in Economics from MIT, and became a tenure-track Assistant Professor of Economics at the American University (AU), Washington, DC. Here, I taught mainly graduate courses and supervised a large number of doctoral dissertations. But I soon realized that my comparative advantage was in applying economic concepts in the real world, not is academic research.

So, I left AU in 1998, and became a self-employed consultant. But, the teacher in me would not quit. Strangers told me I talked like a professor. The people I worked with would often say, "But, this will not work in the real world."

So, I returned to AU after nearly twenty years as an adjunct professor. This time, I wanted to teach economics to graduate students outside the Economics Department.

Which I did. Enjoyed it thoroughly.

Of course, this did not pay my bills. I became a long-standing short-term consultant for the World Bank in Washington, DC. I have also worked for several US agencies. In recent years, I have been working as an economist who estimates the economic damages in cases of injury or wrongful death.

I am looking for something new to do – but as an economist.

www.ingramcontent.com/pod-product-compliance
Lightning Source LLC
Chambersburg PA
CBHW030617220526
45463CB00004B/1316